# Birds of
# Field and Shore

# Birds of Field and Shore

*Grassland and Shoreline Birds of
Eastern North America*

## John Eastman

*Illustrated by Amelia Hansen*

STACKPOLE
BOOKS

Published by
STACKPOLE BOOKS
5067 Ritter Road
Mechanicsburg, PA 17055
www.stackpolebooks.com

Printed in the United States of America

*Cover design by Wendy A. Reynolds*
*Cover illustrations by Amelia Hansen*

10 9 8 7 6 5 4 3 2 1

First edition

**Library of Congress Cataloging-in-Publication Data**

Eastman, John (John Andrew)
    Birds of field and shore / John Eastman; illustrated by Amelia Hansen.
      p. cm.
    Includes bibliographical references (p. ) and index.
    ISBN 0-8117-2699-1 (alk. paper)
    1. Birds—East (U.S.) 2. Birds—Canada, Eastern. I. Title.

QL683.E27 E36 2000
598'.0974 21—dc21                    99-045522

# Contents

# Acknowledgments

"To draw a bird is to experience it," wrote British bird artist Darren Rees. By that criterion, my collaborator, artist Amelia Hansen, is a person of vast nature experience, which has benefited all the books of this series—and our plant series as well. Her interpretation of fine detail makes close inspection of her drawings always rewarding and worthy of return to them. I am fortunate to have her and her talents on my side.

Ecologist Richard Brewer, ornithologist, writer, and professor emeritus of biology at Western Michigan University, and James Granlund, ornithologist, author, and teacher, have read the manuscript of this book—as both have done with my previous books—and again have offered useful comments and suggestions. I thank these distinguished gentlemen and friends, not only for their efforts this time around but also over the long haul. Dr. Brewer also graciously permitted the use of several previously published Hansen illustrations from *The Atlas of Breeding Birds of Michigan,* by Brewer, McPeek, and Adams (East Lansing: Michigan State University Press, 1991).

I thank Dr. Michael B. Stuart for providing access to specimen collections at the University of North Carolina–Asheville.

My friend, naturalist Jacqueline Ladwein, has helped observe and photograph specimens in the field as well as fought the good fight for environmental sense and sensibility as long as I have known her.

Other contributors to this effort in both large and small ways include Jane E. Barrick, Joyce Bertschi, Janea Little, Eric Mills, and Curtis and Shirley McComis.

My durable, loving, and easygoing companion, Susan Woolley Stoddard, has, as always, helped vitally on the practical side of things. Without her, this project—as so many others—would have gone nowhere.

Amelia Hansen dedicates her efforts in this book "To Paul: Thanks for all your kindness and patient understanding. You're my best friend."

# Introduction

This book is the final of a 3-volume series on the most common and familiar bird species of eastern North America—birds that, with rare exceptions, most of us can see in the appropriate season without traveling too far from home. First in the series was *Birds of Forest, Yard, and Thicket* (1997); *Birds of Lake, Pond and Marsh* (1999) followed. Each volume views bird species through the focus of habitat. Separate accounts treat each species from an ecological perspective—that is, as community dwellers coequal with their plant and animal associates in the total complex of their surroundings. A primary aim of this series is to bring news about these birds up-to-date—to convey the results and discoveries of recent research, especially findings of the past 2 decades. My foremost sources, listed in the Selected Bibliography, include records of my own bird observations plus much shared knowledge and opinion from respected birding colleagues.

The 42 species of birds presented in this volume range across a roster of bird families from gamebirds to finches. Many on the list show distinctive adaptations for living in meadow or shoreline habitats. Most occur outside as well as within the regional focus of this book—that is, east of the Mississippi and north of the Ohio River. Many also occur in this region for only part of the year, owing to the physical fact that snow falls and water freezes, rendering food inaccessible or absent throughout much of this region in winter. The birds' adaptation to this problem is to migrate. Most birds that nest exclusively in far northern regions of the continent can be best observed in lower latitudes during these periods of travel to and from their breeding and winter ranges.

Forty-two species represent only a portion of the field and shore avifauna that occur in North America; sandpipers alone number 30 or more species. Rather than strive for total inclusiveness, giving perfunctory accounts of *all* such birds, I have opted for closer looks at some of the core species of these habitats. My particular selection of these is arbitrary; I readily grant that other valid options may exist. A few cases also present other kinds of arbitrary choices. Peregrine falcons, for example, certainly do not fit into the conventional categories of meadow or beach habitats, yet they must be assigned somewhere in a limited human schema such as a book series. Since they commonly nest and hunt along rocky shorelines, I have included them in this book. Likewise gulls and terns, though not nominal shorebirds in the family of long-legged waders, commonly frequent shorelines and coastal areas. And such passerine species as kingbirds, bluebirds, and many sparrows, though not precisely grassland residents in many cases, inhabit open lands containing herb or shrub components of early plant succession. Such open habitats include pastureland and old fields, shrub savannas, dunes, and cropland. I have, in short, slanted some of the usual ecological definitions of field and shore habitats in order to include a number of open-country and shoreline species herein. Along with these birds are included many of the sandpipers, plovers, and grassland species that are strictly residents of field and shore.

This book's taxonomic sequencing of birds follows the DNA classification scheme advanced by Burt L. Monroe, Jr., and Charles G. Sibley in *A World Checklist of Birds* (New Haven: Yale University Press, 1993). One of the least stable elements of a bird's biography these days is its name and relationship slot. Family and subfamily designations swing back and forth, and a bird's "true" name may differ depending on whether you look it up in America or Europe. The Monroe-Sibley system used in this book—and by increasing numbers of ornithologists worldwide—offers a uniform set of criteria based on DNA relationships by which to classify birds, an advantage most other classifications lack. Fashions and partisanships change in taxonomy as in everything else; the recent tendency has been to "promote," or upgrade, many formerly subordinate races or subspecies to mint-fresh bird species—also to restore some formerly lumped groups back to species status. One result has been massive disparities among the various classification systems in the total number of species they finally include in their world checklists.

Such matters, though interesting, only peripherally concern this series. Each species account herein is divided into several sections. Each begins with the bird's English and Latin **names,** usually as given in *A World Checklist of Birds,* though in some cases, to facilitate usage, I have preferred to stick with the conventional American name—for example, ring-necked pheasant instead of common pheasant, bank swallow instead of sand martin. Family and order designations follow. Where 2 or more species of a single family are given accounts, an introductory paragraph on the family precedes the accounts. A brief description of the bird's appearance and sounds follows its names. Section headings include the following:

**Close relatives** identifies the bird's nearest kin.

**Behaviors** describes the bird's characteristic actions, focusing on what an observer may actually see. Included here are the bird's breeding distribution and migrational habits. Descriptions of specific seasonal behaviors and activities follow under seasonal subheadings:

*Spring* is when migrants arrive, singing or other vocal sounds peak, and most North American birds form pair bonds and begin nesting. Many yearling birds return in spring to areas near their birth sites, and most previously mated adult birds return to their previous breeding territories (such homing behavior is called *philopatry,* a term frequently encountered in this book). Many birds remain monogamous breeders throughout a season and some throughout their lives. Seasonal monogamy most often "comes with the territory"—that is, a female bird selects a desirable territory and almost incidentally accepts the male that "owns" it. Yet several score of North American songbird species are known to engage in at least occasional breeding, or extrapair copulations, outside the primary nuptial bond, a total that swells even further when nonsongbird species are included. Nesting data are presented in a boxed paragraph at the end of this seasonal section.

In *summer,* most birds complete nesting activities, song diminishes, and many field and shore species become gregarious and form flocks. Feathers litter the ground in late summer, when annual plumage molts occur in most species, and many migrant birds gather in restless, often large premigratory assemblages (often called *staging*).

*Fall* is another highly stressful season of migration. Some species migrate only to the southern United States; others move much farther, to Central and South America. Some of the Neotropical migrants that travel farthest move from North American summer or fall to South American spring, but they do not renew breeding activities at their destinations.

*Winter* for most birds is a season of feeding, either in flocks or solitarily, depending on the species. For certain species that winter in the North, this may be a season of great hardship and mortality if food becomes scarce, as it often does. Such scarcity may account in many cases for *irruptions,* periodic winter invasions into the United States of such arctic residents as snowy owls and several finch species. Winter distribution of migrants is also described in this section.

**Ecology** focuses on specific details of the bird's relationships to other organisms and to its seasonal environments. Sequenced paragraphs discuss the bird's habitats, nesting, food, competitors, and predators. In addition to threats from competitors and predators, almost all birds carry external and internal parasites (unmentioned in most accounts), mainly protozoans, worms, mites, and insects. The most common skin and feather parasites include fowl mites *(Ornithonyssus),* bird lice (Philopteridae), larval louse or hippoboscid flies *(Lynchia),* and larval blowflies *(Protocalliphora).* Many birds also carry internal parasites, such as roundworms, tapeworms, and flukes. "I suspect that parasites have been very influential in the evolution of birds," wrote ecologist Richard Brewer. (Some interesting research focusing on *Streptomyces* bacteria in feathers suggests that plumage microbes may have played important roles in the evolution of plumage colors, of protection against certain pathogens, and of molt sequencing.)

**Focus,** a catchall section, presents information on origins of the bird's name, the bird's place in native or cultural history, survival data, details of certain adaptations it may show, elaborations on previous sections—anything interesting that fits nowhere else. Latin names of plant and animal organisms other than birds are kept to a minimum; I include them only for specific organisms that bear special ecological relevance to the bird.

Several recurrent terms may need defining:

*Birding* is the methodical field activity of observing birds; *birders* are people who engage in this activity, either as a pastime or for data collection.

*Incubation* is egg heating by a parent bird, accomplished by sitting on the eggs for long intervals over days or weeks; in most (though not all) North American species, incubation is done exclusively by females. Incubating females usually develop brood patches, temporarily bare areas of abdominal skin by which they transfer body heat to the eggs. Some species begin incubation when the first egg is laid, resulting in differential hatching times *(asynchronous hatching)*. In many species, however, incubation starts after the laying of the last or next to last egg in a set, or *clutch,* and hatching occurs more or less simultaneously *(synchronous hatching)*.

*Altricial young* are nestlings that remain in the nest for an extended helpless period and require much parental feeding and brooding, as in most songbirds. *Precocial young* are chicks that leave the nest soon after hatching, follow the parent, and immediately begin feeding themselves, as in most gamebirds and shorebirds.

*Fledging* refers to an altricial nestling's development of feathers and its act of leaving the nest, thereby becoming a *fledgling* until it can feed independently. For precocial chicks, fledging is the act of first flight. Used as a subhead in the boxed paragraph in the *Spring* section of accounts, *fledging* refers to the number of days between hatching and nest departure for altricial young and to the number of days between hatching and first flight for precocial young.

A *juvenile* bird feeds independently but has not yet developed its first winter (usually adultlike) plumage, a molt that occurs concurrently with the feather molt of adult birds in late summer or fall.

*Territory* is, in its broadest definition, the area defended by a singing male or bonded pair of birds. Territories vary in size among species and also among members of the same species. Territory size often depends on the abundance of the species and quality of habitat in a given area. Birds establish their territories by singing and by defensive behaviors against intruders of the same or competing species. Most songbird breeding territories enclose both nesting and feeding sites. Many birds, however, must leave their territories to feed, drink, or bathe; a loose designation for these extraterritorial areas is *home range.* Colonial pairs usually defend much smaller territories than solitary nesters. Nonbreeding territories in some species may include defended food sources, night roosts, and winter foraging sites.

A resident bird's *home range* is the total space it inhabits in a given area; home range encloses the territory but is not defended. Home ranges of separate pairs of a species often overlap.

An *area-sensitive* or *area-dependent species* is one that favors, or thrives best in, large, unfragmented habitat areas.

Birds of field and shore must contend these days with some major habitat problems. In the case of most shorebirds and gulls, water contaminants—many of them initially airborne—or toxic episodes such as oil spills or botulism outbreaks may result in devastating effects. Shorebirds, the feeders and waders of beach strands and mudflats, become especially vulnerable during their migrations. Most are long-distance migrants, and many assemble in enormous concentrations—hundreds of thousands—at key staging areas along their routes; Delaware Bay in New Jersey and Delaware is one such critical area in the Northeast. Coastal development and heavy usage of beaches by humans interfere in spring with the birds' stoking up on horseshoe crab eggs to provide the necessary energy for their travel northward. Recent efforts toward setting aside many of these coastal staging sites as shorebird reserves offer renewed hope for long-term survival of these migrants.

Also of major concern to ornithologists is the current plight of grassland birds. Today a whole roster of species that nest and forage primarily in hayfields and prairies exists in various stages of regional decline and withdrawal, a situation well documented by the North

American Breeding Bird Survey (BBS), the primary monitoring program for North American bird populations. Widespread atlasing and censusing projects over the past 3 decades have confirmed the trend. "Grassland birds," according to a recent BBS report, "show the most consistent declines of any group of birds monitored." The statistics look dismal: Bobolinks have declined almost 40 percent across their breeding range, eastern meadowlarks more than 50 percent, grasshopper sparrows 66 percent. Upland sandpipers, northern harriers, horned larks, sedge wrens, field sparrows—all of these grassland species show declines. In the Northeast, declines of most grassland species since 1966, when the BBS began, register in the high double-digit percentages.

Primary blame for this state of siege is attributed to the changes that have occurred in grassland habitats. These changes reflect shifts in land usage away from agriculture, crop planting and harvest, pasturage—and, when not away from these usages, away from former methods and practices of tillage and harvest. Earlier mowing schedules have become a primary evictor of grassland bird populations, and farming without wholesale application of pesticides, wiping out insects and other invertebrate food for birds, is virtually a lost art. In evicting grassland birds, the farmer loses some of his best friends, economically speaking. In some areas, such as the Great Lakes states, many grassland bird species have withdrawn from depleted farmland habitats to more northern cut-over timberlands where forests are slower to regenerate. In other areas, where the birds do not have such options, they have simply disappeared. Ecologist Peter Vickery's research has shown that open habitats should be at least 500 acres in extent "to support a full array of grassland birds." Few areas east of the Great Plains can any longer provide such support.

The northeastern region of the country, the focus area of this book, is where grassland birds have taken their biggest beating. Some ecologists will tell you that from the historical viewpoint, grassland birds never really belonged there anyway, as they initially came as a result of land clearing and farming by settlers. Yet "there is convincing evidence," as Vickery has stated, "that grasslands were a conspicuous part of the eastern landscape before colonial times."

Large areas kept open by frequent wildfires and beaver work, and through agricultural clearing and deliberate burning by Indians, existed up and down the eastern coastal regions as well as inland. Pollen deposits and historical accounts likewise reveal that ample grasslands existed in this region during the settlement period. For several millennia during and after the last glacial period, unbroken grasslands may have stretched from the Great Plains to the Atlantic coast. Existence of eastern bird populations that had western counterpart subspecies—such as the heath hen (a subspecies of the greater prairie-chicken) and Henslow's sparrow—indicates that eastern geographical isolation of these grassland birds operated for many thousands of years. That many grassland bird populations of this region increased during the eighteenth and nineteenth centuries, however, is probably true. Other factors that are inherent elements of grassland habitats also exist. These habitats are by nature shifting and unstable, and therefore so are their resident species. Fluctuations in density of grassland bird species and vegetation characteristics are numerous and normal. Thus, as one research team wrote, "The shifting pattern of occupancy of grassland birds can be best understood as movements into and out of areas as suitability changes." Grassland areas that show large dips and peaks in numbers of birds with no other environmental changes usually prove less desirable as habitats for the species in question; the peaks in such cases are often overflow populations from more suitable grassland habitats.

Apart from inherent instability resulting from the habitat, however, the age of cultivation, on any large scale, is largely bygone in the Northeast; much former farmland has reverted to forest, and much also lies in ever-widening suburban tracts and industrial parks. Most of the shrinking agricultural acreage that remains is factoried rather than farmed—so intensively planted, sprayed, mowed, and harvested, all by machine and finely calculated grain to the inch, that the landscape more resembles a chemically driven assembly line than a coaxed pattern of seasonal growth. Crops, like chickens, are no longer free-range.

Organized responses to losses of our avifauna begin mostly as fervent dithering—the first, usually lengthiest phase of conservation action. This is the phase we writers handle best—alarmism, critiques

of policy, dire forecasts, the skilled, breathless slant toward apocalypse. Not so long ago, theologians and preachers were our prime
ministers of apocalypse; biologists and science writers have now
supplanted them a hundredfold, often to equally negligible effect
among the populace at large.

Yet some of the sound and fury succeeds, often working to stir
motion. More active phases of grassland conservation are now pro-
gressing here and there. The increasingly popular nationwide land
trust and conservancy movement continues to set aside much
acreage from burdens of incessant human usage. Organizations such
as the National Wildlife Federation, the National Audubon Society,
the Nature Conservancy, the Conservation Reserve Program, and
many state efforts are at last not only deploring but restoring some
of our lost grassland legacy. It helps, too, that "prairie birds are
resilient," as one Illinois biologist pointed out. Species such as dickcissels, eastern meadowlarks, and bobolinks have proved adaptive
to breeding in a variety of restored open-land sites from the Midwest
to New England. Thus one remains hopeful that dickcissels may
again sing in New York State, meadowlarks may again pierce Con-
necticut mornings with their calls, and the whir of a dancing prairie-
chicken may once again become a familiar Illinois sound.

In the meantime, one watches and listens. Visibility conditions
for spotting birds of field and shore, barring snowstorm or deep fog,
are usually good, giving "a clear field for glassing," as birders say.
Hearing the tinkle of horned larks or bobolinks across a field, or the
concupiscent whoop of a prairie-chicken on its lek, is a pleasure of
uniquely American spring mornings. The presence of a snowy owl
just in from the Arctic, sitting solid as a snowbank, or a flock of nervous redpolls that are here today and gone tomorrow, can make a
birder's winter. Walking a beach can bring gulls and shorebirds out of
your binoculars into your life. On South Manitou Island, a speck in
Lake Michigan, I once walked the beach for hours, accompanied the
whole time by 2 least sandpipers that always moved 100 feet or so,
seldom farther, ahead of me. I like to think that I was being useful, a
commensal frightener and mover of potential prey for them. But
maybe, indeed, it was just a simple walk together of 2 different organisms—man and bird—on a beach of our lives. I like to think that too.

## PHEASANT FAMILY (Phasianidae), order Galliformes

This family (often called gamebirds) includes the pheasants, partridges, francolins, grouse, turkeys, and Old World quails—all ground-dwelling, chickenlike birds. Adding the prairie-chickens and ptarmigans (both grouse), North American native species number 11; some 176 species range worldwide. Genes of the red junglefowl *(Gallus gallus)* of Asia appear in many domestic breeds of chicken. Most gamebirds do not migrate and are incapable of sustained flight; their pectoral muscles (the white meat) can generate brief, powerful wingbursts but are easily fatigued. Many show spectacular plumages, the most notable being the peacock (male Indian peafowl, *Pavo cristatus*), an Asian pheasant. Various species also display wattles and inflatable neck sacs. Eggs hatch synchronously in most of the species, and the young are precocial, mobile soon after hatching.

PHEASANT FAMILY (Phasianidae)

---

### Ring-necked Pheasant *(Phasianus colchicus)*

Our familiar ring-necked pheasant is a subspecies *(P. c. torquatus)* of the common pheasant, a native of China. From head to long, pointed tail, it measures almost 3 feet long. The colorful male, with brown body feathers and iridescent head hues, also shows red eye patches and facial wattles, a white neck ring, and leg spurs. Females are mottled brown with somewhat shorter, pointed tails. Crowing males utter a loud, croaking, double squawk ("caw-CAWK"), somewhat resembling the horn of a Model T Ford, followed by a whir of flapping wings. The birds also voice other cackles and clucks.

*An Asian import, the ring-necked pheasant has become an important American gamebird. The colorful males vocalize conspicuously in spring.*

**Close relatives.** Numerous common pheasant subspecies include the green, Korean, Mongolian, black-necked, and Sichuan pheasants. No other *Phasianus* species exist.

**Behaviors.** Its large size and pointed tail immediately identify the pheasant as it struts and forages along country roadsides and hedgerows (only wild turkeys are larger gamebirds). A reluctant flier but silent hider and fast runner (up to 10 mph), it flushes only when a human hunter or other predator comes close. Its pectoral muscles ("white meat") and short, rounded wings enable short bursts of powerful flight, but these muscles are easily fatigued, making pheasants incapable of flying long or far.

Pheasants typically depart their roosting sites, sometimes located in trees but more often in dense, low cover, before sunrise. They forage in fields, rest and preen during midday in shady areas, feed again in the evening, then move back to roosting cover. They dust-bathe in fields or along roads, sometimes on the entrance mounds of woodchuck burrows, sometimes sheltering in such burrows from predator pursuit. Heavy rains or dew often concentrates the birds at field edges—they apparently try to avoid wet vegetation.

Pheasant breeding is *polygynous;* that is, a single male (the cock or rooster) claims a *harem* of females (hens) that feed on his territory. Up to 10 hens may be courted, defended, and bred by a cock, though many cocks mate with only 1 or 2 hens. During nonbreeding

*Field edge habitats frequently host pheasants, especially during rainstorms and in early morning.*

seasons, pheasants are highly social, usually grouped in unisexual flocks that exhibit strong dominance hierarchies.

Ring-necked pheasants range almost across the continent, with heaviest concentrations in the plains states, the upper Midwest, and New England. They are well adapted to cold and do not migrate.

*Spring.* Cocks become increasingly aggressive in early spring and soon disperse from the winter flocks. Often they move into a previous breeding territory of 3 to 9 acres, sometimes much more. Some researchers prefer the term *cruising routes* instead of *territories* for pheasants. As ornithologist Paul A. Johnsgard observed, little evidence exists for "well-defined male territories in this species," possibly accounting for "the great variety in the sizes of crowing territories as judged by various observers." Older, more dominant cocks usually claim the best habitat sites—that is, those offering optimal food and cover. Most cocks do not establish crowing territories until their second year. Yearling cocks (some 30 percent or more of the male population) are often nonterritorial floaters, moving freely through established pheasant territories, remaining unchallenged as long as they do not crow or display. Territorial males crow most vigorously just before sunrise; strut laterally in front of challenger cocks, swelling their wattles and erecting their plumage; or actively chase them. Sometimes the cocks fight, leaping into the air and pecking savagely; fights may last an hour but usually end with

*The cock pheasant's leg spur is probably a fighting tool, sometimes engaged during fierce territorial conflicts with other male pheasants.*

another strutting display in 15 minutes or so. Such skirmishes often occur when a cock follows his wandering harem into another cock's territory.

Small flocks of hens move into prime feeding areas in early spring and bond with the territorial cock by means of his courtship displays, which are similar to the territorial lateral strutting plus chasing and *tidbitting*—a "come-and-get-it" series of clucks from a cock pecking at a morsel. Harem hens are probably monogamous, tending to mate with the same cock in successive years. But fewer than 50 percent of cocks mate with more than 1 hen; the rest attract only a single mate or none at all. Peak mating occurs in May and June. After mating, the hens disperse to begin nesting. The cocks stop defending their territories, which may then be claimed by nearby cocks that are still courting and mating. A hen lays a complete clutch of eggs over a period of 10 to 20 days. As incubation begins, she deserts the harem society. Cocks usually go off on their own during female incubation, playing no further parental role. Hens may quickly desert the nest if disturbed during early incubation. After hatching, they may perform distraction displays if a predator approaches.

EGGS AND YOUNG: 10 to 12; eggs brownish olive; hens occasionally "dump" eggs in nests of other ground nesters such as ruffed grouse, northern bobwhites, mallards, and American woodcocks. INCUBATION: by hen; about 24 days; chicks leave the nest with the hen about an hour after hatching. FLEDGING: chicks can fly several feet when only a week old but continue to be brooded at night by the hen for 2 weeks or so.

*Summer.* Hens raise only a single brood each year, but persistent renesting may extend into August if early nests fail. Broods become fully independent in 12 to 14 weeks, dispersing to feed on their own. Pheasant feather molt begins in midsummer, extending into September or later.

*Fall.* After the breeding season, pheasants gather into mostly unisexual flocks. Hen flocks average 4 or 5 birds and are typically larger than male flocks, which may consist of only 2 birds. In October, the birds tend to move from the open feeding areas they have occupied all summer toward heavier cover—hedgerows, thickets, forest edges.

*Winter.* Flocks often increase in size during cold weather. Up to 30 or 40 birds may roost together, often in brushy or marshland cover, but flock membership appears highly unstable, with individual birds often shifting between groups. Periods of high wind and deep snow, when the birds cannot obtain sufficient food, may result in widespread die-offs. In February, the cocks begin to exhibit aggressive behaviors, manifesting the first signs of flock breakup and spring dispersal.

**Ecology.** The pheasant's typical habitats include open farmlands, old fields, and forest and marsh edges. Cocks favor patches of brushy cover, but many crowing territories consist solely of herb cover. Pheasants favor areas of moderate snowfall, neither hot nor cold climatic extremes. They are especially associated with the calcium-rich soils of the mid-American corn belt. Cultivated stands of grains, alfalfa, soybeans, and other row crops are prime feeding habitats, and stands of switchgrass (*Panicum virgatum*) provide favored food and cover in some areas. Pheasants favor hayfields for nesting habitat, but June mowing takes a heavy toll of birds and nests. A high proportion of successful nesting, wrote pheasant biologist Glenn Belyea, "comes from the relatively few nests in 'permanent' cover—old fields, grassy and shrubby fencerows, and marshes."

Polygynously mated hens often select nest sites just outside the cock's territorial bounds, sometimes in clustered groups of 2 to 8 nests. They scratch a shallow depression, thinly lining it with grasses and leaves.

Although primarily granivorous, pheasants are relatively omnivorous eaters. Chicks up to about 4 months old consume many more insects than do adult birds. This high-protein food includes grasshoppers, caterpillars, beetles, and ants. Corn is the staple food at all seasons in most areas. Soybeans and ragweed seeds plus wheat, oats, and other grains also rank high. Pheasants occasionally damage grain crops, but since most feeding occurs on the ground, they chiefly consume waste grain. Only 5 inches of snow cover may make waste grain unavailable to pheasants, however, so unharvested corn they can reach often becomes an important food resource. Fruit foods include blackberries, apples, wild grapes, elderberries, and wild cherries. Pheasants also need grit for digestion, and they visit sources of gravel, which often accounts for their presence on roadsides.

Competition with other species appears negligible, mainly consisting of brood parasitism. Pheasants not only parasitize other nests on occasion, as mentioned, but are themselves parasitized by dump-nesting chickens, ruffed grouse, northern bobwhites, and neighboring pheasant hens. One pheasant nest I saw contained 17 eggs, obviously a communal enterprise.

Like all ground-nesting birds, pheasants are highly vulnerable to predators, though regional predation figures differ widely. One study listed 14 mammals, 9 birds, and 2 reptiles as known predators. Red and gray foxes are major predators in some areas. Great horned owls, Cooper's and red-tailed hawks, and northern harriers also capture some pheasants. American crows, blue jays, common grackles, skunks, raccoons, weasels, and domestic cats are known nest raiders. Some studies indicate that habitat enhancement, rather than predator control as such, most effectively counters predation. The pheasant's major predator is humans—not only hunters, who take up to 20 million pheasants per year in North America, but also farmers who mow hayfields and burn fencerows during pheasant nesting. Common intestinal parasites include 7 species of the protozoan *Eimeria,* an organism that causes the disease coccidiosis in poultry and livestock.

**Focus.** Any unusual sound, especially in spring, often inspires pheasant cocks to crow. They also seem sensitive to other vibrations. In Japan, it is said, they provide useful early-warning alarms of impending earthquakes, apparently detecting the slight tremors that may precede a major movement. During World War I in England, pheasants became fairly reliable sentinels against zeppelin attacks, sensing far-off bomb explosions as the airships approached. The ring-necked subspecies, though Asian in origin, has become a naturalized resident in many countries around the globe. Ancient Greeks and Romans introduced it into Europe from the river Phasis (now Rion) east of the Black Sea. The Greek word *phasianos,* referring to this river, gives us the bird's genus name and the English name *pheasant.* California received the first ring-necked pheasant from Asia in 1857, and large numbers were introduced into Oregon's Willamette Valley in 1881. In the East, it was first successfully introduced in New Jersey in 1887—not from China but from England. More introductions established the bird in agricultural habitats across the country, except in the Southeast, where pheasants have never thrived. It was first hunted as an American gamebird in Oregon in 1892.

Pheasant hunting with shotguns and bird dogs developed into an American fall tradition replete with expert craft and lore. Some cocks became exceedingly wary and long-lived, refusing to flush when a hunter or dog approaches, testing a hunter's patience and skill. Pheasant populations in many areas, however, seem incapable of sustaining themselves for very long without regular reintroductions of pen-reared birds. Without continuous replacement by game-farm stock, some biologists believe, many ring-neck populations would soon die out. Game biologists once recommended the release of pen-reared hens in the spring in order to augment reproduction, but many now discourage the release of any pen-reared stock into wild pheasant populations. Seasoned hunters agree that periodic introductions of pen-reared pheasants into the wild have genetically corrupted pheasant populations and spoiled the sport of hunting them. Once released, these birds generally become easy prey for gunners and predators, and they show low reproduction and survival rates. Quick-fix pheasant restocking programs became a panacea for many state wildlife agencies and commercial game farms following widespread pheasant decline (of some 67 percent across the continent) from 1971 to 1986; long-term results of these efforts have proved unimpressive. Various reasons suggested for the continuing trend of pheasant decline include changing land-use patterns, high predation rates, and slow recovery after severe winter mortality. Agricultural practices that often destroy pheasant habitat include wetland drainage, shifts from small grain and forage crop cultivation to uniform row crops (corn and soybeans), and herbicide and pesticide use. Also, in the words of Pheasants Forever biologists, "When pheasants were first introduced, the landscape was far different from the one we have today. Farming techniques were primitive, field sizes smaller and crops more diversified. These habitat conditions created a situation ideally suited for the introduction of a farmland species like the ring-necked pheasant." The national organization Pheasants Forever, based in St. Paul, Minnesota, attempts to work closely with wildlife biologists in producing habitats that will result in self-sustaining pheasant populations (www.pheasantsforever.org).

During the past decade or so, gamebird experts, desperate for successes, have focused on importing other strains of common pheasants from Asia (for example the Strauch's or so-called Sichuan pheasant), subspecies they believed were better adapted to the brushy edge habitats that are gradually replacing many eastern and midwestern farmlands. Results of these efforts remain inconclusive to date. Viewing the hunter's dilemma from a scientific perspective, ecologist Richard Brewer wrote that "only the purist and the diehard would suggest that we might have been better off trying to manage our native grouse instead. In a landscape of row crops, the pheasant is better than nothing, perhaps better than we deserve."

Most ring-necks in the wild are short-lived; males average about 10 months, females about 20 (mortality from hunting probably unbalances the ratio to some extent).

South Dakota has chosen the nonnative ring-necked pheasant as its state bird.

PHEASANT FAMILY (Phasianidae)

# Sharp-tailed Grouse *(Tympanuchus phasianellus)*

Measuring about 18 inches long, the brown, speckled sharp-tailed grouse resembles the ruffed grouse in size but is slenderer. The central pair of tail feathers *(rectrices)* is elongated but flat-ended, not pointed as in pheasants. In flight, sharp-tails show conspicuous white under-parts and white-sided tails. On the slightly crested head, a yellowish, erectile comb forms a sort of eyebrow. Sexes look much alike except in spring, when males on their dancing grounds display a purplish, inflatable air sac on each side of the neck. The long central tail feathers of males show linear patterns, whereas hen rectrices exhibit cross-barring. As in many grouse, the legs are feathered down to the toes.

**Close relatives.** Greater and lesser prairie-chickens (*T. cupido* and *T. pallidicinctus,* also called pinnated grouse) are the only other *Tympanuchus* species. These, with the sharp-tail, are often termed prairie grouse. Sharp-tails and greater prairie-chickens (see next account) sometimes interbreed where both species are present.

**Behaviors.** This is one of several grouse species in which male courtship rites occur in the context of a communal dancing ground, or *lek.* The prairie grouse lek is a slightly elevated, grassy area where several males gather and periodically launch into spectacular, ritualized dance movements. Hens walk among the dancers or at the lek edge, seeming to ignore the frenetic activity around them. The lek, however, also serves a much wider function. It provides the major, year-round focal point of sharp-tail existence. Males center their movements and activities around it, and hens usually nest fairly near it. Other so-called lek or "arena" grouse of North America include the prairie-chickens and the sage grouse of the West. As in most grouse species, sharp-tail males are polygamous, form no pair bonds, and perform no parental functions after mating with one or more hens. Sharp-tails reside in sex-segregated flocks for much of the year.

Today the largest sharp-tailed grouse populations reside on the prairie grassland and open brushland of the northern Great Plains. Shifting local populations, however, extend from Alaska eastward to the upper Great Lakes and Quebec. Some evidence suggests that at least partial migrations or emigrations historically occurred—though not necessarily in north-south directions—when most or all of the original range was occupied.

*Spring.* The lek, or arena, is an open but highly compartmentalized piece of ground, a magnet that attracts both old and young sharp-tails. Its size depends on the number of birds using it. Typically 8 to 12 performing males dance on an often snow-covered space

*Sharp-tailed grouse, once among the most abundant of North American gamebirds, remain highly dependent on human land practices for survival.*

50 to 75 feet in diameter. Beginning about mid-March, the birds gather from about dawn to an hour or so after sunrise. Dominant or older males claim the most central positions; younger males occupy peripheral areas. Since hens are most attracted to the central males, a male's position on the lek generally determines his degree of mating success. Thus relatively few males actually mate; a single dominant male in a lek may, in fact, mate with most of the hens and sire most of the chicks. Hens, usually 2 or 3 (but occasionally a dozen or more) per lek, typically approach after males start to dance in the morning, and they depart the lek before the males do. The hens cackle as they approach, a sound that seems to stir display and activity among the gathered males. Early in the season, hens often remain on the outskirts of the lek; then, as activity peaks, they walk among the dancing males, choose and copulate with a dominant male—usually before or at sunrise, and usually only once—then leave. Occasionally a hen will also dance in the lek.

Male dances and other rituals and motions serve as both territorial and courtship displays. The dance, a series of rapid stepping movements (about 18 per second), is performed with the tail cocked erect, wings outstretched, head bowed, and purple neck sacs exposed. The feet stomp in a blur of movement as the birds move in arcs "like the little wind-up toys sold by street vendors," as one observer wrote. The birds vibrate their tails laterally as they move, causing a rattling noise; together with the pattering feet, these movements produce the characteristic buzzing sounds heard on a lek. The males also utter weak, low-pitched, cooing sounds. Flutter-jumping, another display, consists of a short leap into the air and a flight of several feet, often performed as hens approach the lek ("like popcorn on a hot skillet," one observer wrote), followed by several loud, high-pitched call notes. The gobble note—"lock-a-lock"—apparently functions as a territorial warning. Sounds and movements on the lek seem highly synchronous, with males often starting and stopping their displays simultaneously. Flutter-jumping and dancing by a single bird cues similar actions in others. Thus the lek functions not only as a territorial breeding ground for individual grouse but also as an arena for highly social behaviors. Males show strong site fidelity to their leks, often returning to them in the fall and in subsequent years.

Hens make nest scrapes in or near brushy or woody cover before they mate. After copulation on the lek, they usually do not return to it unless nesting failure elicits renesting behavior. Peak nesting occurs in May and early June.

---

EGGS AND YOUNG: average of 12; eggs light brown, speckled. INCUBATION: by hen; about 24 days. FLEDGING: about 10 days.

---

*Summer.* Most sharp-tail hatching occurs about mid-June. The hen leads the mobile chicks away from the nest soon after hatching, usually to areas of fairly heavy cover, then to more open habitats as the chicks age. Broods remain with the females for 6 to 8 weeks, foraging in areas 100 acres or more in size, then gradually disperse. Adult males, in the meantime, wander solitarily or in small, loose flocks within a mile or so of the lek, foraging and resting in thickets and brushy cover.

The annual molt occurs in July and August. Juveniles molt into adult plumage except for the 2 outermost wing primaries (#9 and #10) and their coverts. These feathers remain until the next summer's molt, often becoming faded and worn by that time but providing a useful age indicator. This delayed primary molt occurs in all grouse and ptarmigan species.

Home range sizes in spring and summer average 200 acres or so, then expand in fall and winter to 1,000 acres or more as food resources become scarcer. *Fall.* Sharp-tails gather, often in at least partially sex-segregated flocks or coveys, in late September and October. This is a period of habitat shift from open land to adjacent, relatively brushy areas. Broods and small flocks may join together in groups or *packs* of 40 or 50 up to several hundred grouse, an activity called *fall packing;* prairie grouse range is so fragmented today, however, that large packs seldom assemble anymore. More typically today, several broods merge into a group of about 20 birds, a flock that may increase in size during winter as wandering birds join. Adult males return to the lek in the fall and resume dancing. At least some of the juvenile males join them, establishing lek territories peripheral to the central domains of the older males. In later fall and early winter, many younger males abandon the lek and rejoin female flocks or wander by themselves.

*Winter.* Small flocks of adult male sharp-tails often remain in woody cover near the lek vicinity through most of the winter. Larger flocks consisting of adult and immature hens plus a few immature males appear more mobile, typically ranging up to 5 miles from the lek. Like ruffed grouse, sharp-tails often roost in deep, powdery snow, but unlike ruffed grouse, which usually plunge quickly into such shelter, sharp-tails walk to the site and tunnel into the snow horizontally for several feet, forming a roosting chamber. During extremely cold or stormy weather, they may emerge for an hour or so to feed, then rebury themselves. Unless startled into flight, they usually emerge by walking from the chamber. Flocks begin to disperse as spring approaches, and the birds return as individuals to the same lek where the males established fall territories. The males now resume flocking and dancing. Females likewise return to the lek, attracted by male sounds and movements.

**Ecology.** One Alberta study found that sharp-tails exhibited definite preferences for specific plant communities at different times of day and year. They resided mainly in wooded cover and marsh growth during winter and late fall, the only time they frequently perched in trees. In spring and summer, they favored open areas in

*Sharp-tailed grouse leks often occupy open, slightly elevated areas of sparsely vegetated ground bordered by shrubby growth.*

early morning and evening, taller open cover at midday. Hens with broods usually selected more open cover than males and unmated hens. Semiopen grassland with 20 to 40 percent woody cover or brush is considered optimal sharp-tail habitat, as is 40 acres of open grassland surrounding the lek and bordered by shrub cover. Upland grasses are usually the dominant vegetation of sharp-tail habitats; the entirely open portions of such habitats rarely extend much farther than a square mile. The birds favor clumped aspen growth and breaks in the continuity of height, density, and uniformity of ground cover, and also areas of exposed soil and rocks. As prairie grouse specialist G. A. Ammann wrote, sharp-tails "are found predominantly on surface soils of low inherent fertility. This is not necessarily by choice, but because most of the better soil areas have either been put into agricultural production, or were cleared . . . earlier and reverted to brush or forest cover at a faster rate than the poorer soil areas." Large, open leatherleaf bogs and muskegs also host sharp-tails in some areas. Brushy clearings and mixed groves of trees provide winter browse, protection, roosting areas, and brood-rearing habitat. Lek habitat often consists of a slight rise of ground, usually a half acre to 2 acres in size, in the most open part of the area. Nesting habitats vary widely, ranging from open land to relatively dense shrub stands.

Common plants in nesting habitats may include grasses, aspen, shad-bush, chokeberry, dewberry, and blueberry, among others. Brooding habitat usually consists of somewhat denser cover than nesting habitat but is mainly herbaceous. Recently burned, even still-smoking, areas sometimes attract foraging sharp-tails.

Sharp-tails usually nest directly beneath some sort of overhead cover—a shrub, tree, tuft of grass, or log—or within 10 feet of such cover. The hen scrapes a slight hollow and lines it sparsely with grasses and dry leaves. Most nests lie within a half mile of the lek.

An important element of sharp-tail habitat is food availability. Sharptails "are great browsers," as ornithologist John K. Terres wrote. About 90 percent of the diet consists of plant materials—seeds, buds, foliage, and fruits. The barren appearance of much sharp-tail habitat is deceptive, for many important food plants grow in these sites. In spring and summer, the birds feed heavily on grass blades; leaves of sheep-sorrel, hawkweeds, and clovers; and flowers of dandelions and buttercups. About 10 percent of summer food consists of insects, mainly grasshoppers. Dandelion seeds and leaves also rank as frequent foods. Summer and fall fruits include blueberry, blackberry, dewberry, choke-cherry, pin cherry, and black cherry. Winter staples include buds and catkins of white birch and quaking aspen plus fruits of mountain-ash, sumacs, poison-ivy, hawthorns, roses, and choke-berry. Corn and other grains are also consumed where available.

Sharp-tail competitors include the closely related greater prairie-chicken, which frequents somewhat more open habitats and feeds more consistently on grains. Where both species occur, they may occupy the same leks, and they frequently hybridize. Sharp-tails tend to displace prairie-chickens, possibly reflecting the sharp-tail's greater adaptability to advancing stages of plant succession. As researcher Paul A. Johnsgard noted, both species probably evolved in separate geographical locations from a forest-dwelling ancestor—the prairie-chicken in more eastern and southern oak and savanna habitats, the sharp-tail in more western and northern grassland and forest edges. "There was probably little contact between these two forms until fairly recently," wrote Johnsgard, "when human activities greatly altered the habitats of both species." (An analogous situation occurred in waterfowl with the mallard and black duck; see *Birds of Lake, Pond and Marsh.*) The normal progression of plant succession in eastern North America is the bane of the prairie grouse; fire suppression, reforestation, and anything else that eliminates grassland habitats wipe them out. Thus human land use as well as lack of it both compete with prairie grouse. In some areas, the forester's tendency to view all untreed ground as wasteland pretty well shuts out all possibility of sharp-tail and prairie-chicken existence.

Sharp-tail predators include other birds, mainly raptors such as great horned and snowy owls; Cooper's, red-tailed, and rough-legged hawks; and northern harriers. Coyotes, red foxes, minks, weasels, and house cats are also common predators. Many stealth attacks and kills occur on leks, where the birds are grouped and preoccupied.

**Focus.** Historically, sharp-tailed grouse distribution has expanded and declined throughout the continent, reflecting habitat changes caused by human settlement patterns. Before European establishment on this continent, the bird probably occupied prairie grasslands, as today, and fire-cleared patches in forest vegetation. Thus in the East, sharp-tailed grouse were always temporary residents after fires or logging, their occupancy corresponding to the early stages of plant succession, whereas farther west, permanent grassland habitat enabled them to thrive without radical shifts in distribution.

Throughout much of its range, sharp-tailed grouse distribution remains unstable, reflecting changing habitat conditions. These changes are wrought either deliberately—as in reforestation or controlled burning programs—or as a result of natural plant succession and wildfire, among other environmental events. In relatively few other bird species is habitat dependence so starkly evident. Maintenance of sharp-tail habitats now depends mostly upon human intervention. That prairie grouse still exist at all in north-central North America probably owes mainly to the lumbering and consequent fire history of this region. The birds invaded the extensive tracts cleared by human activities and thrived in the openings and grassland habitats that remained for decades in many areas. Conversely, as reforestation and natural plant succession re-cover many of these formerly stripped lands, the prairie grouse disappear.

Fire was probably the chief influence on historic sharp-tail distribution, even as it is today in many areas. Periodic fire re-creates habitat by interrupting plant succession, reverting it to earlier stages. Fire also releases nutrients that often stimulate a rapid flush of new, nourishing growth, such as smartweeds, ragweeds, sedges, and grasses, on the burned ground. "The best wax for the Sharptail's dance floor," biologist Russell McKee wrote, "is annual fast-moving, shallow-depth wildfires that keep the brush down and the grass dense." Wildlife managers attempting to maintain sharp-tail populations advocate burning once every 5 to 7 years, always in spring before nesting commences.

One population study estimated that a minimum spring number of 280 sharp-tails is necessary for maintaining genetic diversity in an isolated population—as most sharp-tail populations are today, owing to habitat fragmentation. Maintenance of long-distance habitat corridors has been suggested as a way of providing population interchange and diversity.

Human and bird rituals often conjoin in tribal cultures. Today in the Colville Reservation of Washington State, the ages-old communal chicken, or bustle, dance still mimics the lek performances of sharp-tailed grouse, which enjoy protected habitats and high status and abundance on the tribal lands. Sharp-tails became an important food resource for pioneers crossing the plains during the nineteenth century. Stories abound of flocks of thousands attracted to midwestern granaries and hunted from creek bottoms. Today sharp-tail populations east of the Great Plains are declining where not entirely extirpated, owing mainly to state and provincial programs of reforestation. (Some biologists question whether sharp-tails were historically native to these areas at all.) Biologists know how to restore and maintain prairie grouse populations, so their extirpation comes usually as the result of deliberate if unstated policy. Grouse management programs in Michigan, for example—where sharp-tails continue to be hunted despite their special-concern status—conflict with management programs for white-tailed deer, the state's "priority" game species. At the same time, other game biologists are trying to find ways to control the overpopulation of deer in the state. Such conflicted policy aims reveal the kind of guardianship to which we have often entrusted our wildlife resources.

In the Dakotas, Montana, and Canada's prairie provinces, however, large sharp-tail populations still thrive. Winter food-patch planting (corn, buckwheat, clovers) is an important management tool for this species, but one noted researcher, F. N. Hamerstrom, Jr., suggested that many of the food-patch benefits for prairie grouse come largely in summer and are derivative rather than direct. "The exact crop to be grown," he wrote, "is less important than the fact of breaking the sod and stirring the soil," thereby increasing the growth of weedy browse and the presence of insects that accompany cultivation. A half-acre food patch, he claimed, will provide summer food for young grouse over several years after cultivation ceases.

Data suggest that cyclical highs and lows of sharp-tail populations occur in 30- and 10-year cycles that seem to correlate with trends in ruffed grouse and greater prairie-chicken populations. Six sharp-tail subspecies, residing in habitats marked by varying quantities of brushy vegetation, range west from the Great Lakes across the continent. The easternmost subspecies is known as the prairie sharp-tail *(T. p. campestris).*

Extreme longevity for a sharp-tail is 7 years; average survival is about 18 months, though two- and four-year-old birds are not uncommon.

PHEASANT FAMILY (Phasianidae)

# Greater Prairie-Chicken *(Tympanuchus cupido)*

Unlike the sharp-tailed grouse, its close relative the prairie-chicken has a rounded tail, black in males, brown-barred in females. Greater prairie-chickens, about 18 inches long, are brown birds marked by heavy barring on breast, back, and wings. Crown and tail feathers are unbarred in males, cross-barred in hens. Males erect blackish, earlike *pennae* (neck feathers) and inflate orange *tympani* (neck sacs) and flashy orange "eyebrows" during courtship. They also voice resonant, 3-syllable "oo-loo-woo" notes (called *booming).*

**Close relatives.** The lesser prairie-chicken *(T. pallidicinctus),* even rarer than the greater, occupies western short-grass prairie habitats. Both greater and lesser prairie-chickens are also called pinnated grouse. An extinct (since 1932) northeastern subspecies of the greater was the heath hen *(T. c. cupido);* Attwater's prairie-chicken *(T. c. attwateri),* a small Texas subspecies, remains endangered. Sharp-tailed grouse *(T. phasianellus;* see previous account) sometimes hybridize with greater prairie-chickens. Both prairie-chickens and sharp-tails are called prairie grouse; no other *Tympanuchus* grouse species exist.

**Behaviors.** Lek territories, displays, and mating activities are the same as for the sharp-tailed grouse. As in that species, hens visit the leks in small groups, mate once with a dominant male, then leave the lek. When hens are present on the lek, a high degree of excitement prevails—males leap, cackle, strut, boom, stamp their feet, click their tails. Male booming, produced by the syrinx in the throat and amplified by the esophageal tympani, is louder than the sharp-tail's and can be heard 2 miles away on a quiet day. I associate the unique sound with crisp dawns on the Illinois prairie, where I once censused prairie-chickens; ears always led eyes in locating an active lek. Prairie-chickens in flight alternate flapping and sailing, a useful means of identification.

*Spring.* Males may appear on leks as early as January in some areas, but peak booming occurs in April, when most copulations also occur. Hens usually approach the lek singly. As in sharp-tailed grouse, the lek is the only territorial locale, and the oldest, dominant males occupy the central spots. "Theoretically, the territorial system should prevent conflict and make for uninterrupted copulations," wrote researcher Frances J. Hamerstrom, "but over and over again, the immediate vicinity of a seductive hen became a jumble like the pile-up on a football field." Large numbers of competing males on a lek generally result in a decrease of reproduction as aggressive birds interrupt each other's copulations. Some studies suggest that such behaviors constitute a mechanism for population regulation. Wrote Hamerstrom, "The love life of the prairie hen lasts about five days each year," with copulation occurring only on the fifth day. After copulating with a dominant male on the lek, a female wanders away, begins nesting, and has no more contact with a male. Most nesting begins from mid-April to early June. Hens first breed in the year after hatching, but probably few males—though they are physiologically ready to breed—achieve sufficient social dominance in their lek until age two or older. Males remain site faithful to their leks through consecutive years; hens may range in more than one lek but are site faithful to their own areas, usually nesting within less than a half mile of the previous year's nest.

EGGS AND YOUNG: typically 11; eggs olive, finely brown spotted. INCUBATION: by hen; about 24 days. FLEDGING: chicks can fly weakly at about 2 weeks.

*Summer.* Hens often renest if the first nesting fails. Chicks leave the nest soon after hatching, feed themselves, and wander with the hen over several acres. The hen broods her young about half of each day for the first week, seldom brooding them after 2 weeks. As the chicks age, they tend to feed farther apart, occasionally becoming detached from the brood. They usually remain with the hen for about 80 days before their increasing independence results in brood breakup. The annual molt begins after the breeding season and continues through summer.

*Fall.* Following brood breakup in late summer or early fall, juveniles may form separate flocks, or several broods may merge to form larger flocks, or *packs.* Packing seems to result from "a 'snowballing' effect," wrote Hamerstrom; "young chickens stay near their mothers until about September, then these family units merge and are joined by miscellaneous cocks to make flocks of thirty or so. . . . Sometimes, but not every winter, the flocks merge and form *packs,"* consisting of 200 to 300 birds. This flocking and dispersal occur mainly in late September and early October. Some populations remain on or near the breeding area throughout the year, but others may travel randomly for distances of up to 20 or so miles. Hens seem more mobile than males, and many flocks become at least partially sex segregated.

*Greater prairie-chickens share the habitats of sharp-tailed grouse in some areas but rely much more heavily upon cultivated grains for food. Hens such as this one range more widely than males in fall and winter.*

Historically, when prairie-chicken flocks were larger and their ranges more contiguous, longer migrational movements may have occurred. Today their fall movements gravitate toward farmlands, harvested grainfields, and standing corn.

*Winter.* Home range size increases in winter as prairie-chickens range farther for feeding and roosting sites. Both sexes show site fidelity to wintering areas. The birds often roost 20 or 30 feet apart in dense herb vegetation or may bury themselves in deep snowdrifts. Sexes tend to segregate into separate flocks during winter; adult male flocks are the most sedentary, often remaining within a mile or two of the lek.

**Ecology.** Prairie-chicken habitat consists of grassland, specifically extensive areas of tall-grass prairie. The birds "can't stand to be fenced in by fencerow brush or roadside trees," one researcher wrote. One study concluded that a minimal area of about 4 square miles was required to maintain a prairie-chicken colony. In contrast to sharp-tailed grouse, prairie-chickens favor more open sites for leks and nesting and prefer even earlier stages of plant succession. Thus fire was and is an important ingredient of their habitat. "Smokey the Bear has perhaps been the worst enemy of the prairie-chicken," one researcher wrote. Lek habitats are usually slight rises of ground, neither densely vegetated nor entirely bare, typified by

*Dusting sites, bare patches of earth in fields or along roadsides, attract prairie grouse as well as many other grassland birds.*

"low, matted, or sparse vegetation where the footing and visibility are good," according to one report. "Some of the booming grounds [leks] which are in use today probably were used by this species . . . among the huge herds of buffalo that once roamed the Midwest," wrote ornithologist Dan Bowen; "now there are cattle sharing the prairie with these wild birds." For roosting, prairie-chickens favor dry spots in marsh and bog cover. Dusting sites, where the birds bathe their plumage in light, dry soil, may include roadsides, rotting logs, anthills, or mammal burrow mounds. Habitat changes wrought by agriculture have had major effects on this species, but the details are not so simple. For example, although creation of open land by fire or clearing may increase prairie-chicken populations, intensive cultivation of cropland tends to reduce them. The key apparently lies in the proportion of natural prairie to cropland—Iowa prairie-chickens thrived most abundantly during the prairie-cropland transition. About 30 percent cropland seems an optimal proportion. In Illinois, cultivation of redtop grass *(Agrostis)* for hay resulted in increased prairie-chicken populations.

Hen prairie-chickens usually choose nest sites in open-meadow areas where grass cover stands about 7 inches or more tall. The hen scrapes a slight depression in the ground, lining it sparsely with grass, feathers, and small twigs. Nest diameter is about 8 inches. Most nests are sited within a mile of the lek.

Prairie-chickens feed mainly during early morning and evening. Leaves, seeds, buds, cultivated grains, and insects are staple items. The birds graze a large variety of leaves including sedges, sheep-sorrel, knotweeds, clovers, goldenrods, and ragweeds. Dewberries, black cherries, and rose hips are common fruit foods. Historically, prairie-chickens apparently fed mainly on acorns during winter. Corn, oats, sorghum, and wheat gleaned from fields have become the main winter staples. Unlike sharp-tailed grouse, stated researcher G. A. Ammann, "prairie-chickens can't get along during the winter by 'budding' alone." Insects, mainly grasshoppers, are especially important in the chick diet. Fall movement into croplands is probably governed by food availability: "Until the first hard frost knocks down the grasshoppers," one observer wrote, the birds "have no reason to leave the grass." The birds also ingest gravel grit—about 7 percent of gizzard contents—which serves in place of teeth, grinding food items.

Competitive interactions sometimes occur on leks with sharp-tailed grouse, which often tend to dominate where both species are present. Since sharp-tails favor semishrubby habitats, advancing plant succession tends to favor their displacement of prairie-chickens. The species often hybridize, and first-generation hybrids, when back-crossed with a parent species, may reproduce. Ring-necked pheasants also compete and dominate at leks and feeding sites; they occasionally lay eggs in prairie-chicken nests.

Prairie-chicken predators include great horned, snowy, and short-eared owls; Cooper's, rough-legged, red-tailed, and broad-winged hawks; northern harriers; northern goshawks; and eagles. Badgers, red and gray foxes, coyotes, domestic cats, and weasels are frequent mammal predators. Kills on leks, though not uncommon, "are almost invariably cocks," wrote Ammann; given the high male sex ratio (about 1.5 males to 1 female), such mortality is relatively insignificant.

**Focus.** Studies have revealed that genetic diversity becomes reduced in isolated prairie-chicken populations, as now exist over much of the bird's present range. Introduction of outside birds to such leks and colonies helps increase the survival chances of the flock.

The heath hen subspecies became the focus of some of the earliest attempts at wildlife management in North America. Legislation passed in 1791 aimed at protecting the even then rapidly declining bird from market hunting. Loss of habitat plus *undercrowding*—the decline of numbers below an optimal density to maintain a viable population (as expressed in the ecological principle of the Allee effect)—resulted in the heath hen's extinction by 1932.

Dance was an important communal element of Great Plains tribal cultures. The foot-stamping displays of the prairie-chicken may still be seen in patterns of powwow movements.

Probably relatively few prairie-chickens survive beyond 3 years. Evidence indicates that differential longevity rates between sexes may occur, with hens living shorter lives despite lek predation on males.

# 2

## Northern Bobwhite *(Colinus virginianus)*

New World quail family (Odontophoridae), order Galliformes. The northern bobwhite, our only eastern quail, measures about 10 inches long. Both sexes are ruddy brown and short tailed, but males show a white throat and white brow line; in females, these patches are tannish. On juvenile birds, the two outer wing primary feathers are pointed, in contrast to blunt-tipped primaries on adults; juveniles also show a buffy fringe on the tips of the upper primary coverts (the small feathers that overlie the wing primary bases). Distinctive whistled calls (often imitated by starlings) include several 2- and 3-syllable notes. The unmated male's ringing "bob-*white!*" call, the second syllable slurring upward, is the most familiar.

**Close relatives.** Two other *Colinus* species, the black-throated bobwhite *(C. nigrogularis)* and the crested bobwhite *(C. cristatus)*, inhabit Mexico and Central America. The *Callipepla* quails (scaled quail [*C. squamata*], California quail [*C. californica*], and Gambel's quail [*C. gambelii*]) are the nearest living relatives to *Colinus*. Western and southwestern quails include the Montezuma quail *(Cyrtonyx montezumae)* and mountain quail *(Oreortyx pictus)*. Twenty-three other species in this family include the wood-partridges *(Dendrortyx)* and wood-quails *(Odontophorus)*. Old World quails belong to the pheasant family (Phasianidae).

**Behaviors.** "Nature's little chickens," as one writer called them, feed, nest, and roost on the ground. When flushed by a hunter or other predator, they typically scatter, flying only a short distance to cover. Bobwhites are social birds for most of the year. The dominant social unit is the *covey*, a group of 10 to 16 birds once described as "a sort of protection association." One determinant of covey size is the

*The bobwhite roosting circle, or disk, gathers the covey in nighttime protective formation. Assembled here are 3 males and 2 females.*

number of birds it takes to form a roosting circle at night. The birds bunch together, each facing outward and lifting its wings slightly, forming a tight, canopied circle, or "roosting disk," that preserves warmth. Fewer than 7 or 8 birds cannot retain sufficient warmth for a roosting circle; more than 16 may split to form 2 circles. Covey membership is flexible, consisting of mixed sexes and ages, both paired and unpaired birds, perhaps 2 or more family groups. Individuals may join from, or disperse to, nearby coveys, thus regulating covey size. The covey moves, feeds, and rests together throughout the day. It typically forages twice a day, in early morning and late afternoon until dark. The rest of the day is spent loafing in cover, dust bathing, and preening. If an intruder scatters the birds, they reunite by voicing the covey, or separation, call, a loud, whistled "koi-lee." In addition to the calls mentioned, bobwhites have a rich vocal repertoire—some 22 distinct calls signifying alarm, courtship, and aggression. All are uttered in either the covey or breeding context, some in both.

Bobwhites do not migrate, and both individual and covey movements are fairly restricted. With the largest distribution of all quails, they reside from southern New England and the southern Great Lakes west to South Dakota, Colorado, and Texas and south to

*The male bobwhite's covey call brings scattered members of the group back together. Note the bird's large feet, indicative of its ground-scratching feeding habits.*

Guatemala. Northern limits of the breeding range vary with yearly weather fluctuations.

*Spring.* In late winter or early spring, paired birds begin to leave the covey, which soon disintegrates as leftover unmated males also separate. Paired males, which only occasionally call, establish a territory of about 1 acre, on which mating, nesting, and feeding occur. Single males often form territories adjacent to those of mated pairs, calling loudly and often. Male defense against an intruding male consists of a crouching, head-on display with feathers fluffed and tail spread, usually preceding a chase or actual combat. A common behavior between a mated pair is *tidbitting,* or mate-feeding, in which the male picks up a food morsel and utters a soft, rapid "tu-tu" call; the female then takes the food from his bill.

Both sexes build the nest, usually only a scraped depression lined with grasses or weed stems and canopied with woven grasses. The birds may begin and abandon one or more nests in various sites before completing a nest. A bobwhite flushed off its nest by an intruder often performs a distraction display, fluttering and dragging its wings along the ground.

EGGS AND YOUNG: 12 to 16; eggs white. INCUBATION: mainly by female; lasts about 23 days after last egg is laid; hatching synchronous; precocial young. FLEDGING: young birds follow parents from the nest within an hour or so of hatching; parent birds brood the young on the ground for a week or more; young bobwhites can fly in 2 weeks or less.

*Summer.* Bobwhites raise only a single brood but typically renest in summer if predators interrupt the nesting cycle. Juvenile bobwhites remain feeding and roosting in family groups; unmated adult males continue their "bob-*white*" calls into midsummer. Males outnumber females in most bobwhite populations, a gender surplus that provides ready replacement of mated males that die. Calling and territorial behaviors decrease toward late summer.

*Fall.* As bobwhites move to prime feeding areas in the fall, several family groups plus single adults often join to form shifting groups of 30 or more birds—the largest groupings of the year, since weather and predators invariably reduce individual numbers as the season advances. Most bobwhites move only a half mile or so from their breeding sites, but some may travel up to 10 miles. This *fall shuffle* disperses the birds fairly evenly, resulting in the formation of coveys, each of which may occupy an undefended range of several acres up to 30 or 40, depending on food abundance. About 80 percent of the fall population in most areas consists of juvenile birds. By November, the winter coveys are fairly stabilized in both membership and locale. As biologist Walter Rosene wrote, "A covey picks an area that has a food supply and the right kind of ground covering so seeds can be found. . . . A covey will not pick as its winter range a place where all the ground has a thick covering." The birds complete their annual molt of all feathers in October or November.

*Winter.* This season of foremost stress on bobwhites especially affects populations in the northern fringe portions of their range, where their numbers fluctuate widely from year to year. Severe winters can cause local or regional bobwhite populations north of latitude 40 degrees N to suffer radical drops or even total extirpation. Such were 2 winters in the 1970s and 2 in the 1990s, which virtually wiped out bobwhites in many northeastern areas. After such harsh winters, recovery of bobwhite populations may require a series of subsequent mild winters. This quail is the "northern" bobwhite only by virtue of contrast to the distribution of other quail species—it is not and never was well adapted to heavy snows and severe cold. Yet "the coming of winter holds no fear for bobwhites," Rosene observed, "as most of them go through just one winter," and he presumed that "old birds do not remember experiences of the past one." In late winter, as coveys begin to break up, the birds undergo a partial molt of head and neck feathers that continues into spring.

**Ecology.** Bobwhites favor 3 general types of habitat: grassland, cropland, and brushy areas or woodland. Grasslands are the major spring and summer habitat; croplands are frequented for feeding and dusting areas in summer; and brushy areas and woodlands provide food and cover during fall and winter, as well as escape and roosting cover throughout the year. Dew or surface water is an important habitat need, as are dusting sites on roadsides or field edges. One of my teachers, Thane S. Robinson, established the concept of a brushy "headquarters," such as a fencerow, for bobwhite coveys as a vital habitat factor, a center from which the covey emerges to feed and to which it returns to loaf in midday and roost at night. Sign of a quail roosting headquarters consists of 5 or more roughly circular piles of droppings. The birds prefer protected southern slopes or exposures for headquarter sites, and shifts in their locale often seem associated with wind direction and velocity.

In nesting areas, bobwhites favor open, thinly spaced grassy or weedy cover. Bobwhites like to keep their feet on bare ground, tending to avoid heavy ground litter, or duff. Sparse ground-level vegetation, enabling quick, easy movement, marks optimal bobwhite habitat. Bobwhites usually site their nests within 50 feet of roadways, paths, or other open areas, often beside or near clumps of dead grass from the previous summer.

Owing to their popularity as gamebirds, bobwhites' dietary needs "have received more study than [those of] any other wild bird in America," according to one well-known plant food study. Bobwhites secure all their food from an 8-inch stratum of ground level and above. Major food items at all seasons in the Northeast include seeds of ragweeds, corn, smartweeds, foxtail grasses, wheat, bush-clovers, and other legumes. The birds also consume a large diversity of other seeds; they glean waste grains from the ground, thus do not threaten the farmer. Their spring and summer diet shifts to about 30 percent insects, of which beetles make up almost half. Grasshoppers, crickets, caterpillars, spiders, and snails are also common items. In early spring, before insect hatches occur and new seed crops ripen,

food is scarcest for bobwhites. During this period, they often consume green sprouts plus early-setting seeds such as wild geranium
and some panic-grasses. But "snow over three inches deep," wrote
Rosene, "makes seed on the ground unavailable." Then "quail must
depend on seed which has not yet fallen and which they can reach,
or seeds which fall on top of the snow." Feeding habits of other creatures sometimes increase food availability for bobwhites. Blue jays,
for example, sometimes drop acorn fragments from the tops of oaks,
and livestock in fields also dislodges many seeds.

Competitors for food include many seed-eating birds and small
mammals. Probably most habitats that host bobwhites bear enough
seed for all except in winter and early spring, when supplies become
short or less accessible. Eastern or western meadowlarks, which
bear some physical and behavioral resemblances to bobwhites,
often reside in the same habitats (see Eastern Meadowlark).

Bobwhite predators include Cooper's and sharp-shinned hawks,
northern harriers, and great horned and barred owls. Blue jays,
American crows, and wild turkeys sometimes raid bobwhite nests, as
do snakes, red and gray foxes, skunks, opossums, raccoons, weasels,
and domestic cats. Brood parasites—birds that sometimes deposit
their own eggs in bobwhite nests—include chickens, ring-necked
pheasants, and other bobwhite females. The parasitized female usually incubates the added eggs along with her own.

**Focus.** Land clearing and agriculture have benefited the bobwhite, especially in the Southeast, its foremost breeding range.
"Good quail habitat undergoes constant disturbance," according to
one game biologist, "either from farming, grazing, burning, or disk-
ing. The biggest challenge . . . is controlling plant succession." Before
the forests fell, the birds probably existed quite sparsely, residing
mainly along the forest and prairie edges of the West and Midwest.
Indians apparently made only occasional use of bobwhites for food,
probably because of their small size. As bobwhite populations
increased along with new human-created habitats, many colonists
and pioneers trapped them for food, but they were seldom hunted
until the breech-loading shotgun was invented about 1860. Yet bobwhite abundance remained fairly stable until 1940, when shifting

land-use patterns began to alter grassland and cropland habitats. Population trends in the North since 1940 have been downward. The elimination of hedgerows between fields has perhaps increased the stressful effects of harsh winters, thinning out bobwhite populations where they had formerly thrived year-round. Some question also exists about the birds' genetic fitness in certain areas: How many bobwhites on the difficult northern range stem from wild bird stock as opposed to releases of pen-raised bobwhites by hunters and other breeders? In the South, however, this quail remains prolific, the "ideal gamebird" and the favorite excuse of hunters everywhere for a day's outing with prized shotguns and dogs. In the northern range, where winter weather may cause sudden radical declines, quail-hunting seasons are much more sporadic and controversial. Game biologists generally consider quail numerous enough to hunt when censusers hear about 10 bobwhite calls on a 20-stop route.

Relatively few bobwhites survive long enough to breed more than once; average longevity is less than a year, though records exist of bobwhites surviving 7 or 8 years.

# 3

## TYPICAL OWL FAMILY (Strigidae), order Strigiformes

Owls and hawks are collectively called *raptors* because of their grasping talons. Three major owl adaptations—in vision, hearing, and flight—characterize the success of these birds as avian predators.

Frontal eye placement gives owls binocular vision. At night, their pupils dilate hugely, each eye independently; in daylight, the pupils contract in size, though day vision remains acute. Numerous light-receptor rod cells in the retina can detect any glimmer, and a chemical known as visual purple, contained in all bird and mammal eyes, further amplifies and resolves the image. The reflective *tapetum lucidum,* essentially a mirror that increases light intensity in the eye, gives the yellow iris of many owls a reddish eye shine when caught in headlights at night. Owls lack color vision; their world consists of gray and white shades. Since their eyes are fixed like headlights, owls must rotate their heads to see in different directions. Most owls can rotate their heads three-quarters of a turn, and they often bob, sway, and yo-yo their heads when triangulating their gaze on an object.

The owl's hearing apparatus enables some owl species to pinpoint sound sources even in total darkness. Oblong ear slits beneath the skull feathers are lopsided, the right one slightly higher than the left, enabling precise triangulation. Also aiding sound pickup is the facial disk, the concave mask of short, stiff feathers that widely circles the eyes in most owls. This parabolic reflector probably enhances and channels sound into the ears. Despite the owl's hearing acuity, however, its range of hearing is not wide; it has deaf spots and cannot hear sounds below about 70 cycles per second. Ear tufts, or horns, occur only in nocturnal, forest-dwelling owls. Ear tufts have no hearing function; they probably aid in camouflage when the owl is perched.

Having seen or heard its prey, an owl must approach it stealthily. Modifications for dampening sound in flight can be seen on owl wing feathers. Leading edges of the outer primaries have a fringe with comblike projections, trailing edges are soft and elongated, and the feather surface consists of a velvetlike pile. This soundproofing reduces air turbulence over the wing as the bird flies. Calling in an owl at night can be an eerie experience; the bird approaches phantomlike, unheard—suddenly it is just there.

Owls often snap their bills in a series of audible clicks when disturbed or alarmed. Owl sign on the ground beneath perches is fairly distinctive. Regurgitated pellets have characteristic features, and feeding debris—feathers and carcass fragments—often lies beneath roosting trees; splashes of "whitewash" occur beneath nesting trees, where owlets have voided over the nest rim.

Owls have carried a heavy symbolic load through history. Probably because most owls are birds of night, they have been considered omens of death and doom back to ancient Egypt and Rome. The "wise old" owl's reputation of intelligence, patience, and all-seeing awareness contrasts with the actualities of its relatively small brain, slowness to learn, and fiercely predatory instincts. Hatching of young is often asynchronous, and nestlings are altricial, remaining in the nest and requiring parental care for some time.

More than 120 typical owl species range worldwide; 10 breed in eastern North America. In addition to the snowy owl and short-eared owl, described here, others include the eastern screech-owl, great horned owl, barred owl, and saw-whet owl. (For eastern screech-owls and great horned owls, see *Birds of Forest, Yard, and Thicket*.)

---

TYPICAL OWL FAMILY (Strigidae)

---

## Snowy Owl (*Nyctea scandiaca*)

This large (2 feet long or more) arctic owl is all white except for variable dark barring. Its whiteness, large yellow eyes, and habit of perching in conspicuous open places during daytime make it virtually impossible to miss (except when backgrounded by snow). Its broad, rounded wings, 5-foot wingspan, and strong, direct flight are also characteristic. The ear tufts, or "horns," so conspicuous in several owl species, are much reduced, barely existing in snowies. Immatures and adult females show heavier barring than

*The female snowy owl, larger than the male, also shows much more black on its body.*

adult males; females, as in most raptors, are somewhat larger than males. Though they voice a number of ravenlike croaks plus hisses, screams, and booming hoots, these owls usually remain silent except during the breeding season.

**Close relatives.** The snowy owl is the only *Nyctea* species. Snowies are most closely related to the *Bubo* species, which include the great horned owl *(B. virginianus)* and, in Eurasia, the eagle owl *(B. bubo).*

**Behaviors.** Observers in the continental United States see this owl—one of the largest in North America—only in late fall and winter, when it may suddenly appear and remain in a given area for days or weeks. In contrast to most of its relatives, snowy owls are daytime hunters—as any predator in summer arctic regions must be. Their hunting strategy consists of scanning the open ground from an elevated perch, usually a hummock or ridge in the tundra, but when they migrate south, a fence post, telephone pole, or rooftop. They also hunt by coursing slowly, in jerky, swaying flight, across fields and tundra, flying 10 feet or so above the ground. On its territory, especially when owlets are present, the snowy, like most owls, can be vicious, striking an intruder repeatedly with sharp talons. Migrant snowy owls, however, often allow close approach by humans—perhaps because of their unfamiliarity with people. An adult snowy may breed only once every 4 or 5 years, a timing that many observers believe

*The dense feathers on the snowy owl's feet extend protection from cold over the bird's chief predatory weapons, its talons.*

may relate to food supply on the breeding range. Except when nesting and feeding owlets, snowies usually remain solitary. A dense layer of down overlaid by thick plumage that extends over their legs and talons provides insulation in the coldest of weather, enabling the birds to maintain a body temperature of 100 degrees F or more.

Snowy owls inhabit circumpolar tundra regions. Many move southward in fall and winter, and larger-than-usual numbers appear in several-year cycles, or *irruptions,* supposedly reflecting the lemming abundance cycle in arctic Canada. Such irruptions do not occur on a continentwide scale, however; years of east-coast and west-coast highs may differ significantly.

*Spring.* Owing to this owl's remote habitats, many of its life history details still await discovery. One uncertainty involves the degree to which snowy owls return to their arctic homelands following seasons of far-southward movement. Some ornithologists believe that many of these migrants never return but remain wandering far south of their breeding range during the succeeding summer. Probably those that do return to (or remain on) the breeding range become nomadic, breeding only during years and at sites in which they find ample prey.

Monogamous only for a season, snowies pair on the breeding range from late April to mid-May, seldom before their second year of age. Males establish a territory from less than 1 to about 4 square miles in area and defend it vigorously; this is the only time of year when snowies habitually and loudly hoot. The male also performs display flights with deep, undulating wingbeats. On the ground, he spreads his wings and puffs out his plumage, dancing stiffly before his mate, often presenting her with a dead lemming. His deep, booming hoots, it is said, may be heard for several miles. These behaviors continue throughout the nesting period, possibly serving to reinforce the pair bond.

Females select the nest site and develop large, conspicuous brood patches—bare areas of belly skin that warm the eggs during incubation. Incubation begins with the laying of the first egg, and an egg is laid thereafter about every second day until the clutch is complete—a total period of 3 weeks or more if the clutch is large. As egg laying and incubation proceed, the female plumage becomes soiled, much grayer than the male's. Males, in the meantime, continue to hunt, often amassing a stockpile of dead lemmings around the nest.

EGGS AND YOUNG: 4 to 7 if food supply is limited, 11 or 12 if abundant; eggs white, elongated. INCUBATION: by female, which is fed at nest by male; 32 to 34 days for each egg; hatching asynchronous, typically 1 every 2 days. FEEDING OF YOUNG: primarily by male; mainly lemmings; owlets disperse from nest when each is about 2 weeks old. FLEDGING: 7 or 8 weeks.

*Summer.* Owlets develop white facial areas and black, downy body plumage. They grow rapidly on their rich lemming diet. In a large clutch, the first owlet hatched may have left the nest by the time the last one hatches. If food is in short supply, last-hatched owlets often starve to death. Apparent cannibalism of owlets also occurs, as a result of either famine or *siblicide,* when an older owlet kills and devours a younger. After the last owlet abandons the nest, the family group reconvenes and wanders, the owlets still being fed. Reported one owl researcher, "Dispersed young produce an ear-splitting squeal that can be heard a long way," enabling the male to keep track of the scattered brood; he often drops a fresh-killed lemming before each owlet.

Serial fledging of owlets (usually in August) is a laborious process, with each owlet springing from the ground, beating its wings furiously, falling back time and again before managing even short flights. If an intruder appears at this time, and if aggressive defense fails, parent birds may resort to piteous distraction displays, flailing on the ground, squawking and squealing. A flightless owlet in the hand stiffens as rigidly as the rocks of its habitat in a convincing "frozen corpse display." After fledging, young owls apparently remain together with parents for a time. "When and how the parent-offspring bond dissolves is not understood at all," stated owl biologist David F. Parmelee.

Adult snowies begin their annual molt in July, often while still nesting; the molt extends into early fall. Second-year owls, darker and more heavily barred than adult snowies, also achieve their first adult plumage at this time.

*Fall.* Snowy owl seasonal movements have been described as simultaneously nomadic, migratory, and irruptive. Most snowy owls apparently do migrate southward in the fall—occasionally as far as Georgia, Texas, and southern California. In the Great Lakes states, they have appeared as early as September 1, though October and November are more typical times. Yet our biological "handle" on this species remains far from definitive; information on the timing and regularity of their movements remains tentative, even contradictory. In Canada's prairie provinces and the Great Plains, where snowies appear regularly—though in varying numbers—each fall, observers have noted definite sex and age segregations. Immature males seem to travel farthest south, adult females remain farthest north, with adult males and immature females settling in areas between.

*Winter.* The snowy owl's winter range encompasses the arctic breeding range and as far southward as a snowy owl may appear—in other words, an indefinite area with no consistent boundaries. While a few snowies appear almost every year in some part of the continental United States, large numbers periodically invade southern Canada, the northern states, and the Great Plains region. The theory that such movements correspond with 4- or 5-year cyclical lows of arctic lemming populations, however, leaves much unexplained. Recent analyses of Christmas bird counts suggest that migrant numbers fluctuate irregularly and are not necessarily keyed to lemming population cycles. Also, no solid evidence exists that lemming populations bottom out synchronously over the vast arctic landscape. Local lemming abundance certainly shifts, however, at periodic intervals.

Many snowies establish and defend hunting territories in winter, some for months, and females to a greater extent than males. Some observers believe that pair formation may occur in winter, at least among Great Plains snowies. Pairs or small groups sometimes perch within several hundred feet of one another as the birds begin moving northward in February and March.

**Ecology.** Treeless tundra is the snowy owl's domain, and wherever it migrates or wanders in winter, this owl favors areas that duplicate that habitat as closely as possible—fields, prairies, marshes, almost any open area offering an unrestricted view and an abundance of rodent food. On the breeding range, snowies utilize habitual hunting perches, usually large boulders, rock outcrops, or bare knolls. In time, the owl's nitrogen-rich droppings at these perches provide sites for a diverse plant ecology, conspicuous patches of vegetation in the otherwise plant-scant landscape. One botanist on a 1962 expedition collected 36 plant species from these owl mounds, the most common ones being prickly saxifrage *(Saxifraga tricuspidata)* and a shield lichen *(Cetraria nivalis)*. The mounds also trap water and seeds, developing minioases and microhabitats of lush growth in the arctic desert.

Snowy owls usually select a slightly elevated site for nesting, often a bare-topped gravel bank, knoll, or ridge. Here the female scrapes out a shallow depression, left unlined or barely lined with mosses, lichens, or grass plucked from the immediate vicinity. The owls make no attempt to conceal the nest, which in time may become conspicuous as white feathers from the molting adults scatter around it.

On its North American breeding range, the snowy owl primarily consumes 2 species of lemmings: the varying or Greenland collared lemming *(Dicrostonyx groenlandicus)* and the brown lemming *(Lemmus trimucronatus)*. *Dicrostonyx* ranges farther north than *Lemmus.* These rodents, subject of almost as much mythology (namely their supposed mass-suicidal marches off cliff edges) as owls in the medieval age, do undergo swings in abundance, yet the concepts of a 3- to 4-year lemming cycle and a consequent irruptive schedule of snowy owls are now being seriously challenged by researchers as they look more closely at tundra ecology. Do lemming cycles really exist, or do these population highs and lows simply occur randomly? The vast tundra, concluded one 1985 Canadian research team, "would be more realistically viewed as a mosaic of patches varying in size, lemming abundance, and timing of fluctuations. Even the largest of these patches could not have acted as a source area for the irruptions recorded" in North America. The team suggested that fluctuations in weather, rather than tundrawide food abundance, provide a better explanation for snowy owl irruptions.

Even presuming that lemming cycles might simultaneously occur over vast areas (the largest such area claimed covers about 62,000 acres), peak lemming years in the high Arctic may differ from peak years in lower arctic latitudes. The owls, wrote Parmelee, seem "cognizant of the lemming situation long before" the spring snowmelt, spotting the lemmings as they poke their heads outside surface holes in the snow. The lemmings become most visible and accessible to predators just as snowmelt drives them from their mazes of snow tunnels. "For a brief time the land is crawling with wet, bedraggled lemmings," reported one observer. This occurs just as snowy owls begin to nest. An owl pair plus owlets must consume 2,000 or more lemmings per year. Each adult owl eats 3 to 5 or more lemmings daily. In wintering areas, where the owls' diet consists mainly of meadow voles and deer mice, each owl must capture 7 to 12 rodents per day—more than 300 per month—to meet its food requirements. When lemmings or other rodents are in short supply, snowy owls become opportunistic predators, feeding on mammals from shrew to rabbit size and on almost any bird smaller than a medium-size duck. Ptarmigans, goslings, and ducks (especially ducks wounded by hunters, as evidenced by the presence of lead shot in owl gizzards) become common prey when lemmings are scarce. As Parmelee stated, "Few birds are so sensitive to the abundance or scarcity of their food," and their primary choice of lemmings "doubtless buffers predation of other species in years of lemming abundance." A "lemming low" can have far-reaching ecological consequences in arctic habitats as the owls and other lemming predators seek replacement prey. Lemming abundance or scarcity also bears directly on snowy owl breeding density, egg clutch size, and owlet survival.

Competitors for lemming prey include jaegers, arctic foxes, wolves, and other predators. During most owl breeding seasons, lemmings swarm so abundantly on the tundra that probably little food competition exists. But snow cover and lemming lows can radically shift all sorts of equations.

Predation on snowy owls seems relatively uncommon. Jaegers and arctic foxes are probably the foremost nest robbers. In July, nesting passerine birds—especially snow buntings, Lapland longspurs, and water pipits—often mob snowy owls. Power lines, fences, and automobiles pose constant collision threats to these low-flying birds during their winter forays into settled areas.

**Focus.** Snowy owls provide some degree of rodent control during winter in agricultural fields. Owl perching and nesting sites also benefit other organisms. The copious plant growth of the owl mounds attracts lemmings seeking food, and mammal predators seek the rodents here. Here, too, Inuit trappers trap arctic foxes. Greater and lesser snow geese utilize the owl mounds for nesting. More surprising, snow geese and eider ducks often nest semicolonially near functional snowy owl nests, probably benefiting from owl defensive behaviors against arctic foxes and other predators. This commensal relationship between owls and waterfowl is especially intriguing, since snowies are known to attack and kill ducks and geese on occasion. The owls appear to ignore these near-nest tenants, however; apparently they prefer to hunt away from the nest.

The Inuit call the snowy owl *Ookpik.* Other names include arctic owl and ermine owl. Scraped snowy owl bones in Neolithic sites testify that these birds were historically valued as human food, and Inuit hunters still relish the meat. During irruptions, snowy owls sometimes land on ocean ships—"many have reached the British Isles as nonpaying passengers," wrote one observer.

The snowy owl longevity record in the wild is 9 years. A snowy that survives its first year has a good chance of living to breed at least once during its lifetime; probably few live long enough to breed more than twice.

Once a popular winter target, snowy owls by the thousands migrated southward to death by gunshot. Many owls ended as mounted trophies in local museums; today almost any hole-in-the-wall collection of stuffed creatures displays at least one reminder of this period in its snowy owl specimen. Today nobody really knows the size of the snowy owl population, either in North America or elsewhere. Owing to its nomadic existence based on a fluctuating food supply, even reasonable estimates and educated guesses may be far off the mark. Snowy owls are legally protected in all parts of Canada and the United States.

This owl became the official bird of Quebec province in 1988.

TYPICAL OWL FAMILY (Strigidae)

# Short-eared Owl *(Asio flammeus)*

This mottled, tawny brownish-streaked owl ("resembles dried grasses," said one observer) measures 13 to 17 inches long. Spread of its long, broad wings surpasses 3 feet. The upper wings exhibit large buffy patches in flight; a dark "wrist patch," similar to that of rough-legged hawks, shows on each underwing. Females usually look somewhat darker and are sometimes larger than males, which tend to have whitish undersides. Small, barely visible feather tufts rise from the center of the forehead above the whitish facial disk. Dark eye orbits mask the yellow eyes. Vocal sounds include a raspy, squeaking "kee-yow!" heard year-round.

**Close relatives.** Seven other *Asio* owl species reside in Africa and South America. The long-eared owl *(A. otus)* is the only other continental North American species.

**Behaviors.** This owl cruises low over the fields in buoyant, stiff-winged, bouncy flight (often described as moth-like), flapping then sailing with a slightly dihedral (V-shaped) wing profile. Active both day and night, but mainly at dawn and after sunset, short-eared owls hunt mainly on the wing, quarter-

*One of several ground owls, the short-eared owl shows no visible ears at all. The small feather tufts above its eyes are often not erected.*

ing less than 10 feet above ground or hovering higher, coursing over an area much like a northern harrier, a raptor with which it sometimes associates. When it spots prey on the ground, it quickly drops, seizing the prey in its talons. Short-ears also hunt from perches, usually fence posts. These raptors detect prey mainly by hearing, aided by vision. Short-ears also have well-developed capacities for smell, but the role of odor detection in hunting remains unknown. They swallow small mammals whole or first decapitate them. With bird prey, they usually first clip off the wings, sometimes decapitating the bird, but do not pluck the plumage. This owl, fairly social for a raptor, sometimes hunts communally where prey is abundant. Short-ears often roost together on the ground, usually in tufts of dense grass less than a foot high, during nonbreeding seasons.

Short-eared owls inhabit every continent except Australia and Antarctica. In North America, their breeding range extends discontinuously from arctic Alaska and Canada to the southern Great Lakes, Missouri, and central California. Maximum numbers dwell in south-central Saskatchewan. Disjunct populations, fluctuating with prey populations, also exist in coastal areas of the Northeast. In Europe, short-eared owls with a breeding range above latitude 50 degrees N migrate; those that breed below that latitude remain year-round.

*Spring.* Pairs are usually already bonded by late winter. Most northbound migrants travel in March and April, though some may linger on their winter territories into May. Pairs are probably only seasonally monogamous, though polygamy may also occur. A courting male performs elaborate sky dances over his territory, ascending in looping flight patterns up to 200 feet or more. He gives a series of tooting or "hoo-hoo-hoo-hoo" calls at the height of his ascent, then dives, clapping his wings below his body some 8 to 12 times. The female perches on the ground during this performance, occasionally uttering "kee-yow!" calls. Territorial skirmishes and threat displays involve rushing an intruder, wing clapping, bill snapping, and occasional talon grappling with another owl. Females usually breed in their first year.

Short-eared owl *philopatry,* fidelity to previous breeding sites, is apparently irregular—"perhaps not surprising for a species that depends on a fluctuating prey base," one research team wrote. Occasionally, however, a new nest is built atop the previous year's nest. Territory size also depends much on prey abundance, broadly ranging from 5 to 200 or more acres, probably averaging 125 acres or so. Some researchers consider this owl a colonial nester in areas of prey abundance and optimal habitat. Most nesting occurs from April to June, depending on latitude.

EGGS AND YOUNG: typically 5 to 7; eggs white, becoming nest stained. INCUBATION: by female, which is fed by male on nest; 3 to 4 weeks; asynchronous hatching over 1- to 2-day intervals. FEEDING OF YOUNG: by female, with food provided by male; mainly voles, other rodents, shrews, moles. FLEDGING: owlets wander off the nest when 12 to 18 days old, fledge in 31 to 36 days.

*Summer.* Incubating females are reluctant to leave the nest, but if flushed from it, they often defecate on the eggs; researchers suggest that the putrid odor may mask the nest odor or deflect a nosing predator. Female retrieval of an egg that has rolled out of a nest—rolling it back with her bill—has been observed, and female removal of both eggs and nestling owlets from abnormally high tides has been said to occur in coastal marshes. *Siblicide*—the killing of a nestling mate by a sibling—has not been observed, though it probably occurs, as in other raptors where asynchronous hatching results in different-size siblings. Owlet eating of dead nest mates has not been recorded.

How long the parents continue to feed owlets after they leave the nest remains unknown—probably for several weeks. Fledged owlets tend to remain together at daytime roosts, sometimes mingling with other owlet broods. Short-eared owls nest only once per year in most locales, though they presumably renest if the first nesting fails. A complete annual plumage molt begins in August and may last into November.

*Fall, Winter.* Winter migration occurs from the far-northern range but varies from year to year in numbers and distance traveled.

Movements labeled nomadism, migration, and juvenile dispersal seem not very distinct from one another in this species. In North America, southward movements occur from September through November; peak winter movements seem to occur about once every 4 years. Because short-ears depend so heavily upon rodent prey, they usually move as far as they must to find open areas with little or no snow cover and abundant vole and deer mouse populations. Northern-range owls may travel to the southern Great Lakes and New England and as far south as Central America and the West Indies. Site fidelity to previous winter home ranges appears to be more regular than breeding site fidelity. Winter is the social season for short-eared owls, which often associate in small groups at this season. Communal roosting is common, and communal hunting also occurs in abundant prey areas. Pair bonding and wing-clapping courtship displays usually begin in February.

**Ecology.** This is a raptor that frequents open country—grasslands, pastures, dunes, marshes, wet and dry prairie, tundra, open shrubland—in both summer and winter. If the northern harrier is a bird "ruled by a mouse," as one prominent researcher attested, so is the short-eared owl, for its habitats are the same as those of voles and lemmings (and harriers). In winter, when short-ears are most often seen around human habitations, they occupy large, fallow fields. Often they roost in *forms,* patchy clumps of grass marked by black, stringlike feces, egested pellets, and feathers. Young pine plantations are also common winter communal areas; usually the owls roost on the ground beneath the small trees.

One of the few owls that actually construct a nest, such as it is, the female short-ear sparsely lines its scrape in the ground with grasses and feather down. Often the nest is sited on a low elevation such as a small knoll or hummock, seldom in dense vegetation but often partly hidden in a grass clump.

Food items may include any small mammal, but about 80 percent or more of the diet consists of rodents. Success and survival of this owl species depend upon high rodent abundance. Voles are a staple prey (the owls consume 1 or 2 per day), as are lemmings, shrews, moles, and rabbits. The owls are opportunistic predators, also capturing and consuming a variety of nestling and adult birds (32 species in one Wisconsin study) including terns, gulls, shorebirds, and many passerines. Some stockpiling of prey at the nest may occur. Short-eared owl presence or absence in many localities probably reflects the cyclical or random patterns of vole and lemming abundance (see Snowy Owl). Short-ears also consume many insects, especially grasshoppers, June beetles, and cutworms.

Although short-eared owls, snowy owls, and northern harriers often occupy the same habitats and consume the same prey, competition among these raptors appears minimal. When it does occur, it usually consists of food piracy: The snowy owls and harriers chase the short-ears in flight, causing them to drop their prey. Barn owls, where present, may also compete with short-ears for food; in certain areas of New England, nest box programs for barn owls have coincided with short-eared owl decline. Short-eared owls are also well-known harassers and mobbers of other species. Black ducks, great blue herons, gulls, snowy owls, some of the larger hawks, plus crows, badgers, and foxes are common victims of short-ear mobbing. The owls at times become predators and disrupters of common tern colonies. They are in turn frequently mobbed and harassed by crows, gulls, and some smaller passerines.

Nest predators include herring gulls, jaegers, bald eagles, northern harriers, peregrine falcons, red-tailed hawks, great horned owls (which sometimes use short-eared owl feathers for nest lining), snowy owls, and common ravens; striped skunks, foxes, and dogs are frequent mammal predators. Occasionally a large hawk or snowy owl captures a short-ear in flight.

**Focus.** Short-eared owls appear to be declining throughout their North American range, especially in the Northeast. Seven states of this region now list them as endangered, threatened, or of special concern. Habitat loss due to conversion of open land to uniform cropland, recreational areas, housing developments, or forest is usually cited as the main reason for these declines. Yet much apparently suitable habitat throughout this owl's range goes unoccupied by the birds, which indicates that other factors—probably predation and prey scarcity—may also affect their distribution. The birds' nomadic habits and tendency to shift localities from year to year make it especially vulnerable to widespread habitat loss. Rodenticide applications on fields have killed many short-ears as a consequence of vole mortality. This bird's ecological role in controlling rodent irruptions is well documented.

The longevity record in America for a short-eared owl is just over 4 years; in Europe, almost 13 years. The few banding recoveries of this species, however, preclude giving an average or typical longevity.

Like other grassland birds, short-eared owls depend upon the existence of available alternative sites if a current grassland site becomes unsuitable—which, given the fluctuating nature of grassland habitat, including its food resources, it will. If such alternative sites do not exist, the owls become jeopardized.

# 4

## Common Nighthawk *(Chordeiles minor)*

Goatsucker family (Caprimulgidae), order Strigiformes. Recognize the male nighthawk by its dark, mottled brown color, white throat band and tail band, a transverse white bar on each outer wing, notched tail, and long, pointed wings. Females have the wing bars but lack the white tail band, and their throats are buffier. Almost 10 inches long, the nighthawk has a small, soft, flaplike bill, which opens to a wide-mouthed gape; the mouth occupies some 15 percent of its total body area. The nighthawk's squawking "beezt" note, frequently voiced as it courses erratically overhead for flying insects, much resembles the notes of American woodcocks and male common goldeneye ducks. Notes of these other birds are seldom voiced in flight, however.

**Close relatives.** All 5 *Chordeiles* species reside in the Western Hemisphere. Other North American relatives include the Antillean nighthawk *(C. gundlachii)* of the Florida Keys and South America, and the lesser nighthawk *(C. acutipennis)* of southwestern deserts. North American family members, all of which resemble *C. minor* in general form and coloration, include the whip-poor-will *(Caprimulgus vociferus),* the chuck-will's-widow *(C. carolinensis),* the buff-collared nightjar *(C. ridgwayi),* and the common poor-will *(Phalaenoptilus nuttallii).* European *Caprimulgus* species are called nightjars.

**Behaviors.** Few birds have been so defiantly misnamed as the nighthawk—nor, as in this case, has the misnomer been so stubbornly maintained. The nighthawk is neither exclusively nocturnal nor similar to any hawk on earth, though it certainly hawks insects. This sky-roving "aerial scoop" instead bears close physical resemblances to swifts and swallows, also aerial insect catchers. Bill shapes and functions of these birds are essentially alike; nighthawks, however, lack the *rictal bristles* surrounding the gape of its relatives. Nighthawks are primarily *crepuscular*—that is, they fly and hunt most actively during dawn and evening hours, though they can and do fly at any hour of day or night. Well camouflaged when on the ground, they become conspicuous in flight, frequently voicing their nasal beeping note as they fly with quick, erratic wingbeats, often changing course, usually about 100 feet high. This erratic, often batlike flight style gives them the colloquial name "bullbat" in some areas. The piercing note is easily imitated if you can quack like Donald Duck; using it, I have often lured flying nighthawks down to low perches for mutual close inspection. When a nighthawk perches, often on a rail fence or low branch, it aligns itself lengthwise along the horizontal surface. Its squat, hunched appearance (Louisiana Cajuns reputedly called nighthawks "winged toads") and folded wings that extend beyond the tail tip are good identifying features; no other member of its family has such long wings. All members of this bird family have a toothed, or pectinated, long middle toe, a feather comb apparently used for preening the plumage, especially in the head and neck areas. Nighthawks often drink by skimming the surface of a pond, dipping their bills as they fly. When held in the hand, they often release a very pungent defecation.

Common nighthawks are migrators. Their large breeding range encompasses most of North America, north to the treeline and south as far as Panama. Many aspects of this bird's life history remain unknown, providing fertile areas of research for observers.

*Spring.* Fairly late migrators in spring, nighthawks arrive in the southern United States in April; they appear on their northern breeding range in May. Their incessant beeps from the sky make them immediately conspicuous upon arrival. Females may arrive several days before males, often returning to the previous year's breeding sites. Durability of the pair bond beyond a single season, however, remains uncertain. Territory size depends much on the type of habitat: In urban areas, nighthawk territory ranges from about 4 to 7 acres; in rural countryside, about 11 to 13 acres. Occasional loose colonies exist where adequate nesting sites are spatially restricted. Male aerial displays consist of circling and soaring high above the nest site, then suddenly plunging into a fast, 70-degree dive, at the end of which the bird's vibrating wing primaries produce a distinctive roaring sound, variously described as like the whine of a Stuka dive bomber, a "hollow boom," or a "muffled *woof.*" To me, it sounds like a loud, buzzing crescendo, a noise as characteristic of the bird as its squawky call notes. On the ground, the male postures, rocking and calling, in front of the female, spreading his tail and flashing his white throat. These displays continue through the June nesting season. If the nest is approached, the birds may dive at the intruder and perform vigorous distraction displays.

EGGS AND YOUNG: usually 2; eggs glossy, olive dotted with brown. INCUBATION: by female; about 19 days; hatching synchronous; young altricial. FEEDING OF YOUNG: by both sexes; regurgitated insects. FLEDGING: about 3 weeks; juveniles can fly in 18 days, feed themselves in 25.

*Summer.* Nighthawks usually raise only a single brood, occasionally two. Half-grown nestlings display rather intimidating behaviors when disturbed. Opening their prodigious gray-blue mouths, they instinctively lunge toward the intruder—possibly an instance of *Batesian mimicry,* in which a prey species mimics the appearance or behaviors of a predator. (Black-capped chickadee nestlings similarly exhibit this snakelike lunging behavior; see *Birds of Forest, Yard, and Thicket.*) Some nesting continues into early July.

By late July in many areas, nighthawks—among the earliest fall migrants—are assembling into flocks and beginning to move southward. Peak movement in other areas occurs in late August; I recall one mid-August day when, scanning the sky with my binoculars, I spotted a roiling flock of about 30 nighthawks, feeding so high they were barely visible, identifiable only by wing shape and flight style. Their gregariousness at this season may also extend to other behaviors—one observer reported watching a small flock fly upwind during a heavy rainstorm, as if aerially bathing, periodically beating their wings to shed water. Most nighthawks vacate their northern range by mid-September or before. Some migrant fall flocks may number 1,000 birds.

*Winter.* Common nighthawks vacate North America entirely, most by mid-October. Much remains unknown about their winter distribution, though the largest numbers seem to occupy lowland areas east of the Andes in midcontinental South America, ranging into Argentina and southern Brazil. The annual plumage molt apparently occurs on the winter range, extending into January and February. The birds are again winging north by late March.

**Ecology.** For nesting, common nighthawks require open spaces with minimal vegetation—the barer the ground, the better. Burned-over lands, forest clear-cuts, gravel pits, beaches, sand and gravel roadways, young pine plantations, and flat, graveled rooftops of urban buildings provide optimal nesting habitats. For feeding, the birds hunt above fields, open woodlands, and urban streets, though again they seem to favor open areas. Winter habitats, both urban and rural, closely approximate their summer haunts.

The nest hardly amounts to more than a token scrape in sandy ground—not even that much on harder gravel surfaces. No materials are added. Since about 1869, when mansard and flat rooftops began to appear in American cities, the birds have widely adopted these tarred and graveled surfaces for nest sites. Such surfaces heat up like stovetops in direct summer sunlight, and nighthawk daytime brooding mainly consists of shading the nestlings. To cope with such heat, the birds often practice *gular flutter,* a fast

*The common nighthawk, commonly seen and heard in the sky over cities, has adapted well to the flat rooftops of buildings for nesting sites. (From* The Atlas of Breeding Birds of Michigan.*)*

pulsing of the throat skin, with open bill. Gular flutter aids panting, by which many birds, lacking sweat glands, cool themselves by rapid respiration. An incubating female in such locales usually orients her body along the axis of the sun's rays, facing away from the sun. Exclusively aerial insect feeders, common nighthawks are known to consume at least 50 different insect species. Ranking highest in their diet are flying ants, beetles, and true bugs. They also consume many mosquitoes. At night, the birds often forage around artificial lighting—streetlamps, stadium and commercial lighting, beacons, and the like. It has been suggested, but remains unproven, that the nighthawk's incessant beeping notes during flight may be a means of echolocating insect prey (the notes, however, are voiced in daytime as well as at night). Roger Tory Peterson suggested that the rarity of saturniid moth species (such as cecropia, luna, polyphemus, and io moths) in the northeastern United States, perhaps owing to pesticides, may have contributed to the nighthawk's recent decline in this region. The relatively late availability of flying insects probably accounts for the nighthawk's lagging spring migration.

Food competitors are mainly bats, which sometimes chase nighthawks from feeding areas, and, in the bird's southern range, the lesser nighthawk. The lesser and the Antillean nighthawks frequently compete with common nighthawks for territorial space, often displacing them.

Nighthawk nest predators include snakes, owls, gulls, American kestrels, northern ravens, American crows, domestic cats, skunks, coyotes, and foxes. Vehicles take a yearly toll of nighthawks nesting in unpaved roadways.

**Focus.** A summer evening without nighthawks flitting and beeping aloft seems strangely bereft to a birder. Census records show significant declines of this species over the past 3 decades throughout North America. This decrease coincides with widespread pesticide spraying for mosquito control, an action that eliminates many beneficial insects as well as pest species. Another factor may be the increasing replacement of graveled rooftops with smooth, rubberized surfaces, discouraging nighthawk nesting. Installation of gravel pads in the corners of these roofs has proven effective in attracting nighthawks.

To the Zuni Pueblos, nighthawks were holy birds. These natives placed its feathers on ceremonial prayer sticks and also offered them as rain petitions for their crops. Thoreau could empathize with the "superstitious awe" these birds might evoke: An incubating nighthawk that he observed "looked so Saturnian, so one with the earth, so sphinxlike . . . a riddle that might well cause a man to go dash his head against a stone."

Nighthawk life span averages 4 or 5 years, though a longevity of 9 years has been recorded.

## 5

## SANDPIPER FAMILY (Scolopacidae, order Ciconiiformes

This large family, part of the group designated as shorebirds, though not all of them frequent shorelines, mainly consists of wading birds that forage in wetland and wave-zone habitats. Most are slender, relatively long-legged and long-billed birds of subdued, often brownish coloration; plumage patterns often show dark on back, wings, and tail, with white or paler underparts. Many species have well-differentiated breeding and winter plumages. The long, slender bills curve downward in some species (curlews, dunlins, a few sandpipers), upward in others (godwits, greater yellowlegs), but are usually straight. Most species have a spurlike, elevated hind toe *(hallux)* and long, pointed wings adapted to fast flight. Many are also gregarious and exhibit complex aerial and distraction displays during the breeding season. This family is notable for its variety of mating strategies and systems, ranging from monogamy to promiscuity. Sex-role reversal is typical of several sandpiper species. In most species, females are somewhat larger than males. Hatching is usually synchronous, and chicks are precocial, able to feed themselves soon after hatching.

A common habit of many shorebirds, as well as other waterbirds, is perching on one leg, with the other drawn up into the plumage. This may be a heat-conserving adaptation, reducing the amount of bare surface area and potential heat loss, though the birds also do it sometimes in very hot weather as well. Birds of this family range in size from the sparrow-length least sandpiper (birders call the smaller sandpipers "peeps" for their "weet-weet" sounds) to the long-billed curlew, which measures about 2 feet long. Of the 33 North

American species (88 worldwide), only 3 of the most common are presented here. In addition to the close relatives mentioned for each, resident species of the northeastern United States include the godwits, curlews, whimbrel, willet, phalaropes, and dowitchers. The word *sandpiper* means "chirper in the sand."

SANDPIPER FAMILY (Scolopacidae)

## Upland Sandpiper *(Bartramia longicauda)*

Recognize this grassland dweller mainly by its sandpiper form and its prairie and pasture habitats. About a foot long, it lacks conspicuous markings. Brown plumage grading into a white belly, a small dovelike head, thin neck, slight eye ring (giving the bird a big-eyed look), greenish yellow legs, and long tail help identify it. Its whistled notes, however, are distinctive: The "wolf-whistle" call, a breathy, ethereal "whip-whoooleeeooo" voiced mainly in spring, resembles a call of the European starling (which may be mimicking this sandpiper). Other sounds, heard mainly on its territory, include flutelike trills and mellow "kip-ip-ip-ip" notes, often at night.

**Close relatives.** This is the only *Bartramia* sandpiper. It bears close resemblance to the wood sandpiper *(Tringa glareola)* of Eurasia and Alaska; other *Tringa* sandpipers (see Greater Yellowlegs) are near relatives. The only other dry-land shorebirds of its family in North America are the American woodcock *(Scolopax minor*, see *Birds of Forest, Yard, and Thicket)* and the long-billed curlew *(Numenius americanus).*

**Behaviors.** Conspicuous mainly in spring, when they become most vocal, often perch on fence posts and utility poles, and perform high courtship flights, upland sandpipers are open-country birds that rarely reside near water. Owing to their ploverlike behavior— swift runs and sudden stops—on the ground, they were long considered plovers. The upland sandpiper "skims close to the ground to land with tremble of outstretched wings," in the poetic prose of one field-guide author. When alighting, this bird usually holds its wings over its back for a few seconds ("the classic upland sandpiper salute," according to one observer) before folding them. "Whoever

*A sandpiperlike bird perched on a fence post or power pole is probably an upland sandpiper, one of the few shorebirds that favor dry habitats. (From* The Atlas of Breeding Birds of Michigan.*)*

invented the word 'grace,'" wrote Aldo Leopold, "must have seen the wing-folding" of this bird.

Upland sandpipers occupy a large breeding range, spanning the continent from Alaska to Labrador and south to Maryland, Illinois, Oklahoma, and Oregon. Their foremost population center is the Great Plains, mainly North Dakota grasslands.

*Spring.* All upland sandpipers apparently migrate north through Central America from their winter range. Many are paired by the time they arrive on their breeding range in mid-April to early May. Most of them are probably *philopatric*—that is, return to their previous breeding sites—but the often ephemeral nature of their habitats makes this species, like most grassland birds, highly vulnerable to changes wrought by plant succession and agricultural practices. Pairs are often loosely colonial. Territories typically range from about 2 to 15 acres per nest; some may occupy 50 or more acres, the size probably depending on population density and habitat quality. In addition to territories, adjacent loafing and feeding areas are communally used by several pairs.

Two types of courtship flight may be seen: Males fly slowly in high, wide circles over the territory, voicing whistled notes and the distinctive wolf-whistle call, often plummeting like a rock to the ground after this display; and a low, fluttering and gliding flight over the territory. These displays continue through the breeding season, probably reinforcing the pair bond. Nesting usually begins in early May. Parent birds rarely approach the nest directly, alighting some distance away and moving to it on the ground. When approached by an intruder, "each incubating bird has its own flushing distance," wrote nest researcher Hal H. Harrison. Some flush when the intruder is 6 feet away; others sit closely, even permitting themselves to be stroked on the nest.

EGGS AND YOUNG: typically 4; eggs pinkish buff with reddish brown spots. INCUBATION: by both sexes; about 24 days. FLEDGING: about 32 days.

*Summer, Fall.* Chicks remain closely attached to parents until they fledge. Both old and young birds begin grouping by late July. "By August," wrote Leopold, "they have graduated from flying school, and on cool August nights you can hear their whistled signals as they set wing for the pampas, to prove again the age-old unity of the Americas." Adult birds begin molting their body plumage in August, completing the wing and tail molt on the winter range.

Like most shorebirds, upland sandpipers are summer or early fall migrators. Small flocks move southward during August, with stragglers remaining into September. Most have departed the continent by late October. Their far destination is South American grasslands, especially the Argentine pampas and areas in Uruguay and Paraguay. Fall migration routes spread over a wider front than the spring movement, heading across the Caribbean as well as through Central America.

*An upland sandpiper chick explores the world—in this case, the other side of the road. (Drawn from author's photograph.)*

*Winter.* Conditions of change in this bird's South American winter range may have greater bearing on its population status than habitat changes in its breeding range (though South American ornithologists tend to disagree with this). The wintering area is much smaller than the breeding range (for the bird itself, of course, there is no winter; it travels from North American summer to South American spring). Continued pesticide use there, which limits the insect food supply, plus other agricultural practices place this species under particular stress during winter.

The birds undergo another molt of body plumage before winging north in March.

**Ecology.** This resident of the short-grass prairie requires large, open fields—both dry and wet meadows, alfalfa and clover fields, pastures, mowed areas adjacent to expressways and airports—with absent or sparse shrub growth and a few elevated perches such as fence posts or utility poles. Upland sandpipers favor generally level and untilled land, preferring fields of mixed grasses and legumes containing abundant insects over uniform crop stands and pesticide-treated fields, which the birds tend to avoid. This is a highly *area-sensitive* species—that is, it requires *contiguous* grassland habitat of about 20 acres or more for nesting; habitat fragmentation into smaller plots discourages nesting. For feeding and loafing sites, upland sandpipers favor unharvested hayfields, grain stubble, and grassy airport runway margins. Communal loafing sites are usually sparsely vegetated.

*Large expanses of short-grass prairie sites—especially areas that contain fence posts or utility poles for perching—are optimal upland sandpiper habitats.*

Built on the ground in often thick grass cover, the nest consists of a dried grass cup about 5 inches across placed in a shallow scrape with standing grass arching over it, hiding it from above. Females usually begin building in vegetation 6 to 14 inches tall.

Chiefly insect eaters, upland sandpipers consume huge amounts of grasshoppers, crickets, and weevils, which make up almost half the total diet, plus many other beetles, true bugs, moth caterpillars, spiders, snails, and worms. Truly this bird is the farmer's friend, especially in its consumption of injurious insects. The 3 percent of the diet that is vegetarian consists of grass and weed seeds plus waste grain. According to reports published early in this century, upland sandpipers were said to exhibit an intriguing habit of food transportation. Snails of the genus *Physa,* often as many as 20 or 30, were found clinging beneath the wings upon the birds' spring arrival on the Gulf coast. Presumably placed by the birds themselves, this unique instance of food caching (if such it was) has not been recently recorded but may still bear investigation.

Farmers have been slow to recognize the benefits of upland sandpiper presence. In most places where it exists today, this bird has become largely dependent on human land-use practices. Mowing in May and June drives it out, as does intensive, uniform crop farming of almost any sort. Yet its rapid exploitation of grassy fields and pastures makes it an ideal candidate for habitat-management programs concurrent with normal farming operations. Competition with creatures other than humans appears minimal. The birds coexist with moderate cattle grazing in many areas. In one upland sandpiper nesting area familiar to me, bird associates include northern bobwhites, Henslow's and grasshopper sparrows, bobolinks, and eastern meadowlarks. On the winter range, the southern lapwing, a plover, is said to be a food competitor in some areas.

Information on predators of this bird is slim. Presumably their nests are vulnerable to northern harriers and to a variety of mammal predators including ground squirrels, skunks, raccoons, foxes, and coyotes. Cattle occasionally trample the nests in pasture habitats, and the nests are sometimes parasitized by brown-headed cowbirds. "In farm country," wrote Aldo Leopold many decades ago, this bird "has only two real enemies: the gully and the drainage ditch. Perhaps we shall one day find that these are our enemies, too."

**Focus.** Ornithologists have fiddled considerably over what to name this bird that seems to bridge the plover and sandpiper families; within living memory, it has worn the labels Bartramian sandpiper and upland plover. Significant agreement has finally established that it is a real—if ploverlike—sandpiper.

When market hunting began to result in marked decline of the passenger pigeon in 1880, the upland sandpiper largely replaced it as the market bird of choice. Forest clearing and agriculture had expanded upland sandpiper range eastward from the Great Plains. Thousands arrived each spring; to judge from early accounts, it was probably the most numerous prairie bird. A few decades of mass slaughter largely extirpated it from areas where it had formerly flourished.

Although migratory bird laws finally halted the carnage by 1918 and slow trends of general increase in numbers and distribution have continued since the 1930s, the species has not yet recovered from the assault by our forefathers. Also, as much former eastern and midwestern farmland has been replaced by second-growth forest or suburban housing, upland sandpiper populations—along with several other grassland bird species—have in many areas shifted northward, where much cut-over timberland remains relatively open. Whether these increases in northern populations have balanced the declines in other areas remains unknown. Wildlife specialists interested in creating and maintaining optimal habitats for this bird advise a 3-year rotation of rotary mowing and prescribed burning.

This bird's habitat needs—and the fact that grasslands have become increasingly endangered habitats on both its summer and winter ranges—make it a useful indicator species, one to be monitored closely—and one to consider when public and private land management decisions are made. "A more fitting symbol of rural America is hard to imagine," researcher David Wilcove wrote. Aldo Leopold's essay "Back from the Argentine" in *A Sand County Almanac* (1949) probably gives the best brief portrait of this bird, known to Leopold as the upland plover.

Banding recovery of a 5-year-old upland sandpiper has been recorded.

SANDPIPER FAMILY (Scolopacidae)

# Greater Yellowlegs *(Tringa melanoleuca)*

Recognize this shorebird by its relatively large size (about 14 inches long); its thick-jointed, bright yellow legs; its mottled gray-brown back and wings; its whitish underparts quite heavily streaked and speckled in spring plumage; and (in flight) its white rump and tail. The long, 2-inch bill has a slight upward tilt, not always conspicuous in all yellowlegs. Yellowlegs' toes are webbed at the base. The distinctive call is a ringing, 3-note whistle: "tew-tew-tew."

**Close relatives.** Fifteen *Tringa* sandpipers exist worldwide, 3 in North America. The lesser yellowlegs *(T. flavipes)* appears a smaller version of the greater; the solitary sandpiper *(T. solitaria),* at 8 to 9 inches long, is the smallest of the trio. The redshanks *(T. erythropus, T. totanus),* the greenshank *(T. nebularia),* and the wood sandpiper *(T. glareola)* are related Eurasian species.

**Behaviors.** Commonly seen during its migrations to and from its far-northern breeding range, the greater yellowlegs is more easily identified than many of the shorebird tribe, owing to its bright leg coloring and unmistakable calls.

This was my spring project bird for college ornithology, and I spent many solitary hours afield observing its characteristics and noting its behaviors. Feeding in the shallow pond margins and muddy rocks, it often presents a comical show as it frantically pursues swimming prey. "The amount of energy expended in its erratic pursuit patterns," I wrote, "probably necessitates all

*One of the more easily identified sandpipers because of its distinctive calls and leg coloring, the greater yellowlegs commonly stops along shorelines during its long migrations to and from the tundra.*

the amount of food thus captured. Whether the bird follows only one swimming creature or becomes distracted by a host of them, the visual effect is a fast display of double-takes, sudden turns and dashes, abrupt halts and about-faces, all accented by rapid stabs and splashes of the bill."

Sometimes the yellowlegs also feeds by bill-sweeping and skimming the water surface. Not a mud prober, it pecks and snatches in the water for food, usually wading in the shallows but sometimes in depths up to its belly. Another frequent behavior, especially when alarmed, is "hiccuping," a spasmodic bobbing of the head and the whole body at times, becoming more rapid as alarm increases. These motions also precede occasional regurgitation of indigestible food pellets.

Frenetic feeding sessions are broken by 10- or 20-minute rest periods, during which the birds stand motionless (often on one leg) on the gravel bars or beaches. Loud whistling notes often precede flight, the bird continuing to call as it takes wing. When alighting, it stands for an instant with wings extended, then folds them down, hiccups once or twice, and begins feeding. Frequently vocal but not as gregarious as the lesser yellowlegs, the greater yellowlegs usually feeds or rests solitarily or in small, widely spaced flocks.

This species breeds in a wide band across the continent from Newfoundland to Alaska, northward from about latitude 50 degrees N to the forested edge of the tundra.

*Spring.* The main period of spring migration encompasses mid-April to early May. Flying both day and night along seacoasts and interior routes as well, greater yellowlegs travel high in small flocks, settling in wetland habitats—often sewage lagoons or wildlife refuges—for days or weeks en route. Migrant populations may build to 50 or more birds in such areas. (The most I observed at one time in my own pond study area was 9.) Then one day they are gone; fast flying (about 40 mph), most arrive in their breeding range by mid-May, but small numbers of nonbreeding birds may remain along coastal areas of the United States and Canada through summer.

Probably most of the migrants become paired before or during their journey. (I witnessed several apparent pairs on my study area but saw no courtship behaviors; even the paired birds widely separated when feeding.) Territory size remains uncertain, but the birds are extremely vocal in their nesting areas. Often heard is a yodeling whistle—"too-whee" or "whee-oodle"—given in flight. Nesting begins in May, extending into June.

> EGGS AND YOUNG: 4; eggs brown spotted, wreathed with brown at larger end. INCUBATION: probably by both sexes; about 23 days. FLEDGING: 18 to 20 days.

*Summer.* Greater yellowlegs nest only once per year, although they often renest if the first nest is destroyed. Broods remain with parents until they fledge. Because of this bird's remote nesting sites, relatively little is known about their postnesting activities. Like many other sandpipers, yellowlegs apparently abandon their territories to gather in loose flocks at prime feeding areas. By early July, many adult yellowlegs are moving southward, followed by juvenile birds some 2 or 3 weeks later. Visual differences between adult and juvenile birds are obvious: The fresh-plumaged juveniles look very dapper in contrast to the worn-feathered adults. Populations gradually build in prime feeding habitats southward of the breeding range as birds continually arrive and often remain for weeks. In August and September, adult birds replace their body feathers; the winter plumage shows whiter, less speckled underparts than the breeding plumage.

*Fall.* Yellowlegs may loiter in feeding marshes along their migration paths well into October or even later. Most, however, have departed the northern United States by early November, except along the continental seacoasts south of New York and Oregon, where many remain through winter. Some yellowlegs (perhaps mainly juveniles) travel only to the Gulf coastal states to winter. Most, however, move much farther, settling on wetlands throughout South America to its very tip at Tierra del Fuego.

*Winter.* Small flocks of greater yellowlegs maintain and defend winter feeding territories. As with those of many shorebirds in winter, however, these territories are flexible and shifting, depending upon food availability at any given time and place. The birds molt and replace their wing and tail feathers now. Beginning about February, another molt of body feathers also occurs, giving the birds their breeding plumage of speckled breast and flanks. By early March, most of the population is again winging northward.

**Ecology.** This is a bird of the shallow wetland margins—pondsides, gravel bars, island and marsh edges, mudflats, meadow pools, even roadside ditches. For nesting, yellowlegs favor open semitundra and high tundra sites—specifically, areas of boggy muskeg with scattered trees, small ponds, and rock outcrops. The winter range encompasses coastal marshes, pampa marshes and ponds, and other wetland areas.

Nests, usually sited close to a pool or small pond, often lie on a sphagnum moss hummock partially sheltered by a branch or log or on a drier ridge. The nest is hardly more than a slight depression barely lined with grass or leaves. According to one experienced observer, "a yellowlegs never nests on ground which is too soft. . . . There must be soil or dry, hard peat."

Yellowlegs primarily eat fish; minnows, killifishes, and topminnows are common prey. The birds also consume aquatic insects, worms, snails, crustaceans, and tadpoles. They occasionally eat berries such as cranberry as well.

Although greater and lesser yellowlegs share the same breeding range and migration habitats and often nest in close association, competition between them is probably minimal. Greaters migrate slightly sooner than lessers in spring. Lesser yellowlegs favor drier nesting sites, and their diet consists mainly of insects. During migrations, greater yellowlegs frequently associate with blue-winged teal; wherever I see a blue-wing, I can often count on seeing a yellowlegs feeding shoreward nearby. The frequency of this association is well known, but whether their synchronous appearance indicates any ecological significance remains uncertain.

Information on predators of this species is slim. The ground nests are presumably vulnerable to foxes, coyotes, and other mammals. Raptors may capture chicks and adult birds at times.

**Focus.** The generic name *Tringa* derives from the Greek for "a water bird with a white rump."

Before the passage of migratory bird laws in 1917, yellowlegs, along with most shorebirds, fell in large numbers to market hunters during fall migrations and on their winter range. "I knew an old gunner," wrote ornithologist Arthur C. Bent in 1927, "who celebrated his eightieth birthday by shooting 40 yellowlegs." Bent mourned the passing of "the delightful sport of bay-bird shooting."

In any wetland where they are present, yellowlegs often perform the role of sentry species, alerting ducks and other waterbirds to danger by their sharp vigilance and ready calls. Its old nicknames "telltale" and "tattler" reflect this habit. "Many a yellowlegs," wrote Bent, "has been shot by an angry gunner as a reward for his exasperating loquacity." Although the bird is still legal game in some states, relatively few are hunted today.

SANDPIPER FAMILY (Scolopacidae)

# Spotted Sandpiper *(Tringa macularia)*

This most common and widespread of all sandpipers measures 7 or 8 inches long. Its gray-brown back and wings and white underparts are "generic sandpiper" patterns, but its breeding plumage—round, dark spotting covering the white breast and flanks—is distinctive. Birds in unspotted winter plumage often exhibit a white, fingerlike mark extending up from the breast in front of the wing bend. Females are slightly larger than males, showing more conspicuous breast spotting. A sharp, whistled "*peet*-weet-weet!" is often sounded as the bird takes flight.

**Close relatives.** Fifteen *Tringa* sandpipers exist worldwide. North American species include greater and lesser yellowlegs *(T. melanoleuca, T. flavipes)* and the solitary sandpiper *(T. solitaria).* The common sandpiper *(T. hypoleucos)* of Eurasia closely resembles the spotted sandpiper.

**Behaviors.** This bird and the killdeer are probably the best-known, most widespread shorebirds in North America and also—when the sandpiper is in breeding plumage—the easiest to identify.

*The spotted sandpiper, probably the most common American sandpiper, wears spots only in spring and summer. In its winter plumage, it often fades to "generic sandpiper" patterns and is much harder to identify. (From* The Atlas of Breeding Birds of Michigan.*)*

On the ground, spotted sandpipers teeter constantly, bobbing the tail up and down, as if the bird is "a bit too delicately balanced," observed Roger Tory Peterson. In flight, the birds show stiff-bowed wings with shallow, fluttering wingbeats "vibrating like taut wire," as one observer wrote. The feet of spotted sandpipers are better adapted for grasping small objects and for perching than those of its kin; its toes are closer together, and its hind toe *(hallux)* is more developed. These birds can swim and dive, though they usually remain ashore, wading infrequently in the shallows. Like solitary sandpipers and killdeers, they always go ashore to defecate. One researcher suggests that this habit exists "to prevent the spread of parasites, or to avoid fouling and clouding its foraging area." (The infinitives, unfortunately, imply intentionality, to which most ornithologists would not subscribe.)

The spotted sandpiper is one of the few bird species that exhibit almost complete sex-role reversal, with a mating system called *serial polyandry*—literally "many males." (Other polyandrous shorebirds include the northern jacana and Wilson's, red-necked, and red phalaropes.) Females establish and defend territories and initiate serial courtship and mating with 2 or more males; males do most of the incubation and brooding of chicks. Many intriguing biological and social aspects of this mating system occur (see Focus), a system predicted by Charles Darwin before it was known to exist.

Spotted sandpiper breeding range spans the continent from the Arctic south to Virginia, Oklahoma, and southern California.

*Spring.* "The river seems really inhabited when the peetweet is back," wrote Thoreau. "Its note peoples the river, like the prattle of children once more in the yard of a home that has stood empty." Spotted sandpipers exhibit *differential migration*—that is, age- and sex-segregated differences in timing of migration and distance traveled. Older females arrive first, usually in late April or early May, followed a few days later by older males and yearling females. Yearling males arrive last, often about mid-May or later. Females, site faithful *(philopatric)* to previous nesting sites, immediately claim a territory, the size of which depends upon the density of sandpiper population. In certain areas, more than 100 pairs may crowd into only a few acres, in which case female territorial encounters continue more or less constantly. Where the birds are more thinly dispersed, the female may establish a territory 3 or more acres in size. Arriving older males also return to previous nesting sites—and thus, probably often, to the same mate. "Some females," wrote researcher Lewis W. Oring, "acquire mates through the quality of their territory, while others compete physically for males." Sometimes females recruit stopover migrant younger males. Female rivalry can be fierce, with episodes of chasing, pecking, and gouging; they tend to invade adjacent territories and attract any resident male to their own. Males thus attracted also compete among themselves for dominance on subterritories within the female territory. Once a male settles on a female territory, courtship and mating are swift, sometimes occurring within a few minutes of male arrival. The female struts in front of the male with ruffled neck and drooping wings, often on a stretch of open shoreline or atop a shoreline log, and copulation may directly follow. Males probably do most of the nest building, such as it is, and the mated pair usually remains monogamous until egg laying occurs. Then the female abruptly abandons both nest and mate and renews courtship or battle for another male, repeating the process up to four more times in a breeding season. This procedure could actually be termed serial monogamy, but occasionally a female may mate with 2 males within the same day or so *(simultaneous polyandry)*. Females often help incubate the final nest of the season; inexperienced yearling females, which rarely attract more than a single mate per season, also share nesting duty. "Multiple mates," as one researcher points out, "enable a female to increase her reproductive output by freeing her from the responsibility for incubation and care of the young." Individual males incubate and raise only 1 brood per season.

EGGS AND YOUNG: typically 4 per nest; eggs brownish buff with heavy brown spotting. INCUBATION: mainly by male; about 3 weeks. FLEDGING: about 3 weeks.

*Summer.* Nesting may extend into July, fledging into August. Spotted sandpipers perform frantic distraction displays when nests or chicks are threatened. Chicks and the attending parent soon abandon the territory, moving toward water or less densely vegetated areas. In mid to late summer, juveniles wear clear white breast plumage in contrast to the adults' spotting. As adults molt into winter body plumage, they too become unspotted, so differences between age groups are no longer obvious. The birds gather in small feeding flocks from July into September. Some of the birds (probably unmated yearlings) begin southward migration in July.

*Fall.* Migration occurs usually in small flocks and mainly at night through September and October. Some of the birds move only to Florida and Gulf coastal areas and along the seacoasts south from South Carolina and southern British Columbia. Many others migrate to the West Indies and South America as far as Chile and northern Argentina.

*Winter.* Settling in both coastal and interior wetlands, spotted sandpipers molt wing and tail feathers soon after their arrival. Later, just before or during spring migration in March and April, they also renew their body feathers, acquiring their spotted breeding plumage.

**Ecology.** Its adaptability to a variety of wetland habitats from seacoast marshes to mountain lakes helps account for the spotted sandpiper's abundance and wide distribution. Often favoring open areas near water, it frequents shorelines of ponds, lakes, and streams, as well as temporary or seasonal pools and standing water. Small islands are common residence sites. One research team labeled the spotted sandpiper a pioneering species, able to exploit brief, disturbed, or early successional habitats, moving elsewhere when flooding occurs or wetland plant succession advances.

Adaptable in breeding sites as well, spotted sandpipers usually nest in thick vegetation, often tall, rank marsh grasses or sedges well back from the water's edge. Sometimes, however, they build far from water in hills or pastures, on sandy knolls, beneath a shrub, log, or roadside bank. Nests, often loosely colonial because of the bird's polyandrous habits, consist of scrapes in the ground lined thinly with grasses, weeds, or mosses.

The spotted sandpiper's main diet consists of insects. This bird is well known for stalking and snatching flying insects—flies, dragonflies, and mayflies, among others—out of the air. It also consumes many other aquatic insects, plus grasshoppers, crickets, caterpillars, and beetles. Worms, crustaceans, snails, and small fishes are also taken. It eats little if any seeds or plant food.

Spotted sandpipers face little competition from other species, probably owing to their wide habitat adaptations. But competition from other spotted sandpipers can be intense.

Minks probably rank as this bird's major nest predator. Mice, weasels, and ground squirrels also raid the nests, and northern harriers, peregrine falcons, and northern shrikes sometimes prey on adult sandpipers and chicks. In one 3-year study, deer mice and meadow voles punctured many eggs, resulting in spotted sandpiper egg losses of up to 30 percent. Brown-headed cowbirds occasionally parasitize the nests, and flooding also becomes a hazard at times.

**Focus.** The spotted sandpiper's polyandrous mating system has attracted much research effort. Lewis W. Oring and others found that males have higher levels of prolactin (a mainly female hormone associated with incubation) than females, and that male testosterone levels dropped at the onset of incubation. The researchers also discovered that a female need not repeatedly copulate in order to lay succeeding egg clutches after her first. In many instances, a female may actually thwart copulation with a second or third male even after soliciting it. She can store sperm from a previous mate up to 31 days, using it to fertilize one or more succeeding clutches whether or not she has copulated with the incubating male on the nest. Thus many later-season nests are tended by a cuckolded male that is not the biological parent. Oring suggested the survival value of this system: Females "essentially always pair first with older males," which have demonstrated their genetic fitness (since, in birds, survivability itself is a good indicator of such fitness). Since spring arrival of older males precedes that of yearling males, "the early bird gets the sperm." As the season advances, females increasingly pair with yearling males, but "by storing the sperm of their first mates, the females retain sperm of older males, which is, on average, of higher quality." Also, as ecologist Richard Brewer pointed out, "a young male hatching eggs fertilized by an earlier bird is getting something out of it—experience—that is, practice on somebody else's genes." And, by surviving for 2 years or more, a male becomes a biological as well as behavioral parent. (Spotted sandpipers that survive their first year live, on average to age three plus; occasional birds survive to age nine.) Females, concluded Oring, "are in control of mating." Yet their control is far from absolute, since in the study cited, only a minority (11 percent) of offspring were the product of stored sperm. Apparently, stated Oring, sperm storage is not foolproof, "or not every old male is of high quality." Also, "not every second or third mate is young." The chronic shortage of available males during the later breeding season, since most males are incubating, leads to increased competition among females for mates. This is why females, though capable of producing 20 eggs per season ("equivalent to a human female producing a five-hundred-pound infant," stated Oring), produce an average of only 8. These circumstances strongly indicate a system still in flux, still evolving toward an optimal survival strategy. The combination of a long breeding season with abundant food availability plus heavy predation has been postulated as a reason for the evolution of serial polyandry in birds.

Spotted sandpipers remain common throughout most of their breeding range owing to their wide habitat tolerance. Because of their tendency to travel in small flocks, they suffered less depredation from nineteenth-century market hunters than did many other shorebirds.

# 6

## PLOVER FAMILY (Charadriidae), order Ciconiiformes

Plovers are wading shorebirds. They somewhat resemble sandpipers except that they are chunkier with shorter necks and have larger eyes. Their bills are also shorter and slightly enlarged toward the tip (pigeonlike). The feet of most plovers have only minimal webbing and lack a functional hind toe *(hallux).* All plovers are strong fliers, run fast, and can swim. Unlike sandpipers, plovers run in starts and stops. Hatching is synchronous, and the young are precocial, able to feed themselves soon after hatching. The word *plover* probably derives from the Latin *pluvia,* meaning "rain"; *plovier* was Old French for "rain-bird," but why plovers came to be associated with rain in the first place remains a mystery.

Of the 66 plover species worldwide, 8 reside for at least part of the year in North America. Dotterels and lapwings are also plovers. Other family members include the oystercatchers, stilts, and avocets.

PLOVER FAMILY (Charadriidae)
***

## Killdeer *(Charadrius vociferus)*
The 9- to 11-inch-long killdeer is easily identified. Distinctive marks include the gray-brown back, white chest and belly marked with 2 black, transverse breast bands, and a rusty-orange rump (best seen in flight). Sexes look alike. Its loud, repetitive "kill-*dee!*" calls, voiced mainly in flight, make this bird conspicuous wherever it is present.

**Close relatives.** Thirty *Charadrius* species exist worldwide, 6 in North America. These include the snowy plover *(C. alexandrinus)* of

*A killdeer always reveals its presence by its loud, ringing calls and conspicuous behaviors on the ground.*

Gulf coastal areas; the piping plover *(C. melodus),* an endangered species; the Wilson's plover *(C. wilsonia);* the semipalmated plover *(C. semipalmatus);* and the mountain plover *(C. montanus)* of the western United States. The dotterel *(C. morinellus)* is a Eurasian species. Related family members in North America include the black-bellied plover (called grey plover in England) and American golden-plover *(Pluvialis* spp.).

**Behaviors.** Though classified in a shorebird family, this common plover, probably the most widespread American shorebird of all, dwells more often in uplands than in wetlands. Not shy or secretive, it noisily advertises itself, is in fact hard to miss if present. On the ground, like most plovers, it moves by rapid runs (up to 5 mph) and sudden stops. Often killdeers alight behind plows, consuming the beetle larvae exposed in the fresh-turned soil. Their flight, on long-pointed wings that show a white, lengthwise stripe on each, is somewhat wavering and erratic. Killdeers, usually seen as singles or pairs, seldom associate in large flocks during the breeding season. Small groups, however, often join at communal feeding areas even during the breeding season; intruders may arouse a clamor that attracts other killdeers, resulting in a sort of mobbing behavior similar to that seen in some passerine birds.

Killdeer breeding range spans the continent from southern and northwestern Canada to Mexico and the Gulf coast.

*Spring.* Among the earliest migrants of all American birds, many killdeers have arrived on their snow-spotted breeding range by mid-March or earlier, though migration peaks in early April. Males precede females, usually to their previous territories of an acre or less; they immediately begin making circular flights, up to a half mile in diameter, above the territory, and also stand on ground elevations while voicing "deah!" and "killdee!" calls. As females arrive, usually (but less often than males) to their previous nesting territories and thus frequently to the same mates, activity becomes noisier and more frantic. The birds chase and yell. Males often perform a backward kicking motion called sham nest scraping, creating small, scraped-out depressions at various places in the territory. Paired females also join in this behavior, the birds tossing bits of grass or pebbles over their backs as they scrape. Frequently voiced now is the stutter call, a long, chittering trill also voiced in territorial and alarm situations. Females choose one of the several nest scrapes, usually adding little if any lining. Nesting often begins in early April.

Killdeers are noted for their broken-wing distraction displays—tilting to one side, fluttering along the ground, uttering piteous cries—when nest or chicks are threatened. One observer reported that killdeers on his property vigorously attacked his tractor but performed only distraction displays when he was afoot.

EGGS AND YOUNG: typically 4; eggs buff, heavily blotched and spotted, sometimes wreathed at large end. INCUBATION: by both sexes, males often at night; about 25 days. FLEDGING: about 30 days.

*Summer.* Killdeers often raise 2 broods per breeding season and also renest if the first nest is destroyed. In the southern breeding range, where hot temperatures prevail, incubating killdeers sometimes soak their bellies in water before sitting on the nest, thus cooling the eggs. Chicks may be brooded for several hours after hatching, then permanently vacate the nest.

Females may begin incubating a second nest while males guide and care for the first-brood chicks. Second nestings may extend through July. Parents and chicks gradually abandon the territory, moving to prime feeding areas with heavier cover, often joining several killdeer families in such sites. The long-legged chicks wear only a single dark breast band, in contrast to the adult's two.

Adults begin their annual plumage molt in July, sometimes extending into fall. The birds gather into flocks of up to several hundred in July and August, usually in wetter, more typical shorebird habitats than where they nested. At such feeding and staging sites, the birds sometimes display to each other, appearing to defend temporary individual feeding territories. Southward migration begins as early as July in some areas.

*Fall, Winter.* Killdeer migration is a long, protracted affair, extending through September and October, with occasional birds lingering into December—or even over winter in open-water areas. The birds fly high in small flocks during migration, usually in daytime and at speeds of 25 to 50 mph, often voicing their calls. Many killdeers fly only as far south as they must to find open water and a reliable food supply. Often they associate with other plovers and sandpipers, both as they travel and on wintering sites.

In the eastern United States, winter populations exist from Long Island and the Ohio River to the Gulf. Migrants also travel south to Central America and northern South America. Nonmigratory populations reside in the West Indies and coastal Peru and Chile.

Killdeers begin a second molt of body plumage in February, often extending into spring.

**Ecology.** Killdeers require different habitat types for various phases of their annual life cycle. For nesting, they favor dry uplands—flat, open areas with sparse vegetation but with nearby concealing cover and standing pools of water that are not too far distant. Killdeers nest on beaches, old fields, gravel roads and parking lots, even lawns, golf courses, and flat rooftops. Postbreeding habitats include wetter, marshy areas such as sod farms and mudflats. Open, grassy areas plus beaches and mudflats, where killdeers often associate with other shorebirds, are the primary winter habitats.

The nest is only a shallow, barely lined scrape on open ground. Despite the lack of concealing vegetation, the eggs are so well camouflaged amid the gravel or cinder debris of the site that spotting the nest is not an easy task—virtually impossible without close observation of parental behaviors to help narrow the search.

*Ground debris plus the eggs' cryptic coloration successfully conceal the killdeer's nest, which is hardly a nest at all.*

Killdeers mainly eat insects, which constitute 75 to 98 percent of the diet. Foremost items include beetles, caterpillars, grasshoppers, ants, mosquito larvae, caddisflies, and dragonflies. Spiders, ticks, earthworms, snails, and crayfish are also consumed. About 2 percent of the diet consists of weed seeds.

Competition with shorebirds or other organisms appears negligible in most areas, owing mainly to the killdeer's adaptable range of habitats. The bird's avoidance of southern Mississippi and Florida Gulf coast wintering areas, however, suggests to some observers that the presence of semipalmated and black-bellied plovers in these areas may limit the killdeer's winter distribution. Yet killdeers seem to occupy other Gulf coastal areas that those plover species avoid, such as the Florida panhandle and the Mississippi River mouth. These differences in distribution probably have more to do with habitat preferences than with competitive exclusion. Naturalist Edwin Way Teale pointed out the killdeer's function as sentinel "lookout bird," its loud alarm calls alerting smaller shorebirds to the approach of potential predators.

Potential nest predators include numerous birds and mammals. Opossums, raccoons, skunks, foxes, ground squirrels, domestic cats, and mice sometimes prey on the eggs. Raptors such as short-eared owls capture many birds in the killdeer's winter range. Probably the killdeer's foremost (usually accidental) predator is man; the bird's choice of nest sites often subjects it to intrusion by vehicles or human foot traffic, as well as by treading cattle. Chicks hatched on rooftops with enclosed parapets often starve, and others that fall off may not survive. Tall towers are collision hazards, as for many migrants.

**Focus.** Land clearing and creation of open spaces by industry and agriculture have obviously benefited the opportunistic killdeer, which often resides in areas of human habitation and activity. Probably its present populations far exceed presettlement numbers; its range expansion has likely followed cow, plow, fire, and axe—as well as bulldozer blade and heavy industry—all over the continent. Numbers in some states have increased by some 50 percent in just the past 3 decades. The killdeer's preference for upland breeding habitats, including much so-called waste ground, makes it less vulnerable than most shorebirds to the loss of wetland habitats.

While killdeers are conspicuous enough when flying or performing distraction displays, their plumage pattern of alternating black and white banding on head and breast provides disruptive coloration in their typical nesting sites of gravel or stony surfaces.

Killdeer longevity sometimes exceeds 10 years, but 5 or less is probably typical.

PLOVER FAMILY (Charadriidae)

# American Golden-Plover *(Pluvialis dominicus)*

Recognize this beautiful shorebird by its killdeer size (about 10 inches long) and, in breeding plumage, by its dark, golden-scaly back and crown. Its black face, breast, and belly and a broad white stripe extending from the forehead down the sides of neck and breast also identify it. In winter plumage, the bird looks quite different: plain brown above, lighter below, relatively featureless even in flight. Sexes look much alike except that females often show less clearly defined head and neck striping and have distinctive white cheek patches. The birds voice "queedle," "coodle," and "quee-ah" calls.

**Close relatives.** Only 3 other *Pluvialis* species exist: the Pacific golden-plover *(P. fulva)* of Alaska, Eurasia, and Australia; the Eurasian golden-plover *(P. apricaria);* and the grey or black-bellied plover *(P. squatarola),* almost worldwide in distribution. American and Pacific golden-plovers were, until 1993, considered subspecies of the lesser golden-plover *(P. dominica),* now an obsolete nomenclature.

**Behaviors.** Most of us see golden-plovers only during migrations, when they fly low over the ground in compact, fast-shifting flocks. To an early-spring birder starved for migrant sightings, no finer vision exists than a golden-plover flock rising from or alighting on a fresh-plowed field, its gold-spangled plumages shimmering like rich brocade.

Like many shorebirds, golden-plovers often stand on one leg when resting or roosting. Much communal feeding occurs off the territory.

American golden-plover breeding range is almost entirely arctic, extending from Baffin Island westward through Alaska and the eastern tip of Siberia. Southward, it reaches only to northern Manitoba and British Columbia.

*Spring.* Migration peaks in the upper Midwest and southern Canada in May, with most golden-plovers arriving on the arctic breeding range from mid-May to early June. Migrants travel through Central America into Mexico and Texas, also cross the Caribbean and Gulf of Mexico to Louisiana and Florida, then move in broad fronts up the Mississippi, Missouri, and lower Ohio River valleys into Kentucky, Michigan, Illinois, and the Dakotas.

*American golden-plover flocks sweep through midwestern farmlands on their migration to the arctic breeding range.*

Most of these seasonally monogamous birds arrive on the breeding range unpaired. Males show a high frequency of *philopatry* (site fidelity) to territories from year to year; females are less site faithful, though they may return to the same general locale. Males immediately establish territories of 25 to more than 100 acres, depending on site and breeding density, defending them by aerial displays, notably the butterfly display—slow, measured wingbeats at 30 to 300 feet high while voicing repetitive "chu-leek" calls. Then the male rapidly descends to the ground and utters a whistled "wit-weeyou-wit" call. Males frequently chase each other, then do the butterfly display; occasionally these displays escalate into actual pecking and grappling on the ground. Each territory has a gradient of defense—the closer to the nest, the more intense the pair's distraction displays and defensive behaviors. Flight displays may also attract females. Common pair-bonding and courtship behaviors include head-to-tail rocking motions of both sexes, nest scraping by the male on tundra or snow surface, and wing stretches by the male. Copulation may quickly follow. Egg laying occurs mainly from late May to mid-June.

EGGS AND YOUNG: typically 4; eggs cinnamon to buff, spotted and blotched with brown and black; well camouflaged on ground. INCUBATION: by both sexes, female mainly at night; male may initiate incubation; off-duty males usually forage on or near the territory, while off-duty females usually depart the territory and feed elsewhere, sometimes at considerable distances from the nest; about 26 days. FLEDGING: about 3 weeks.

*Summer.* American golden-plovers raise only a single brood per year. Parent birds lead the chicks to foraging areas, performing distraction displays when threatened or aerial attacks on potential predators. When the chicks fledge, parents may abandon them, or the entire family group may join other family groups to form foraging flocks.

Adult molting, begun during incubation, requires almost a third of the year, one of the longest molting periods for any bird. As molting advances through July, males and females become progressively more similar in plumage.

Peak departure from the breeding range occurs in August, though some adults begin leaving in late June. Some southward migration (especially of juveniles) duplicates the spring route, but many golden-plovers travel offshore along the Atlantic coast, often flying nonstop to South America.

*Fall.* Juveniles tend to linger longer on the breeding range (late August to early October) and stop off more frequently during migration than adults. Golden-plovers arrive on their winter range from late August to December. The primary winter range consists of the Rio de la Plata grasslands and pampas in Argentina, southern Brazil, and Uruguay.

*Winter.* A few golden-plovers overwinter in Central America and along the Florida coasts. The birds are probably site faithful to their wintering areas, and many, though not all, defend daytime feeding territories to which they return each winter. In midafternoon, both territorial and nonterritorial birds join at water sources for bathing and drinking, and the birds also roost in flocks at night, often along swamp and lagoon edges.

Annual molting into the breeding plumage occurs on the winter range and during the northward migration, which begins in late January, coinciding with the annual river flooding cycle in Brazil. This northward exodus, peaking in February, apparently shifts westward of the fall route, traveling the upper Amazonian river valleys in Bolivia, Peru, and Colombia. Mass staging does not occur; the birds move both day and night in flocks of varying sizes.

**Ecology.** Dry, rocky tundra uplands with short, sparse vegetation are the main breeding habitats of American golden-plovers. Foremost winter habitats are grazed grasslands and wetlands. During migrations, golden-plover flocks may be seen feeding and resting in pastures and burned and plowed fields, at airports, and on golf courses, mudflats, and beaches. Fall-migrating juveniles seem to favor wetter, marshier areas than adults. Soybean stubble fields of Amish lands in western Indiana are also frequented by migrating golden-plover flocks—the Amish disdain for pesticide use results in a larger abundance of soil insects. Extensive deforestation in Amazonia, though it has eliminated many habitats of migrant songbirds, has produced new, open habitats for migrating and wintering plovers.

The nest, one of several shallow scrapes made by the male either on bare ground or amid reindeer lichens, is lined with other lichens (often *Thamnolia vermicularis*), sometimes also grasses and leaves. Nest diameter is 4 or 5 inches. Nests usually last for several years, but reuse of them has not been observed.

Golden-plover diet consists mainly of small invertebrates—grasshoppers, crickets, beetles, soil insect larvae, spiders, earthworms, snails, and crustaceans, plus many others. Crowberries, blueberries, and grass seeds are important foods where present.

American and Pacific golden-plovers share *sympatric,* or overlapping, breeding ranges only in western Alaska; the latter species favors lower, moister, less rocky, more densely vegetated sites for nesting. Competitive interactions more frequently occur with other shorebirds: Golden-plovers defend their territories against black-bellied plovers, dunlins, rock and western sandpipers, common snipes, and Lapland longspurs. Short-billed dowitchers seem, at least in some places, relatively well tolerated by breeding golden-plovers and may benefit them by their vigilant alarm calls when danger or disturbance threatens. On the winter range, territories of American golden-plovers and buff-breasted sandpipers often overlap with no apparent conflicts.

Predators on adult golden-plovers include rough-legged hawks, gyrfalcons, peregrine falcons, and snowy and short-eared owls. Parasitic and long-tailed jaegers prey on chicks. Siberian research indicates that "lemming lows," when lemmings become scarce in the arctic range, may indirectly but severely affect golden-plover predation and breeding: Raptor and arctic fox diets may shift largely to eggs and chicks, thereby affecting shorebird populations. Trampling by caribou herds has been known to destroy golden-plover nests on occasion; these deer also eat eggs and chicks at times.

**Focus.** American golden-plover populations appear relatively stable, though far below their early-nineteenth-century abundance. Excessive sport and market hunting, especially during spring migration, devastated this species for a century from about 1810, almost wiping it out. Numbers rebounded after the Migratory Bird Treaty Act of 1918 ended hunting of these birds, but long-continued habitat loss and exposure to contaminants on the South American winter range have slowed population recovery and continue to threaten it.

The American golden-plover, it is claimed, carries at least 52 local and regional aliases in North America, reflecting the bird's wide popularity with nineteenth-century gunners. Black-breast, brass-back, bullhead, field plover, muddy-belly, and squealer are only a few of the names.

If robins and bluebirds are harbingers of spring in most of North America, Eurasian golden-plovers perform the same role for Icelanders in May. "The Golden Plover has arrived to sing away the snow," lilts an old song.

Longevity data, available only for Pacific golden-plovers, probably apply similarly to American golden-plovers. The oldest survivor on record was aged at 15 years, but longevity of 5 or 6 years seems more typical.

# 7

## GULL FAMILY (Laridae), order Ciconiiformes

Gulls and terns inhabit inland waterways, as well as the seacoasts. These are predominantly white birds with varying head and wing markings and sometimes colorful bills and feet, the latter webbed. Their gregarious behaviors, vocal sounds, and graceful flight make them especially conspicuous around harbors, beaches, and bays. They are colonial nesters, and sexes look alike. Hatching is asynchronous in both groups, often resulting in brood reductions as older chicks attack younger ones. Chicks are precocial, though they remain quite sedentary for their first few days.

Both gulls and terns, along with many other seabirds, have a remarkable adaptation called *salt glands,* paired interior structures located in front of the eyes and connected to the nostrils. These glands ooze excess salt in highly condensed solution from the bird's system, enabling it to drink seawater without ill effect.

Gulls are not especially powerful fliers, tending rather to ride the wind on their long, narrow wings, soaring on air currents and thermal updrafts. So precisely do their movements reflect the shifting winds that meteorologists have learned much about ocean air currents from gull observations. Gulls sometimes hover above the water surface to pick up food and also frequently swim. On the water, they mainly feed from the surface, rarely dive. The relatively short gull bill may be thin or quite heavy, depending on the species, and it is slightly hooked on the end. Many species show yellow bills marked with a reddish spot on the lower mandible during the breeding season. Tails are generally square or rounded, and most species have black wing tips. Gulls require 2 to 4 years (again depending on the species) to achieve full adult plumage, and 1-, 2-, or 3-year-old subadult gulls, which show intermediate brownish or mottled plumages, are hardest to pin down as to species. As ornithologist Kenn Kaufman pointed out, "gulls are much *more difficult* to identify at rest than in flight. Many of the best field marks, especially for immatures, involve details of pattern of the wings and tail" that cannot be seen when the wings are folded.

Omnivorous and opportunistic scavengers and predators, gulls have "gone inland" in many areas, finding ample sources of food in sanitary landfills, mall parking lots, and other sites of affluent (and effluent) waste.

Forty-four *Larus* (gull) species exist worldwide, 19 in North America. American gulls range in size from the glaucous and great black-backed gulls *(L. hyperboreus, L. marinus),* more than 30 inches long, to the 11-inch-long little gull *(L. minutus).* Small ocean gulls also include 2 species of kittiwakes *(Rissa* spp.). The word *gull* derives from a Celtic term referring to the bird's wailing cries. Mormons in Salt Lake City erected a monument to the California gull *(L. californicus)* for stemming grasshopper plagues in 1848 and 1855.

Terns differ from gulls in several important respects. They appear generally smaller than most gulls, look more streamlined, and have longer, sharp-pointed bills, which often tilt downward as they fly. Tern tails are forked, some deeply (hence this bird's colloquial name "sea swallow"). Unlike gulls, terns seldom swim—their feet are smaller and weaker than those of gulls—but hover and plunge headfirst for food. In flight, they beat along steadily on long, pointed wings, seldom soaring like gulls. Breeding plumages of most species display black caps and at least partially orange-red bills. Most species are basically white-plumaged, but a few, such as the black tern *(Chlidonias niger)* and sooty tern *(Sterna fuscata),* are extensively dark-colored. Noddies *(Anous, Procelsterna* spp.) are dark terns of the tropics.

Mainly fish eaters, terns do not share the scavenging habits of their gull cousins, thus are not as often seen in areas of human habitation. Some tern species suffered huge losses from plume hunters around the turn of the century, their plumage being faddishly coveted for the millinery trade.

North American terns (13 species of 44 worldwide) range in size from the Caspian and royal terns *(Sterna caspia, S. maxima),* more than 20 inches long, to the 9-inch-long least tern *(S. antillarum).* Gulls and terns are closely related to the jaegers *(Stercorarius* spp.), skuas *(Catharacta* spp.), and skimmers *(Rhynchops* spp.). The word *tern,* meaning "sea swallow," originated in Scandinavia.

GULL FAMILY (Laridae)

---

# Ring-billed Gull *(Larus delawarensis)*

Similar in white appearance to the herring gull but smaller (about 19 inches long), the ring-billed gull also differs in having yellowish or greenish legs and a black ring encircling the bill near its tip. In flight, the ring-bill shows more black on the wing undersides. Its squealing calls are higher pitched than the herring gull's.

**Close relatives.** Other North American *Larus* species (16 total) include the herring gull *(L. argentatus,* see next account), laughing gull *(L. atricilla),* and Bonaparte's gull *(L. philadelphia).* The common gull *(L. canus)* of Eurasia closely resembles the ring-bill.

**Behaviors.** Gregarious like all gulls, ring-bills often associate with other gull species except in their breeding colonies—and even these may lie adjacent to herring gull or (in the West) California gull colonies. The ring-bill is the typical gull of the Great Lakes and other northeastern inland waters, though its breeding range spans the continent from northern Canada to the Gulf, and it appears on both seacoasts as well (it divides into eastern and western populations at the 96-degree meridian of longitude).

Many of the ring-bill's most conspicuous behavioral characteristics apply to other gulls too; few traits exclusive to this species are apparent. The ring-bill's flight is more buoyant and agile than the herring gull's, but feeding behaviors are much alike. The gulls forage on the water, on the wing, and on the ground. On water, they are surface feeders, skimming or dipping their heads to seize subsurface items; they sometimes hawk flying insects; and they forage in fresh-plowed fields, pastures, and garbage dumps, often in large flocks. In shallow water along beaches, they may stomp their feet, driving small, scurrying invertebrates into motion. "Ring-bills," wrote gull observer Larry Penny, "are adept at catching moving things like shrimp and small fish from near the top of the water column. When feeding, they often 'porpoise,' lifting their backs up while putting their heads down, eyes and bills under water, all the while moving forward." Ring-bills also carry objects aloft, drop them, then swoop to catch them, perhaps an activity adaptive for capturing flying insects or other prey. Unlike herring gulls, however, they apparently do not crack hard-shelled food items by dropping them from aloft.

Gulls have evolved a large repertoire of ritualized social behaviors and calls, several of them easily seen and heard in any sizable flock. But despite their highly social milieus, individual gulls are often combative and, in the breeding colony, fiercely territorial. At feeding sites, they show aggressively competitive behaviors, loudly chasing and mobbing any gull carrying a food item, and food piracy is common. Ring-bills often steal from waterfowl, especially diving ducks, by swooping directly at a just-surfaced bird that has a fish or other morsel; the duck dives, expelling its prey, and the gull grabs it. ("Evolution pays no attention to the commandment 'Thou shalt not steal,'" wrote one gull researcher.) They also commonly raid nests of neighboring gulls and other waterbirds, consuming the eggs. They attack straying gull chicks and may even cannibalize them. Thus, in many ways, the gull flock almost seems a society of anarchists when the birds are competing for food or space. Yet when a fox or human predator enters a breeding colony, crowds of gulls noisily gather and hover overhead, conspicuously marking the predator's locale, not attacking but tracking its presence for all gulls—some even attracted from distant flocks—to see and evade.

*Spring.* Ring-billed gull migration extends over a lengthy period, with older adult birds arriving in March and April, first- and second-year birds into May (some of the younger group often do not migrate, remaining on the southern winter range). Flying in flocks of 6 to more than 300 birds, at altitudes up to 1,400 feet, many eastern ring-bills move up the Atlantic coast to Chesapeake Bay, thence westward to the Great Lakes. Others travel up the Mississippi River, diverging northeast to Lake Michigan. The birds (especially males) show strong

*A ring-billed gull breeding colony, this one occupying a dike between sewage
lagoons, is a noisy, tumultuous scene as birds constantly come and go and engage
in territorial rivalry.*

fidelity to previous colony sites and to nesting areas within the colony.
Pairing, often with a previous mate, occurs just before arrival or during territory formation. As the gulls converge at the colony site (large
colonies may number up to 80,000 birds), pairs segregate into rigorously defended territories of about 11 to 40 square feet.

Territories increase by several square feet as incubation proceeds and again when chicks hatch, probably compensating for nest
failures in the colony and consequent available space. An unmated
territorial male advertises his availability by calls and head-tossing
displays when a female lands near him. This species is unique among
the larger gulls in the fact that 2-year-olds often breed (most other
gulls begin breeding at age three), but the younger gulls usually
begin nesting up to 2 weeks later than their elders.

In any large ring-bill colony, some small percentage of pairings
are between females; these birds build nests, and both members of
the pair lay eggs, resulting in *superclutches* of 5 to 7 eggs per nest.
Males readily copulate with these pairs, so at least some of the eggs
are fertile, but males do not incubate or help raise the chicks from
these matings. This phenomenon, where it exists, may reflect an
unbalanced sex ratio (shortage of males).

Nesting extends over a long period: I have found eggs in ring-bill colonies as early as mid-April, and younger birds may still be nesting in early July. A large, floating, nonbreeding population of ring-billed gulls also exists. Unattached to any breeding colony, they feed and roost in flocks throughout the season at shifting locales.

EGGS AND YOUNG: typically 3; eggs olive-gray blotched with brown. INCUBATION: by both sexes; about 3 weeks. FEEDING OF YOUNG: by both sexes; mainly regurgitated insects and fish; downy chicks feed themselves from parent bill or from regurgitant on ground after first day until fledging. FLEDGING: 4 to 6 weeks.

*Summer.* Ring-billed gulls nest only once per season. Parent birds apparently recognize their own chicks by sight, not sound; the reverse is true for chick recognition of its parents. Many chicks that wander off the parental territory die when adjacent territorial gulls attack them. Occasionally 15- to 20-day-old chicks form *creches* (combined groups) of 10 or so at the colony edge, feeding on stolen regurgitant from nearby territories.

Family groups and territories rapidly disintegrate after fledging, and juveniles depart the colony about 11 days after they begin to fly. Adults also disperse, usually to prime feeding areas such as garbage dumps, shallow bays, golf courses, and stubble fields. Some ring-bills fly northward, as far as the Yukon and James Bay, before heading south for the winter.

During the gull's second summer, its gray upper parts have become somewhat lighter, its wing tips become solidly black, and its tail shows a blackish terminal band. Annual molt of all feathers proceeds more or less continuously from March to October. Adult winter plumage is much like summer plumage except for slight graying on the crown and nape.

*Fall.* Ring-bills are shifting southward from their northern continental breeding range by late summer and early fall. The gray-brown juveniles acquire their first winter plumage—largely grayish upper parts plus a narrow white band at the tail end—by late fall. In

*Ring-billed gulls require 3 years to attain full adult plumage. Juveniles such as this one are commonly seen in many ring-bill flocks.*

October and November, tens of thousands of ring-bills mass in western Lake Erie, forming the largest concentration of this species in North America. Most are gone by December, though some linger through winter. Most of the eastern population flies eastward to the Atlantic coast, where the birds spend the winter; the largest numbers congregate on the Atlantic side of Florida (though juveniles favor the Gulf side), and also along the Gulf coastal states. Small numbers of subadult birds move to the West Indies and Central America. Fall migration in this species proceeds more leisurely than spring migration.

*Winter.* Although most ring-billed gulls winter along the Atlantic and Gulf coasts, with many returning to specific wintering sites, large numbers (depending on severity of the winter) often remain in the southern Great Lakes area and on interior lakes and rivers where open water and sufficient food exist.

From February to April, the birds molt head and body plumage. Third-year birds acquire their full-white head plumage at this time. Many adult ring-bills begin northward migration in late February.

**Ecology.** For breeding habitat, ring-billed gulls favor bare or sparsely vegetated islands and shores of freshwater lakes, though some also nest on coastal oceanic islands. Rocky peninsulas and dikes in sewage lagoons are also common habitats. Sometimes the birds create their own nesting habitat by killing the vegetation in woodland edges with their fecal droppings (whitewash) and occupying the newly opened areas. This mainly occurs on wooded islands.

*Nests of ring-billed gulls usually consist of sparse debris supporting the 2 or 3 eggs. Neighboring nests in the colony may lie only a foot or so apart.*

Conversely, later stages of shrub willow and red-osier dogwood growth sometimes force the birds out. Habitat changes or disturbances may lead to colony abandonment of one island for another. Ring-bills, as ornithologist Frank Graham, Jr., noted, "are of necessity a footloose population," being well adapted to "boom-and-bust periods" resulting from habitat instability and catastrophic change. Winter habitats on or near coastal areas include harbors, docks, reservoirs, landfill sites, and shopping malls.

A thin mat of dried grasses or debris, sometimes lined with fine grasses and a few feathers, holds the eggs. Some pairs use almost no nesting material. Nests measure about a foot across. They may be placed as close as 12 to 15 inches center to center, and densities of 2,000 nests per acre are not uncommon. Sand, rocky beaches, bare rock, concrete slag, and (recently) flat urban rooftops are typical nesting sites. If an egg rolls out of the nest, the birds may attempt retrieval or simply rebuild the nest around it. When a mate disappears, the other usually abandons the nest, as well as any further breeding attempts for that season.

Like all gulls, ring-bills are food opportunists, feeding mainly in the morning and just before sunset. Fishes, insects, earthworms, grains, and lakeshore carrion rank high in the diet. Alewives and smelt are common prey, as are grasshoppers and other flying insects. "This is the species that follows the plow," wrote gull researcher James P. Ludwig, "feeding on worms, grubs, beetle larvae, and mice." According to Ludwig, "contaminants in the Great Lakes seem to have affected this gull relatively little, probably because a significant proportion of its food does not originate in waters of the Great Lakes." Meadow voles and deer mice are favored prey in garbage dumps, where thousands of ring-bills may gather to forage, often in association with blackbirds, starlings, turkey vultures, other gull species, and (in the southeastern range) cattle egrets.

Ring-bills seldom pirate food from other gull species but often steal from each other and from starlings and waterfowl. Occasionally ring-bills consume eggs of nesting associates, such as terns and cormorants. Probably the ring-bill's foremost nesting competitors are Caspian and common terns and double-crested cormorants, but since the gulls outnumber these birds in most areas and are more opportunistic feeders, the competitive edge usually falls in their favor, and they often crowd out these species.

Ring-bill predators are many. Eggs and chicks fall prey to herring gulls, American crows, common ravens, red foxes, coyotes, skunks, raccoons, weasels, and minks. Great horned and snowy owls and mammal predators attack both chicks and adults. "Nesting on islands," wrote researcher John P. Ryder, "may be an evolutionary response . . . to mammalian predators." The mere presence of a predator in the colony may result in abandonment of many nests and consequent exposure of eggs and chicks to cooling and predation. Repeated human intrusion into colonies can likewise disrupt incubation and lead to desertion of nests. Ring-bill pairs will attack any chick not their own if opportunity offers; parental instinct is hardly communal in these colonies.

**Focus.** To John James Audubon, this species was "the common American gull," so abundant did he find it in 1840. From that time until the 1920s, however, ring-bills declined precipitously. Hunters sought their plumage for the millinery trade and their eggs for food, and human encroachment seriously disrupted their nesting habitats.

By 1900, ring-bills had become largely extirpated from the eastern United States; most of the depleted population retreated to unsettled areas of the prairie states and provinces. The federal Migratory Bird Treaty Act of 1918 gave this species, along with many others, a new lease on life. Ring-bills had reestablished in the Great Lakes by 1926. The introduction and spread of rainbow smelt and alewives in these waters, and the increased availability of island habitats during low-water cycles—plus adaptability of the birds to human-altered habitats, including landfills and garbage dumps—resulted in slow increase. In the late 1950s, the ring-bill population exploded, intensifying in the 1970s, as gull dispersal rates increased and food resources (mainly human generated) soared.

The population explosion of Great Lakes ring-bills exemplifies the effects of an ecological course of events that began with the invasion of sea lampreys via the Welland Canal in the 1950s. Lamprey parasitism decimated the large predatory native fishes, which had stemmed alewife invasions; alewives streamed unchecked into the lakes, producing huge overpopulations and annual die-offs that littered beaches and provided bountiful food for the gulls, with consequent increase in colony numbers and size.

Today an estimated 4 or 5 million ring-bills exist; some 70 percent of them nest in Canada, 30 percent in the United States, and the species continues to expand northward. This bird, wrote Ludwig, "has staged the greatest population increase sustained over the longest period of time of any Great Lakes species." Conservationists worry that its negative effects on tern nesting may require control measures to reduce its numbers. The ring-bill's reputed predation on waterfowl eggs and young, however, remains largely unconfirmed. Around airports, where ring-bills often feed, flocks pose flight safety problems. Ring-bills rank with pigeons in some urban areas for nuisance defecations. The bird's current abundance has given it definite pest status.

If ring-bills survive beyond their second year (less than 20 percent of eggs become breeding-age gulls), their chances for a longevity of 2 decades or more are good; the survival rate of three-year-olds approaches 90 percent. In any large ring-bill flock, first-year and adult gulls outnumber second-year birds, which are the least abundant age group owing to multiple hazards and inexperience. Different patterns of age-group dispersal, however, may lead to locally observed age ratios that do not precisely reflect those of the species as a whole.

GULL FAMILY (Laridae)

# Herring Gull *(Larus argentatus)*

Measuring about 2 feet long, adult herring gulls have white heads, underparts, and tails; a pearl gray mantle (back and wings) with black wing tips; and pinkish legs and feet. The heavy, yellow bill shows a red spot near the tip of the lower mandible. Immature herring gulls—that is, birds 4 years old and under—exhibit varying degrees of darker plumage. This bird's "hiyah hiyah," "ow ow ow," and "klee-ah klee-ah" cries, along with other squealing and wailing notes, are familiar sounds of beach and port.

**Close relatives.** All other *Larus* species are closely related (see Ring-billed Gull).

**Behaviors.** Visibly larger than the ring-billed gull, the herring gull is the gregarious, widely distributed "seagull" (a generic vernacular term—no gull species of that name exists). This bird's complex behavioral traits, especially during the breeding season, were notably observed and reported by Dutch biologist Niko Tinbergen in his classic *The Herring Gull's World* (1953), a book that helped establish the scientific study of animal behavior *(ethology)*. Tinbergen observed entire repertoires of ritualized motions, postures, calls, and other interactions of this gull, providing one of the most richly detailed biographies of any bird species.

In flight, herring gulls make ample use of air currents and updrafts of their windy environment, often soaring effortlessly, slightly adjusting the bend or plane of wings and tail as they glide. Few birds are so intimately united with the wind as these and other gulls; they exhibit a visible poetry of motion. If you have ever been on a ship forging into a headwind and watched the accompanying gulls, you have seen their ability to keep pace with the ship by expert use of updrafts from the vessel.

Their social interactions in the flock are not so poetic. Except between a breeding pair, they exhibit no cooperative behaviors, often pirate food from one another, and their noisy squabbles, especially when feeding, are incessant. They readily attack (or occasionally adopt) stray chicks in the breeding colony and also consume eggs from unguarded nests of their own and other species. Roosting flocks on a sandbar or wharf, however, appear sedate as they bask in the sun. On the water, herring gulls swim and float

*The herring gull, which exhibits both sedate and fiercely competitive behaviors, is a familiar resident of most Northern Hemisphere coastal areas.*

buoyantly, feeding mainly from the surface. Occasionally, spotting small fishes, they plummet ternlike from the air in a splashing dive, but this is not a common behavior. Their buoyancy prevents them from diving deeper than a few feet.

One familiar feeding strategy of herring gulls is to carry a mollusk (usually a clam) aloft, then drop it. If the shell breaks on the ground (or ice), the bird lands and consumes the inner flesh; if the shell does not break, the gull retrieves and drops it again, sometimes repeatedly. One study found that adult herring gulls average 1.6 drops for breaking open a clam, and that yearling birds require 2.3 drops. Sometimes the birds carry their prey far inland in executing this maneuver. Many of them, however, can't seem to distinguish a hard, shell-cracking surface (rocks) from softer ground (sand), so the strategem often proves unsuccessful.

Herring gulls are common in the Northern Hemisphere throughout the world. In North America, they breed across the continent from the Arctic Circle south to the Great Lakes, New England, and coastal North Carolina. The herring gull provides a prime example of a ring species—that is, a species that varies over a circular range (in this case, circumpolar or Holarctic) to the extent that at each end of the circle, where the divergent subspecies rejoin (in northern Eurasia), they no longer interbreed. The *Larus* ring species complex probably evolved when parts of the ring distribution became fragmented and reproductively isolated during Pleistocene glaciation, then again became continuous.

*Spring.* A partial molt of body feathers occurs in March and April; fourth-year birds acquire full adult plumage at this time.

Adult herring gulls exhibit strong site fidelity *(philopatry)* to their natal and previous breeding colonies, often returning to the same territory they occupied the previous year, usually in April and May. Younger gulls, arriving later than the already paired adults, usually form territories at edges of the colony where competition from older gulls is less intense. But many subadult birds—gulls under age four or five—do not return to their home colony until they reach adulthood. These gulls wander widely in the intervening years and may show up almost anywhere in North America or Europe. Tinbergen believed that herring gulls usually pair for life but that mates probably do not remain together after breeding seasons. Yet, he wrote, "observations seem to show that both partners find and recognize each other in spring" weeks before they return to the previously occupied territory; "this shows an amazing faculty, not only of recognizing individuals, but also of memory."

Most herring gulls begin breeding in their fourth or fifth year. Females initiate pair formation within the social context of what Tinbergen termed the *club,* a dense association of unmated birds that gather in specific areas at the colony edge. Males attract flying females to land in the club by voicing the yelp or long call, an extended series of "ow ow" and "kyow" notes. Courtship behaviors include mutual displays—head tossing, pecking motions, foot scraping, feeding of the female with male regurgitant, and other actions. Herring gulls require larger territorial space than ring-bills—some 30 to 50 yards in diameter. Threat displays at territory borders consist of upright strutting and grass pulling, sometimes actual fighting. Pairs at this time spend only a part of each day on the territory, regularly flying from the colony to feeding areas, sometimes for distances of 10 miles or more.

Both mates soon begin scraping slight ground depressions on the territory; eventually they focus attention on one of them and construct the meager nest. Nesting usually begins in May.

EGGS AND YOUNG: typically 3; female-female pairs sometimes lay superclutches of 5 to 6 (often sterile) eggs; eggs olive or bluish, blotched with brown and gray. INCUBATION: by both sexes, relieving each other every few hours; about 26 days; chicks hatch over a 3-day period, are brooded in the nest for several days. FEEDING OF YOUNG: by both sexes (males more often before fledging, females more often after fledging); chicks initiate feeding by pecking at red spot on adult bill; mainly regurgitant of small prey items. FLEDGING: 5 or 6 weeks.

*Summer.* Herring gulls raise only 1 brood per year. Both fledglings and adults remain on the colony site through much of the summer. Fledglings continue to beg and be fed by parents for up to 6 months, a much longer period of feeding than in most bird species. Many fledglings, however, gather in groups, or *creches,* on the colony perimeters, where they forage by themselves and beg from any nearby adult.

Individual gull dispersal from the colony begins in late July, but most of the birds remain relatively near the breeding area, reassembling into large flocks only at abundant food sources. A wider general dispersal occurs in August, when the birds undergo their complete annual molt. The white adults' new plumage, marked with indistinct, brownish head and neck streaks, will be replaced with new white head and body feathers the following spring. Juveniles acquire a quite uniformly brownish plumage in August. As they age through 3 winters, successive spring and summer molts gradually lighten the head, bill, underparts, and rump. Experienced gull observers can usually identify an immature gull's year of age by these subtle though distinctive variations in plumage—particularly the wing pattern and amount of gray in the mantle.

*Fall.* Migrational movements in this species are age segregated. First- to third-year immatures are the foremost migrators. The youngest birds appear to move farthest south to milder climates, usually in October through mid-November, with second- and third-year birds traveling relatively less far. Most of the adult population remains throughout the year near the breeding area. Subadult gulls concentrate along the Gulf and southern Atlantic coasts, but many also winter inland in large lakes or reservoirs.

*Winter.* Adult herring gulls can be seen in the Great Lakes area throughout winter, foraging wherever open waters and other food sources permit. In the northern coastal states, many herring gulls move offshore during late fall and winter, finding richer food resources in the warm Gulf current than along shore. "A winter flock," observed Tinbergen, "seems to be made up of individuals, not of pairs." The birds defend winter feeding territories—usually areas of beach or intertidal flats—from other gulls. By March, the adult gulls begin to drift back to their continental breeding colonies.

**Ecology.** Secluded islands are the herring gull's foremost colonial breeding habitats. Major requirements are areas free of mammal predators and nest sites sheltered from prevailing winds. Feeding habitats include open sea, lake and ocean coastal areas, harbors, and inland landfills and garbage dumps. Roosting and loafing sites include beaches, landfills, parking lots, fields, and airport runways.

The nest, a scraped depression lined with grasses, mosses, and debris, measures a foot or two across. Occasionally, where remote island habitat is lacking, herring gulls nest solitarily in trees and on rocky ledges and rooftops. For nesting, herring gulls favor open, grassy sites near water, often in proximity to clumps of herb or shrub vegetation. Such nesting habitat is often shared with cormorants.

Omnivorous and opportunistic scavengers, herring gulls consume almost anything organic. Marine invertebrates (mollusks, worms, crustaceans, starfish, sea urchins), fish, insects, rodents, and carrion are common animal fare. Herring gulls follow plows on land for worms and grubs, trail ships and fishing boats for food and wastes thrown overboard. They also pirate food from other waterbirds. If opportunity offers, they attack undefended eggs and chicks of adjacent nesting gulls, terns, cormorants, puffins, and other birds; such predation appears uncommon, however, except where human intrusion into colonies disrupts normal behaviors, often causing the birds to vacate their nests temporarily. In company with other gull species, plus blackbirds, starlings, and others, herring gulls forage extensively at landfills and garbage scows. Several studies indicate that food from garbage dumps has much lower nutritive value for gulls than fish or fishery waste. Chicks fed by adults on garbage items show significantly lower growth and survival rates, thus belying the theory that the spread of landfills and garbage dumps significantly accounts for gull increases. At sea, herring gulls often associate with feeding groups that may include kittiwakes, cormorants, shearwaters, dolphins, and whales. Predatory fishes such as tuna may drive smaller fishes to the ocean surface, where the gulls capture many. Juvenile gulls in the Gulf of Maine often associate with surfacing humpback whales in fall and winter, feeding on fish driven to the surface by the whales. Herring gulls also consume algae and wild berries on occasion.

Mixed-species colonies are fairly common, with herring and other gull species and terns populating the site. Herring gulls defend their territories only from other gulls. This gull's foremost competitor in New England and Canada's Maritime Provinces is the great black-backed gull *(L. marinus)*, which sometimes hybridizes with it, often competes for nesting habitat and territorial space, and also robs its nests. Herring gulls have also hybridized with glaucous, glaucous-winged, lesser black-backed, and common black-headed gulls, indicating at least potential competitive interactions. Food competitors include all other gulls present plus predatory fishes and sea mammals.

Island breeding habitat restricts the number of mammal predators on gull colonies. At sites other than islands, red foxes, raccoons, minks, and rats consume gull eggs, and domestic dogs and cats kill chicks. Birds are more common predators: gull species, common ravens, and American crows on eggs; great black-backed and other gulls, great horned and short-eared owls, northern harriers, and herons on chicks. Adult gulls occasionally fall prey to bald eagles, peregrine falcons, gyrfalcons, and great horned owls, plus sharks and harbor and gray seals. Some herring gulls become tangled in nets and fishing lines. Waste litter of plastic six-pack covers, in which birds strangle, has killed many gulls. Pesticides in lake ecosystems (especially DDT and DDE, as estrogen mimics) cause a skewed sex ratio (shortage of males) and consequent formation of female pairs that produce sterile egg clutches. Water pollution and contaminants, especially in the Great Lakes, resulted in much egg and chick mortality during the 1960s and 1970s, becoming somewhat alleviated in the 1980s. Yet herring gulls show remarkable physiological toleration of such toxins as PCBs, dioxins, and botulinus in amounts that are lethal to other waterbirds.

**Focus.** Shifts in herring gull abundance and distribution over the past century may have more numerous and complex causes than the human-created garbage sources so often cited as the simple explanation. No reliable figures exist for herring gull population size before European settlement in North America. During the nineteenth century, however, the birds were widely hunted for their plumage, used in millinery, and their eggs were widely sought as food, resulting in gull declines of massive proportions. Audubon considered the species rare; in 1900, only an estimated 8,000 pairs existed, all of them in Maine. Numbers recovered slowly after passage of the 1918 federal Migratory Bird Act prohibited hunting and egging (though gull egging remains legal in Canada).

From the 1930s through the 1960s, herring gull populations rapidly increased. In addition to the proliferation of garbage dumps during this period, equally or more important causes of increase included gull protection; the increase of commercial fishing activities, which generated large amounts of fish waste and reduced the abundance of large predatory fishes that compete with gulls for small fishes; and drastic decline of competitive whale and seal populations, again reducing competition for small fishes (especially capelin and sandlance) and invertebrates. Overfishing and new landfill techniques may account for the current leveling off of herring gull abundance in many areas. Also, based on figures from various studies from 1979 to 1984, the maximum fledging success of 3 chicks per pair lags below 25 percent in this species.

Today Massachusetts and Maine are the foremost herring gull states, but herring gull abundance has apparently peaked there, and may even be declining in the maritimes and New England. Causes are attributed to eggers in Canada and the southward expansion of great black-backed gull populations. Once the exclusive breeding gull of the Great Lakes (now ranking second after the ring-billed gull), herring gull populations continue slow growth there. In recent years, colonies have expanded southward along the Atlantic coast. Despite these relatively modest trends of increase, herring gulls have evoked considerable clamor besides their own in certain coastal New England areas. Recent government poisoning programs in Cape Cod— intended to eradicate thousands of herring gulls, thus making habitat available for terns and the endangered piping plover—met with storms of protest from local residents, whose motto became "save the seagulls." Studies show that such extermination programs usually don't work very well except in extremely localized situations; the gulls that are left simply expand their territories to fill available space, resulting in no appreciable gain of habitat for other species (bringing to mind ornithologist Pete Dunne's maxim: "That environment is maintained best which is juggled least").

Eider ducks and puffins benefit from gull vigilance and attacks on predators. Gull eggs have long been staple food items for human coastal dwellers. Gull expert Frank Graham, Jr., vouched for their pleasant taste, "which has a hint of the sea in it." Gull egging is still pursued on the birds' northern range outside the United States.

Typical adult herring gull longevity is 15 to 20 years, though ages over 30 have been recorded. As with most birds, chances for survival increase with age (up to a point), a fact reflected in the variously plumaged age classes seen in a gull flock (see Ring-billed Gull).

GULL FAMILY (Laridae)

# Common Tern *(Sterna hirundo)*

Recognize the common tern by its white, deeply forked tail; black cap; grayish back and wings; and sharp-pointed, red-orange bill with black tip. A black wedge in the outer primaries, pointing in from the trailing edge of the wing, is distinctive. In juvenile and winter plumage, the bill is black, and the black cap covers only the eyes and rear head, the forehead being white. Feet are orange-red. The bird's harsh, gargling call ("ke-arrr") slurs downward; it also voices other staccato and shrill notes.

**Close relatives.** Common terns closely resemble arctic, Forster's, and roseate terns *(S. paradisaea, S. forsteri, S. dougallii)* in several features. Twelve *Sterna* species (including those mentioned) breed in North America; 32 others exist worldwide. Royal and Caspian terns *(S. maxima, S. caspia)* are the largest American terns (20 or more inches long), least terns *(S. antillarum)* the smallest (9 inches). Also related are black terns *(Chlidonias niger)* and the noddies *(Anous, Procelsterna* spp.).

**Behaviors.** This bird remains the most widely distributed tern in the world. As with so many birds named common, however, its occurrence is currently spotty, and its declines in abundance, especially in North America, have made its label a misnomer. (Opinion: Bird names should avoid reflecting temporal abundance status.)

Graceful in flight, slimmer and more streamlined than gulls, terns are gregarious and colonial like their cousins and often associate with them, both in coastal feeding areas and in their breeding colonies, called *terneries,* though the earlier-nesting gulls often tend to usurp ternery sites.

Tern feeding methods also differ from those of gulls. Primarily fish eaters, terns spot their prey while flying 10 to 20 feet above the water, then plummet headfirst straight down, splattering the surface as they hit but seldom diving more than 1 or 2 feet, often immersing only the forepart of the body. The entire procedure lasts 2 or 3 seconds at most. A grabber, not a stabber, the bird holds its captured prey crosswise in the bill tip, then carries it to the colony or deftly turns it headfirst and swallows it. Long outer feathers *(streamers)* of the tern's flexible, forked tail (accounting for the vernacular name "sea swallow") act as rudders during those steep dives, precisely calibrating the bird's angle of descent—a marvelous coordination of eye and tail movement, and marvelously entertaining to watch. Like gulls, terns also dip in the surface to feed. Unlike gulls, however, terns are poor walkers and swimmers, their feet being smaller and weaker, though they float buoyantly on water. They seldom feed on

*Although terns and gulls show resemblances, this head profile of the common tern reveals its distinctive bill shape and head pattern.*

land and do not omnivorously scavenge like gulls. In the ternery, "their clamoring, their maneuvering, their minor acts of aggression, are incessant," as naturalist John Hay observed. A tern carrying a fish is always subject to interference and piracy from another tern.

Primarily birds of the ocean coasts, common terns also range inland to large freshwater lakes. Terneries occupy islands and beaches from the Rocky Mountains eastward, extending from northern Canada to the Great Lakes and the Carolinas, and across Eurasia as well. These birds are long-distance seasonal migrators.

*Spring.* Strongly site faithful *(philopatric)* to their terneries, adult common terns arrive days or weeks before younger ones. Northern migration is a somewhat protracted movement, with birds arriving in late April through mid-May at irregular intervals. They appear in no hurry to begin nesting, often roosting and feeding in nearby areas for days before actually occupying the ternery. Some terneries host roseate and arctic terns along with commons. Terneries range in size from tens to thousands of birds.

Most of the adults are already paired when they arrive—the birds apparently pair monogamously for life—and they often claim the same territory they have previously occupied. Depending on density of pairs, territories range from 2 feet or less to 6 feet in diameter, average size being about 4 feet. Common terns also establish feeding territories, often located 5 miles or more from the ternery. A typical feeding territory of a pair extends 100 to 300 yards along the shoreline and about 200 feet offshore; it is strongly defended from other terns. Before incubation begins, pairs spend about a third of the day on these territories, feeding and loafing.

Terns begin breeding at age three or four. Unpaired later-arriving males often occupy peripheral or less desirable territories. Subadult terns (those under 3 years old) are scarce in the colony; apparently few terns migrate from the winter range until they reach adulthood and are able to breed.

Courtship behaviors, between both paired birds and unpaired singles, are various and complex. A ternery is a milling, clamorous, hyperactive scene, with birds constantly coming and going, performing strutting displays on the ground and gliding displays in the air (most notably the "pass ceremony," in which each mate alternately lags behind, then overtakes the other in flight), plus mate feeding, chasing, squabbling, and foot scraping on the territory. Terns are nervous birds, usually appearing in a state of constant activity and excitement in the ternery. Yet by means of this incessant motion and excitement, the tern society settles itself, pairs gradually sort out and arrange themselves, and nesting commences, usually by mid-May to early June.

Terns strongly defend their territories, especially after incubation begins, often mobbing predators and diving at human intruders, sometimes even striking them. Possibly adding insult to injury, a common aspect of this defensive behavior is defecation at the low point of the dive, showering the intruder. But terns en masse also exhibit directly contrary behavior, sometimes at the least provocation, such as a strange noise or sudden movement, and sometimes for no discernible reason. The entire colony, or a portion of it, rises without a vocal sound and moves silently out over the water, usually flying in a low, compact flock before wheeling about and returning. These silent outflights, called *dreads,* may "occur under so many different conditions, and often for such apparently contradictory reasons," wrote John Hay, "that it is hard to assign them a function."

Because predation, loss of habitat, and competition with gulls have depleted tern populations in many areas—and because impulse or disturbance can cause them to abandon their nests for hours at a time, leaving eggs to cool or overheat in the sun and become exposed to predators—human intrusion into terneries is prohibited by law in most places.

Common terns with clutches smaller than 3 eggs often roll one or more stones into the nest, thus making up the "right" number of eggs to accord with the bird's 3 brood patches. Presumably this action relates to stimuli affecting incubation behavior.

EGGS AND YOUNG: usually 3; eggs buff or brownish, brown spotted, often wreathed with brown; downy chicks are brooded on territory for about a week. INCUBATION: by both sexes, female more than male; sitting bird is fed by mate; about 22 days, up to a month if birds are disturbed. FEEDING OF YOUNG: by male for first week, by both parents after that; small fishes. FLEDGING: about 3 weeks.

*Summer.* Common terns raise only a single brood (with occasional exceptions), but nest disruption often results in renesting attempts, extending the season in some cases into July. Many of these later nests prove unsuccessful, owing in part to decline of hormonal stimuli and attentiveness of parent birds as the season advances. Parent birds are seeking fish during most daylight hours at this season, making countless trips to and from the ternery. The well-camouflaged chicks usually hide in areas of the territory when the parents are absent, rapidly assembling around an arriving parent carrying a fish. Many fish brought to the chicks, especially during their first week or so, are too large for them to swallow; tern colonies are frequently littered with uneaten fish carcasses for this reason. Most parent terns quickly adjust to the needs of their young, bringing smaller prey. As chicks age, they may wander outside the territory. Neighboring adult terns may peck at them but seldom kill stray chicks; occasionally they even feed them. Chicks from several broods sometimes gather in groups, or *creches,* off their territories, returning to them when parent terns arrive with food. Fledglings soon accompany parents on fishing flights, but they often continue to beg and be fed through summer. Fledging proceeds through July and much of August.

By late summer, most terns have abandoned the ternery; the few unfledged chicks that remain are likewise abandoned. Red bills darken as the adult birds begin their annual plumage molt in August and September. This molt is often temporarily arrested during migration, which occurs from mid-August to early September. Erosion of the black forehead feathers, with their white bases, accounts for the gradual change in head plumage.

*Fall.* Common terns usually migrate in small flocks, sometimes consisting of several family groups. Large flocks of more than 1,000 birds, however, also occur at times. Such flocks, often mixed with roseate terns, occupy island staging areas in New England until mid-October. Most of the birds have reached their winter quarters by early November. Many young of the year will not return to their birthplace ternery for 2 or 3 years. The summer molt resumes on the winter range; winter adult plumage and subadult plumages look much alike.

Common tern winter range extends from the southern Atlantic and Gulf coasts through Central America to Peru, Brazil, and northern Argentina.

*Winter.* Common terns continue their long, progressive plumage molt that began in summer into February or March. Another partial molt, mainly of body and some wing feathers,

*Common tern plumages differ depending on the time of year one sees the bird. The black and white breeding plumage (top) appears in spring and summer; winter head plumage (bottom) looks grayer and less distinct.*

begins in December; it overlaps with the prior molt and is completed before the birds migrate again in March or April. Now the adult birds appear in the full black and white breeding plumage, first gained during their third winter. Bills redden again as the rejuvenation of sex hormones pushes the birds back to the ternery.

**Ecology.** The common tern occupies a wider geographic range of habitats than other tern species, residing from arctic fringes to the tropics—"a remarkable variety for a bird that basically needs clear water with fish in it and a piece of bare ground to nest on," as tern expert Rob Hume remarked. The tern's world is "the junction between the water and land," whether on inland lakes or ocean coast. Vital components of common tern habitats include bare sandy or gravelly margins of islands or peninsulas for nesting and unsilted waters for feeding, since successful capture of prey depends upon visibility. But "outside the breeding season," wrote Hume, "the quality of the land becomes less of a problem. . . . All they need apart from fish is a place to perch now and then, and a safe place to spend the night." Rafts, piers, buoys, moored vessels, floating logs, and other objects or structures become frequent perching and roosting places.

One of several foot scrapes made on the territory during the courtship period becomes the common tern's nest. Sometimes the birds add bits of debris, strands of seaweed or grass, or small twigs. Sparse vegetation (such as marram grass), if any, characterizes the site; occasionally terns colonize rocky or grassy shorelines as well.

Some 90 percent of the common tern diet consists of small fishes, the birds capturing whatever kinds become most abundant at a given time and place. Sand launces, pipefish, menhaden, and alewives are common prey. Length of most prey averages 2 to 4 inches. Fishes that school and shoal near the surface—whether driven up by larger fish predators, by tidal currents, or by water temperature inversions—become the most vulnerable to capture. One feeding tern often attracts others; some ornithologists speculate that the white, highly visible plumage of many colonial seabirds may have evolved as a feeding adaptation that benefits the colony. If fish are in short supply, terns also consume crustaceans, such as shrimp, and insects.

The foremost common tern competitors, mainly for nesting space, are gulls—especially ring-billed and herring gulls. These species, which begin breeding earlier in spring than the terns, often co-opt relatively scarce beach and island nesting habitats before the terns arrive. The gulls' omnivorous feeding habits also give them a competitive edge, as does their greater tolerance for water contaminants. Probably humans, however, compete even more aggressively than gulls (gull overpopulations are, in many cases, an indirect consequence of human-caused environmental changes). Overfishing plus development and heavy usage of beach shorelines have driven out the terns from many former terneries. Terns' ability to coexist with the kinds of human activities that occur along vast stretches of our continental and inland beaches is conditional at best, as demonstrated by the trend of decline in this species over the past several decades. Nothing is sadder to a lover of these beautiful waterbirds than a ternless ternery in spring.

Opportunistic gull predation on tern eggs and chicks sometimes occurs where gull and tern colonies abut. One destructive predator is the great horned owl—not so much because of its sudden nocturnal capture of a tern on the nest, but as a result of wholesale dreads. Alarmed incubating or brooding birds, unable to defend the colony at night, flee en masse, exposing eggs and chicks to often fatal chill and to other predators before their return. Short-eared owls, ruddy turnstones, and black-crowned night herons sometimes raid terneries. Island habitats usually preclude most mammal predation; in other beach habitats, however, raids by foxes, coyotes, skunks, weasels, rats, dogs, cats, and snakes may, similarly to owls, adversely affect the colony beyond the initial predation itself. Ants sometimes kill newly hatched chicks.

**Focus.** Commercial fishermen know this bird as the "mackerel gull," the "striker," or the "medrick," among other local names. They watch it closely, for wherever terns are feeding, chances are good that mackerel or tuna have driven smaller fish prey to the surface, and there the net harvester wants to be. As both terneries and fisheries diminish in the Atlantic and Great Lakes alike, however, such direct bird-human coactions become increasingly rare. Great Lakes common terns are listed as threatened; numbers there have declined about 70 percent since 1960, reflecting high water levels of the past several decades that have flooded out many terneries, plus toxic contaminants in the lakes. Efforts to restore tern habitat have included the creation of man-made islands for nesting, erection of predator and people fences, brush-cutting on small islands that once hosted terns, and control of competing gull populations. Some wildlife refuges attract terns to restored habitats by placing decoy terns and playing tapes of tern calls. These and other measures have sometimes resulted in temporary local increases of terns, but all are essentially stopgap solutions. Size of the ternery may be an important aspect of breeding success; small terneries are generally less vigorous and successful than large ones.

Terns simply cannot tolerate high levels of human activity around their terneries. Troops of sunbathers and trains of speedboats and beach buggies, along with water pollution and overfishing, effectively usher terns out of existence. Tern experience causes us to conclude that the future for birds that do not adapt well to people does not look bright for our world.

Whatever the perilous status of these birds today, it remains improved from the early years of this century, when plumage hunters all but eradicated this species from North America. The tern's long tail streamers were valued for ladies' hats (1 of every 1,000 Americans in 1900 was employed in the millinery industry). From flocks of 100,000 common terns on New England beaches in 1870, numbers had dropped to only a few thousand pairs 20 years later. Tern slaughter continued until about 1910, when public fashion for elaborate headdress dwindled (male Audubon Society lecturers had harangued audiences on such topics as "Woman as a bird enemy"), probably owing as much to economics—rising prices and fallen demand—as to conservationist oratory and new laws.

Once past the high-mortality period of their first 3 years, common terns are fairly long-lived. Ages of twenty and above are not uncommon, though average life span is about 12 years. Terns have amazing powers of flight and endurance. In January 1997, a common tern banded as a chick in Finland the previous summer was recovered in Australia—a world-record bird trip of more than 16,000 miles; gale winds no doubt helped propel it on its journey.

# 8

## Northern Harrier *(Circus cyaneus)*

Hawk family (Accipitridae), order Ciconiiformes. Measuring almost 2 feet long (about crow size) with a 3- to 4-foot wingspread, northern harriers (formerly known as marsh hawks) cruise low across field and marsh with wings slightly uptilted like a turkey vulture's dihedral. Slim-bodied with long, banded tails and long, rounded wings, the harrier shows a white rump spot on the back, its most distinctive mark; yellow eyes, bill, and feet; and an owl-like facial disk, which gives the small-billed head a hooded appearance. Males (sometimes called "gray ghosts") are silver-gray with light buff chest and belly and black wing tips; the slightly larger females are sparrow brown above, streaked brown beneath. Juveniles, darker brown above than adult females, exhibit a copper-red chest and belly. Older immatures and adult females look much alike. Vocal sounds include a shrill, nasal "kee kee kee" and flickerlike notes.

**Close relatives.** Thirteen *Circus* species range worldwide, but the northern harrier, known as the hen harrier in Eurasia and Africa, is the only one in North America.

**Behaviors.** A large bird slowly quartering and tilting 7 feet or less above the ground is probably a harrier; its large white rump patch confirms it. Harriers hunt on the wing, dropping to seize a mouse or other prey, relying not only upon superb vision but also on acute hearing. The flattish facial disk probably helps focus sound, as in owls, enabling the birds to hunt in lower light levels than most daytime raptors. Northern harriers also perch-hunt at times, hover-hunt with beating wings, stoop (dive on prey from aloft), and soar high, often rocking unsteadily in the wind. The wingbeats, often seen even when the bird soars on thermal updrafts, are slow and regular, quite distinctive to observers familiar with harrier flight patterns. Northern harriers have been observed flying as high as 3,000 feet during migrations. This is one of the few North American hawks that show *sexual dimorphism* (male-female differences) in plumage;

*A male northern harrier clutches its prey, a white-footed mouse. Note the facial disk similar to that of owls. Unseen in this profile view is the white spot on the bird's lower back.*

the only one that is frequently *polygynous* (1 male mates with 2 or 3 females); and the only one that regularly nests on the ground and in colonies.

Northern harriers are circumpolar, breeding in Eurasia as well as North America. Their breeding distribution spans our continent from Alaska to Newfoundland, south to North Carolina, Texas, and southern California. Only harriers on the northern range migrate; snow cover, and thus food accessibility, probably accounts for this movement.

*Spring.* Harriers exhibit the most protracted migration periods of any North American raptor, appearing on their northern range from late February through early June. Adult males precede females by days or weeks, and subadults arrive last. The birds usually travel singly or in small groups of 2 to 5 birds, move both day and night, and favor coastal routes rather than inland thermals along land ridges. Male yearlings' reddish breast feathers, now fading to white, begin to resemble adult female plumage.

Adults that have successfully reared broods in a certain site are *philopatric,* tending, as if imprinted, to return to that site. Site fidelity is low, however, for birds that have experienced nest failures. Thus previously mated pairs may reappear in the same nesting area, but relatively few of the birds—even males that remain monogamous for the season—pair again with the previous mate.

"Harriers are like the men of Islam," wrote researcher Frances Hamerstrom; "most of them have one wife, but if they can afford it, more." Polygyny in local harrier populations seems to be triggered by the combination of a surplus of females (the unbalanced sex ratio typical of these birds), shrinking habitats that crowd the birds, and an abundant food supply. In such circumstances, even yearling females may become polygynous partners, whereas yearling males, usually chased out by older breeding males, may breed monogamously with a yearling female. Females apparently select their mates based on the quality of male courtship feeding and display behaviors.

Territory varies with habitat quality and nest density, ranging from less than 1 acre to more than 200 acres in size. Typical territories seem to average about 1 square mile. Home range, mainly undefended feeding areas, may extend 2 miles or more, increasing in size as the chicks age; each bird typically has its own habitual feeding site within that area. Although solitary nesting pairs are not uncommon, prime habitats may host loose colonies of several to a dozen or more nests. Nests are rarely spaced less than 300 feet apart, though females of a polygynous harem may nest closer together.

The male harrier's aerial courtship displays, known as sky dancing, are spectacular. They consist of multiple U-shaped loops and barrel rolls high over the territory. (Males also sky-dance during migration.) Females occasionally join in. Males seldom approach the nest after incubation begins, spending all their time hunting and perched. As a male carrying prey nears the territory, the female flies up from the nest. He drops the prey item; she catches it in her talons and returns to the nest with it, usually landing some distance away and approaching the nest on foot.

Incubation usually begins by early May on the northern range. The birds frequently abandon nest and territory if disturbed before eggs hatch.

EGGS AND YOUNG: typically 4 or 5; eggs bluish white, usually unmarked, sometimes brown spotted. INCUBATION: by female; about 31 days; hatching asynchronous; chicks altricial. FEEDING OF YOUNG: by female, which tears prey (mainly rodents and birds) brought by male into small bits; if female dies, male piles food on the nest but does not tear prey or feed chicks. FLEDGING: about 30 days or more.

*Summer.* Parent harriers vigorously defend their nests when chicks are present, even attacking human intruders occasionally. Female chicks often have a better survival rate than male chicks, producing the skewed sex ratio commonly seen in harriers. *Siblicide* (killing, often indirectly by starvation, of one chick by another), though quite frequent in most hawks, seldom occurs in harriers. "Partly grown harriers," wrote Hamerstrom, "tend to scurry away upon hearing the shrill cries of their smaller nest mates," perhaps a mechanism that increases the younger chicks' chances for survival. The family unit remains together through summer. Even after fledging in July, juveniles do not begin to hunt but continue until migration time to catch prey dropped by the parents. Juveniles spend much time in play, chasing one another, often pouncing on corncobs or other objects. Males and—after the young have fledged—females roost solitarily at night (and often during the day) on the ground, usually at some distance from the nest.

Adult birds undergo their annual plumage molt from July to September; females sometimes begin molting flight feathers while they incubate. Yearling harriers now molt into their first sexually dimorphic plumages, though they do not gain fully adult appearance until the following summer. Fall migration of immatures usually begins in August or September, about 3 weeks after fledging, followed by adult females and, lastly, males through October and November.

*Fall.* The birds dally, as during their spring migration; most travel singly. Harriers from the arctic range seem to migrate farthest, many to Central America, Venezuela, and Colombia. Most northeastern harriers, however, fan out across the southern two-thirds of the United States. A few remain on the northern breeding range over winter in places where depth of snow cover permits them to find prey.

*Winter.* Harriers often form temporary individual territories of varying size (averaging about 160 acres) on their winter range, defending them from other harriers from several hours to 15 or more days. But they often gather at communal night roosts, sometimes shared with short-eared owls (also ground-dwelling birds). The roosts are often traditional sites but fluctuate in size as the birds wander; about 20 harriers is an average roost size. Harrier migrants are often moving northward by late February.

**Ecology.** Northern harriers are birds of open lands, making them relatively easy to spot. They favor wet meadows with rank grasses but also occupy fields, marshes, savannas, and prairies. Apparently the most important habitat element is an abundant vole population; indeed, good vole habitat (weedy fields, hayfields, clear-cuts) generally indicates good harrier range. Since harriers spend almost 60 percent of their foraging time perched, they also require low perch sites—fence posts, small shrubs, boulders, or ground elevations—in their home ranges.

The female constructs the nest, often from materials brought by the male. Females sometimes return to the previous year's nest, adding materials. New nests are often flimsy, built of sticks and coarse plant materials, lined with feathers and finer grasses. In wet ground, the nest may be placed a foot or more above soil or water. Nest outside diameter is 15 to 30 inches. The birds usually select sites in tall, rank sedges or grasses, sometimes hummocks, often in marsh vegetation or sphagnum bogs. One study found willows, goldenrods, and sedges the most common plants in harrier nesting areas.

In optimal habitat, the harrier's diet consists of about 95 percent voles, also called meadow mice *(Microtus),* and white-footed mice *(Peromyscus leucopus).* A feeding strategy in some areas is harrier seizure of vole nests, which resemble upside-down, grassy bird nests

*The meadow vole, chief prey of northern harriers, experiences population highs and lows, which in turn affect harrier and other predator populations.*

on the ground; many times the voles are at home in the nest. Vole populations rise and plummet in about 4-year cycles, greatly influencing local harrier breeding abundance in any given year. Evidence exists that a floating population of harriers—Hamerstrom calls it a "gypsy cohort"—can take rapid advantage of high vole abundance to settle and nest. Vole numbers far exceed the harrier appetites in years of abundance. As Hamerstrom wrote, "harriers probably have about the same effect on [vole numbers] that a man has on mosquitoes when . . . swatting them at dusk." Efforts to convince people that rodents would demolish crops if not for raptor predation, she believed, are "primarily propaganda to 'justify' the existence of raptors" as friends of man. The voles' effects on harriers are far more significant than vice versa. Hamerstrom's research established that abundant vole populations increase the likelihood of harrier polygyny and breeding in brown-plumaged, first-year males. She suggested, moreover, that something in the intestinal flora of voles may stimulate harrier gonads, acting as an aphrodisiac, since the birds consume the intestines of small mammals primarily during onset of the breeding season. Harriers opportunistically capture and consume other prey as well: insects (mainly grasshoppers), snakes, frogs, sparrows, red-winged blackbirds, meadowlarks, ground squirrels, and rabbits. Where voles are in short supply, harriers also feed on carrion, and they occasionally capture ducks and raid poultry yards. A raptor associate and sometime competitor is the short-eared owl, which often nests, forages, and roosts in habitats similar to the harrier's. The owl territories may overlap those of harriers, usually with few conflicts. Harriers hunt during the day, whereas the owls hunt both day and night. Both birds consume rodents, which could lead to food competition in areas of low prey populations (though the vole-cycle mechanism probably governs bird abundance). Harriers tend to pirate food from the owls rather than vice versa, usually by causing the food carrier to drop its prey. And red-tailed and rough-legged hawks pirate from harriers. The harrier's biggest competitors are humans; drainage and filling of wetlands, fire suppression allowing plant succession to advance and thus shrink suitable habitats, and pesticides sprayed on fields account for the harrier's endangered status in several states.

Harrier predators are fairly numerous, as with most ground-nesting birds. Egg raiders include American crows, northern ravens, skunks, and raccoons. Great horned owls, red-tailed hawks, red foxes, coyotes, domestic dogs, and raccoons devour chicks; cattle and white-tailed deer sometimes trample nests. Carrion beetles (Silphidae), attracted to meat scraps in the nest, also attack and sometimes kill chicks. Like most raptors, harriers are frequently harassed or mobbed by other birds—sparrows, European starlings, American crows, blackbirds, swallows, and American kestrels, among others.

**Focus.** Harrier populations fluctuate widely from year to year in many areas, reflecting cyclic prey abundance. Grassland habitat loss and pesticide contamination have also affected harrier populations, resulting in widespread decline of this once-common species since about 1960. Various recovery schemes have been proposed: reversing the loss of wetland and grassland habitats; placement of perching posts in open field habitats; creating more vole habitat by increasing hay acreage. "Few people put their minds on how to maintain good mouse habitat," noted Hamerstrom; it requires periodic ground disturbance, as in burning, plowing, or mowing.

The name *harrier* derives from the sixteenth-century English word *harien,* meaning "to pillage and torment." British birders call female harriers "ringtails" for the barred tail feathers. "Frog hawk" was Thoreau's frequent name for the harrier, but he thought "kite" would be a better label. Unaware that harriers nest on the ground, he once spent an afternoon searching for its nest by climbing several pine trees. "The sight of a marsh hawk in Concord," he wrote, "is worth more to me than the entry of the allies into Paris."

Studies have determined that some 60 percent of harriers die in their first year, mainly from accident, predation, and starvation. Annual adult mortality is about 30 percent. Harriers sometimes live to age sixteen or more, but mean age at death is about 16 months.

## 9

## FALCON FAMILY (Falconidae), order Ciconiiformes

This family of raptors consists of 63 species worldwide: falcons, caracaras, forest-falcons, falconets, kestrels, and bobbies. The 7 North American species, in addition to the 2 following accounts and listed relatives, include the crested caracara *(Polyborus plancus)* of the southern United States. Falcons are not classified as hawks, though as raptors, they are often considered generic hawks.

Like hawks, falcons are predatory and have hooked bills, taloned feet, and superbly keen vision. Unlike hawks, falcon wings are long and pointed (except in caracaras), built for speed, not soaring. Falcon bills show a notchlike tooth toward the tip, an adaptation for severing the neck vertebrae of prey. Among raptors, only falcons have "sideburns"—one or more vertical black bars on the sides of the head. Both sexes wear similar (though often not identical) plumage; as in most raptors, females are slightly larger than males.

Characteristic hunting technique of most falcons is the steep power dive, or *stoop,* frequently knocking bird prey out

*The tomial tooth—the notched bill of falcons such as the American kestrel (top)—is a feeding adaptation, also seen in a few other predatory species such as the loggerhead shrike (bottom).*

of the air with a blow of fisted talons. When perched, falcons often bob their heads and tails. Few falcons construct nests, usually adopting cavities, ledges, or stick nests of other species for their own egg laying. Hatching is synchronous in most species, the nestlings altricial. The ancient art and sport of falconry (using mainly peregrine falcons but also others plus some hawk species), in which falcons are trained to retrieve captured prey, was pursued in many civilizations and continues, by special permit, to the present. Falconry has its own lexicon and terminology. To falconers, for example, *falcon* always refers to a female bird; males are called *tiercels*. Today many raptor ornithologists are also avid falconers.

The word *falcon* originates from the Latin root *falx,* meaning "sickle," referring to the shape of the curved talons or hooked bills of these birds.

FALCON FAMILY (Falconidae)

## American Kestrel *(Falco sparverius)*

The smallest (9 to 12 inches, about killdeer size) and most common North American falcon, the American kestrel, also called sparrow hawk, has distinctive markings. On each side of the head, two black, vertical "sideburns," one of them running through the eye, frame white cheek and chin patches. The top of the head is blue with a rusty cap, usually brighter in males than females. A pair of black spots on the rear of the head, called *ocelli,* or false eyes, may deter possible predators from sneak attack. Males have a rusty back, bluish gray wings, and a rusty-colored tail with a black terminal band; underparts are spotted. Females have rusty wings, back, and tail, all marked with black barring, and brown-streaked underparts. Kestrels voice their alarm calls, rapid, high-pitched "killy killy killy" or "klee klee klee" notes, mainly near the nest.

**Close relatives.** The genus *Falco* includes, besides the kestrel, 5 other North American falcons: the Aplomado falcon *(F. femoralis)* of the Southwest, the merlin *(F. columbarius),* the gyrfalcon *(F. rusticolus),* the prairie falcon *(F. mexicanus),* and the peregrine falcon *(F. peregrinus;* see next account). Thirty-two other falcons range worldwide. The common kestrel, or windhover *(F. tinnunculus)*, of Eurasia is a slightly larger, gray-tailed version of the American kestrel. **Behaviors.** Kestrels are easily seen in their open-country habitat as they hover-hunt on rapidly beating wings or perch-hunt from power lines and poles. In flight, the almost 2-foot wingspan curves back in sickle shape; a reliable field mark for male kestrels is the line of translucent dots along the rear edge of the wing. Another characteristic is the kestrel's habit of bobbing its tail when perched. The birds are buoyant in flight, gliding more than most falcons, and can also soar on thermal updrafts. Kestrels capture most of their prey on the ground, seizing it in their talons and carrying it to a perch. Primarily solitary birds, kestrels apparently mate for life, but even during the breeding season, mates spend most of their time apart.

American kestrel breeding range spans North and South America from the arctic treeline to Tierra del Fuego. Only the northernmost breeding populations—from the northern Great Plains, northern New England, and northern Great Lakes—migrate.

*Spring.* Many, if not most, migratory kestrels have already arrived on their northern breeding range by early spring—"after the horned larks and shortly before the bluebirds," one observer noted. Previous breeders are *philopatric,* returning to their previous territories, which vary extensively in size, depending on quality of habitat; 100 acres is probably minimal. Females, arriving some days later than males, often wander in and out of several male territories before settling on the mate's territory, and extrapair copulations with one or more males are common during this period. American kestrels are noted for their frequency of 7-second copulations—up to 15 times a day over a 6-week period, beginning days or weeks before the female's fertile period. Females can store viable sperm up to 12 days in their oviduct tubules before fertilization occurs. But whereas copulations are frequent, actual fertilizations by males other than the bonded mate apparently are not.

In addition to aerial dive displays by males, mate feeding is an important courtship and bonding behavior. A male spends hours afield hunting, transferring prey to his mate at habitual perch sites on the territory. Before egg laying begins, the female stops hunting; her mate supplies all the food until a week or so after the nestlings hatch, a total period of 2 months or more. Egg laying on the northern range usually begins in April.

---

EGGS AND YOUNG: usually 4 or 5; eggs white or pinkish, finely dotted with brown. INCUBATION: by both sexes (male about 4 hours per day, when female vacates to feed and preen in morning and late afternoon); about 30 days. FEEDING OF YOUNG: by female for first few days, from food brought by male, then by both sexes; mainly grasshoppers. FLEDGING: about 30 days.

---

*Summer.* Fledglings, which leave the nest from about mid-June to early July, remain perched in the nest vicinity for about 2 weeks, being fed by the parents and brooded in the nest cavity at night. Over the next few weeks, they learn to hunt for themselves, sometimes merging with other kestrel families or all-juvenile flocks of up to 20 birds. Kestrels nest only once per year in most northern habitats, twice in the southern range.

Juveniles resemble adults but show dark streaking on the breast. During late summer and fall, most juveniles molt into adult plumage. Annual plumage molt of adults begins in midspring and occurs over the entire summer period; females typically molt weeks ahead of males. The molt is usually complete by early September, as the birds begin migrating. Some late-summer migrators, however, are still molting as they travel.

*Fall.* Peak movements of northern-range kestrels occur in mid-September and early October. Falcon migration relies on fast, direct flight rather than on thermal updrafts that reflect ridge topography, as in most hawks. Kestrels migrate in groups of 3 or 4 or in small, loose flocks over a broad interior front and along the seacoasts. Unlike other falcons, they seldom fly far over open water. Many northeastern kestrel migrants augment the resident kestrel populations directly south of the breeding range; many also winter in the southeastern states, especially coastal Florida.

*Winter.* Resident kestrels in the middle and southern United States may remain year-round in their breeding areas or on winter territories, but many also wander, seeking feeding sites elsewhere.

Solitary now, the birds establish and defend individual winter feeding territories of 100 acres or more. In Florida, males tend to forage in edge areas, margins of slash pine woodlots, eucalyptus plantations, cypress swamps, and citrus groves; females seem to favor more open, sparsely vegetated sites. Researchers believe that female kestrels are dominant over males, at least in winter, forming territories in prime feeding habitat and forcing males into more sideline, edge habitats.

Many male kestrels begin moving northward by late February and early March.

**Ecology.** American kestrels favor open farmland habitats—pastures, hayfields, grasslands, and fields of row crops. Hence they were probably uncommon in the northeastern United States before settlement and land clearing. Marshland, forest openings, clear-cut forest areas, and bogs also host kestrels at times, and median strips of expressways are common foraging sites. Habitats must also contain nest cavities and perch sites, such as power lines and poles, roadside and hedgerow trees. This species has also adapted to urban and suburban areas; kestrels often perch-hunt amid the ample house sparrow populations around skyscrapers and warehouses.

*A woodpecker-excavated cavity in a dead tree, often one that stands by itself in an open area, provides a typical nest site for a kestrel.*

Natural tree cavities, old tree excavations of northern flickers and pileated woodpeckers, vacated holes in cliffs, and crevices in old barns and outbuildings are typical kestrel nest sites. These birds never excavate their own holes. The female selects the site after inspecting a number of cavities located by the male. Many previous breeders probably return to cavities they have previously used. The birds bring in no nesting material; the female lays eggs atop whatever debris already lies on the floor of the cavity. Kestrels perform no nest sanitation and do not carry away nestling fecal sacs. Chicks shoot their feces onto the cavity walls, where they quickly dry. Dermestid beetles (Dermestidae), prevalent in most kestrel nests, scavenge food scraps.

Summer and winter diets vary according to prey availability. The birds capture most of their prey on the ground, though they occasionally forage aloft for aerial insects and capture birds on the wing. Insects—mainly grasshoppers and crickets—are the chief summer foods; in winter, more small mammals, such as voles, and birds up to flicker size are captured. Other food items include lizards, snakes, frogs, upland sandpiper chicks, and bats. In urban habitats, kestrels feed mainly on house sparrows, sometimes raiding ivy-covered walls of buildings where the sparrows nest and roost. Kestrels often cache food items for periods up to 7 days, usually in grass clumps or niches in tree limbs. The birds cache dead rodents top side up; the rodents' own protective coloration helps conceal them.

Nest cavities, often scarce in kestrel habitats, are sources of most interspecific competition, mainly from northern flickers, European starlings, and squirrels. Biologist Terry Root has pointed out the inverse relationship kestrels exhibit with northern shrikes; although shrikes are not raptors, they exploit most of the same winter habitat types and prey as kestrels. The chief difference that largely precludes competition between them is the kestrel's preference for warmer areas. "Perhaps these two ecologically similar species are avoiding each other," suggested Root.

Kestrel predators are relatively few. Blue jays sometimes mob them, and larger raptors (mainly sharp-shinned and other accipiter hawks) occasionally capture them.

**Focus.** Kestrel populations have shown modest trends of increase during the past several decades; recent researchers estimate that more than a million breeding pairs inhabit North America. Probably only about half of the chicks survive to fledge; typical longevity is 2 to 5 years, though some have survived in the wild to age 11. Kestrels are extremely sensitive to cold, rarely remaining in wintering areas where temperatures plunge below 20 degrees F. Tolerant of heat, they even inhabit deserts in the Southwest, obtaining most of their moisture requirement from their diet.

Probably the foremost limitation on kestrel numbers in otherwise adequate habitats is the lack of suitable nesting cavities. Losses of American elm trees from Dutch elm disease have depleted a once-common nest tree for kestrels. Placement of kestrel boxes or roofed nail kegs in open habitats near wet areas has helped restore kestrel populations in many areas. Boxes containing wood chips in the bottom should measure 16 by 12 inches with a $3^1/_2$-inch-diameter hole, mounted on 10- to 15-foot cedar poles placed along fence lines or highways and facing into open fields. Since kestrels and eastern bluebirds occupy similar habitats and both use nest boxes (with different-size entrance holes), the helpful house provider should "choose one species or the other," recommended naturalist Emma B. Pitcher; "a hungry kestrel might hassle or even eat a bluebird."

Beginning falconers in America often train themselves by using kestrels before attempting to train larger hawks or falcons.

The name *kestrel* derives from the Old French *cresserelle*, in turn originating from the Latin *crepitare*, "to rattle, creak, or crackle," supposedly suggestive of the bird's call.

FALCON FAMILY (Falconidae)

---

# Peregrine Falcon *(Falco peregrinus)*

Once called the duck hawk, this second-largest North American falcon (next to the gyrfalcon) measures 15 to 20 inches long, about crow size. It has a black hood; dark slate blue, finely barred upper parts; and brown spots and barring on chest and belly. Its most distinctive field mark is its white throat extending to the sides of the neck, the white divided by a black sideburn that drops below the yellow-rimmed eye. The long, pointed wings extend in an almost 4-foot wingspan; the tail is long and relatively square cornered. Both sexes wear similar plumage, though females grow to a third larger in size.

Immature birds, longer tailed than adults, are brown and heavily streaked but also show the black sideburns. Peregrines voice rapid "cack cack cack" and squeaky, flickerlike or gracklelike "*wee*-chew *wee*-chew" notes around their nests.

**Close relatives.** See American Kestrel.

**Behaviors.** "Few works of nature or man equal the sight of a Peregrine in the wind," wrote one observer team. Famed for the speed of its steep hunting dive, or *stoop* (claimed by some observers to exceed 200 mph), the peregrine may either pluck its prey out of the air or deliver a killing blow with fisted talons, circling back to seize the falling victim before it hits the ground. Sometimes, overtaking a bird in flight, it rolls over in the air, grasping its victim from below. In a stoop, the peregrine's body forms a characteristic anchor shape with swept-back wings; then the bird pulls its wings tight to its body, decreasing air resistance as it plummets. Recent studies have concluded that actual stooping speeds fall well below the calculated theoretical maximum—more moderate speeds facilitate the birds'

*A stooping peregrine falcon is a sky streaker, one of the fastest creatures on earth. Its streamlined shape and posture cut air resistance as it pursues its prey, usually a flying bird.*

maneuverability in the air. "Peregrines often tower (pull up) to regain altitude quickly," wrote one research team, "to initiate another blow, and can attack the same prey many times." The peregrine's kill success rate is much better than that of most raptors, about 1 in 3 tries on average. After capture, it flies to a habitual perch, where it proceeds to pluck the feathers of its prey and tear it to pieces. The peregrine hunts from high aloft over open country or city, scanning the air and ground beneath. In ordinary flight, its quick, shallow wingbeats often resemble those of a pigeon (one of its chief victims), common loon, or cormorant. A peregrine soaring overhead may also resemble a broad-winged hawk in shape and outline. In their nesting areas at night, peregrines roost separately from each other in cliff niches, often facing the cliff wall.

The peregrine falcon inhabits every continent except Antarctica—indeed, it has the widest natural distribution of any bird in the world, rivaled only by ospreys and common ravens. But its North American distribution is extremely local and spotty. Americans in the Northeast see peregrines mainly during migrations or at urban nesting sites, sometimes through office windows on the thirtieth floor. Their foremost nesting areas, shrunken from a once-extensive breeding range, include arctic regions of Greenland, Canada, and Alaska; the Rocky Mountains; and along the entire United States Pacific coast. Much smaller breeding populations exist in scattered locales throughout the continent and in some 25 North American cities where the birds have been introduced, with varying degrees of success, as biological controls on pigeon populations. Perhaps more often, the motivation has been less practical, the birds being viewed mainly as desirable raptor residents of a clifflike habitat with pigeons serving as a built-in food supply.

Long-distance peregrine migrators are chiefly those that breed in the Arctic; elsewhere they tend to wander in winter or reside year-round.

*Spring.* Migratory peregrines, traveling alone or in pairs, arrive on their breeding range in March or early April. Although the birds mate for life, individual mates usually travel and arrive separately at the nest site occupied the previous year. Most migration progresses along the seacoasts, though overland movement also occurs.

Peregrines are strongly territorial, but territory size is not well defined. They defend an area of several hundred yards around the nest, as well as feeding and hunting perches that may be located much farther away. Home range—the primary hunting area—measures some 6 to 19 square miles and may overlap with home ranges of other pairs. Neighboring nests are usually spaced several miles apart, occasionally much closer. Courtship activities consist of soaring together; cooperative hunting, in which one mate separates a prey bird from a flock and the other captures it; acrobatic dives, loops, and rollovers at streaking speed; and mate feeding, the transfer of a prey item from male to female, either on a perch or in the air. Courtship activities may continue year-round between a pair but occur most frequently in late winter and early spring.

As in most birds, a nonbreeding, floating population of unknown size exists, providing replacement mates when one of a pair dies. The male brings in most of the food during incubation and early nestling phases.

---

EGGS AND YOUNG: 3 or 4; eggs white or pinkish, heavily brown blotched. INCUBATION: mainly by female, replaced by male for brief periods; about 35 days; female broods chicks almost continuously for first 8 to 12 days. FEEDING OF YOUNG: male brings food, female feeds young; mainly insects plus bird prey plucked of feathers and decapitated by male before delivery. FLEDGING: 6 weeks or more; males fledge before females.

---

*Summer.* Hunting prey for the nestlings (which are called eyasses by falconers)—and later, fledglings—is full-time work for parent birds throughout summer. At about 4 weeks of age, nestlings are so large and aggressive that the parents simply drop food at the nest, no longer trying to feed them directly. Fledglings remain food dependent on the adults for several weeks. They roost in the nest vicinity, chasing other birds and each other. As territorial defense wanes, peregrine families vacate the nest sites and often wander widely. Family groups of migratory populations may remain together until migration, or the birds may individually disperse before they move southward.

*Fall.* Migratory peregrines travel solitarily in September and October. Historically, northeastern peregrines moved west to east rather than north to south, wintering along Atlantic coastal marshes. Both fall and spring migrations coincide with the seasonal movements of smaller birds, which peregrines capture en route. Peregrines sometimes fly far out to sea during migrations, capturing birds and eating them on the wing, also perching on ships to eat and rest. Today most of the northeastern urban-dwelling peregrines do not migrate. Arctic populations migrate mainly to Central and South America as far as Argentina and Chile.

*Winter.* Scattered peregrines also winter along the American seacoasts and from the southern Great Lakes and New England northward.

**Ecology.** Wetlands, lakes, and rivers are areas that tend to concentrate bird prey, and high, rocky habitats—cliff ledges, high bluffs, steep slopes—that overlook such areas are the peregrine's traditional nesting areas, still used by wild populations. Both natural and urban habitats bear close similarities to those of a chief prey species, the common (rock) pigeon or rock dove. Peregrine adaptation to city landscapes for nesting and feeding is hardly a recent phenomenon— these raptors ventured into urban areas long ago, mainly in winter. In Europe, they have occupied castle and church towers for centuries. Probably, indeed, they have resided in cities almost as long as pigeons have, though never as numerously. Peregrines also favor gravel shores or beaches for bathing.

The peregrine nest, or *aerie,* usually consists of only a scrape in the soil or rock crumbs of a cliff or building ledge or niche—one of several scrapes in various locales made by the male. After selecting a particular scrape, the female enlarges it into a shallow saucer about a foot in diameter and an inch or so deep. The pair adds no nesting materials. Often the site chosen is a cliff face midway between top and bottom. Water towers, grain elevators, and bridges, in addition to tall buildings, are favored urban sites. Below the aerie, the birds' droppings, or *whitewash,* can often be seen, sometimes coated with an orange lichen growth. Peregrines usually change nest sites from year to year but may use the same general locale or cliff face for decades. Where cliff or tall building sites are lacking, the birds seem fairly versatile opportunists. In the Arctic, they often nest on tundra mounds; in the southern United States, they may use tree hollows or broken tops of tall cypresses, sycamores, and cottonwoods. They also sometimes occupy vacant nests of eagles, hawks, and common ravens.

Peregrine prey consists almost exclusively of birds, usually plucked before eating. Pigeons are staple items, having replaced the now-extinct passenger pigeon. But peregrines also capture, usually by aerial attack, a large variety of waterfowl, shorebirds, and songbirds—even other raptors such as northern harriers and American kestrels. Plovers and sandpipers become common prey in many coastal areas. The birds also capture flying insects such as dragonflies and migrating monarch butterflies but take mammals infrequently. During the breeding season, male peregrines commonly cache many food items—usually bird carcasses—in cliff ledges near the nest, thus providing a fallback source in case of poor hunting weather.

No significant competitors exist, though other cliff-nesting falcons (mainly gyrfalcons and prairie falcons) might potentially compete for sites.

Likewise, few predators attack peregrines. Mammals, even those that can gain access to aeries, usually shy away from the birds' fierce defense. Great horned owls are known to prey on young peregrines, and common ravens may occasionally threaten nests. Pigeons, commonly and often harmlessly infected with trichomoniasis, may transmit the protozoan parasite with lethal effects when peregrines consume the flesh. But the peregrine's deadliest, most insidious predator is man, mainly via pesticides and other chemical contaminants. Urban peregrines also frequently collide with walls, windows, and vehicles.

**Focus.** The word *peregrine* derives from the Latin word for "wandering." Peregrines have never been abundant anywhere in the world, owing to their habitat requirements and high status on the food chain. Only an estimated 350 pairs existed in the eastern United States during the early 1940s. Falconers, who probably know more about them and observe them more closely than anybody else, were the first to notice radical population declines correlating with the widespread use of DDT pesticides beginning about 1954. This trend of nest failure and aerie desertion—as DDE, the metabolized breakdown product of DDT, resulted in thinning and breakage of eggshells—continued into the 1960s. By 1964, not a single peregrine could be found east of the Mississippi, and population declines elsewhere on the continent and in Europe were dramatic. Data from worldwide peregrine censuses also rang initial alarm to the fact that not only peregrines but many other raptors atop the food chain stood in desperate straits, several heading for total extinction. In 1969, peregrines were officially listed as endangered in the United States; 3 years later, DDT was banned in America and subsequently in most industrialized nations. Since then, restoration programs in eastern North America—mainly by means of *hacking,* the introduction of unfledged peregrine chicks into likely sites to which they become imprinted—have achieved notable results, and many states again have nesting pairs. Not all ornithologists approve of such procedures. "Much of the hacking has been done outside the original range of the bird and with subspecies of peregrines not present in North America," wrote James Granlund, explaining why many introduced peregrines fail to migrate. Also, peregrines' occasional capture of passing migrants and their raids on terneries and piping plover colonies have aroused second thoughts about restoration efforts in some quarters. Recovery, though heartening, progresses slowly; peregrines remained a federally endangered species until 1999, when about 2,000 breeding pairs existed in eastern North America. The most stable, secure populations—mainly those in arctic Alaska and Canada—are those least affected by environmental contaminants such as dieldrin and PSBs.

Peregrines have been the falconer's favorite species since the sport began, mainly because they are relatively more easily trained than other hawks and falcons. Some writers claim falconry, or "hawking," as the oldest sport in the world, dating at least from ancient Egyptian times. It became the aristocratic sport of kings in medieval Europe. Training a falcon to retrieve game is tedious, meticulous work. "Affection is lost on these creatures," one falconer wrote, "fear is unknown, punishment useless. Food is the only lure." Sooner or later, most falcons escape the falconer and return to the wild. From falconry, which employs a large, specialized vocabulary of its own, come the terms *cad* and *codger* (as in old), derived from *cadge,* the perch on which the *cadger,* a senior falconer consigned to a helper role, carries the bird afield; and *booze,* from the falconer's *bowse,* to drink. Today only a few thousand licensed falconers practice the archaic sport in the United States, and falconry permits are not easily obtained—nor should they be. Still, it is true, as one naturalist-falconer wrote, that "those who have made the most significant advances in protecting and recovering endangered raptors have not been ecologists, not wildlife managers, not animal-rescue organizations, but falconers, many of whom are both scholars and hunters." By far the most useful and substantive peregrine research to date has been done by falconers and biologists in Britain.

Adult mortality in peregrines probably ranges around 10 to 15 percent per year. A life span of 2 decades, if hardly typical, is not uncommon in these birds. But only about half of all peregrines survive their first birthday.

# 10

## Eastern Kingbird *(Tyrannus tyrannus)*

Tyrant flycatcher family (Tyrannidae), order Passeriformes. About 8 inches long, the eastern kingbird has a black head, back, wings, and tail, which is broadly white banded. Chin and underparts are white, but the reddish crown patch is rarely seen. Sexes look alike. Characteristic sounds include a twittering, high-pitched sputter of notes and a single, emphatic "tzee!"

**Close relatives.** Twelve other *Tyrannus* species inhabit South America, the West Indies, and the southern United States. North American species include the tropical kingbird *(T. melancholicus),* Couch's kingbird *(T. couchii),* Cassin's kingbird *(T. vociferans),* the thick-billed kingbird *(T. crassirostris),* the western kingbird *(T. verticalis),* the scissor-tailed flycatcher *(T. forficata),* and the grey kingbird *(T. dominicensis).* Some 540 species of this exclusively New World family exist, most of which reside in South America.

**Behaviors.** Flycatchers introduce the order of perching birds, or passerines, about 60 percent of all bird species. Passerine birds show a distinctive *anisodactyl* foot, in which 3 toes point forward and 1 backward, all joining the foot at the same level—a foot adapted for perching. The passerine foot relates to many behavioral characteristics, enabling these birds to specialize in certain ecological roles, or *niches,* that might otherwise remain unexploited by birds. Except for flycatchers, most passerines are classified as songbirds, or *oscines.* Flycatchers, though many sing by any conventional definition, possess fewer syrinx or voice muscles than true songbirds and are therefore labeled *suboscines.*

North American flycatchers show somewhat flattened bills bearing *rictal bristles,* or whiskers, at the base. Strong ligaments connecting upper and lower jaws snap the bill shut, as if spring-loaded, on a flying insect. Flycatchers use a sit-and-wait strategy, launching forth in brief, looping flights from a perch to capture insects.

Perched on a fence or atop a shrub, usually 4 to 12 feet above ground, the kingbird sallies out to capture large flying insects, then returns to the same perch or another. It also hawks and hover-hunts, seizes insects from vegetation, and gleans insects in the tree canopy or from the ground. Its bickering notes and low, conspicuous perches, combined with its open habitats, make this one of the most easily observed birds of the countryside.

One characteristic kingbird behavior is its habit of attacking almost any larger bird—crows, ravens, and hawks are frequent targets—that flies over its territory, usually diving and striking it from above. Seen at a distance, a crow or hawk being chased by a smaller bird is a common sight, and often the attacker is a kingbird. These attacks sometimes occur 100 feet in the air—kingbird territory has been likened to a vertical cylinder shape— and often continue far outside the territory. Usually the intruder is just passing over with no predatory aims; often I've watched with amusement as a raven, minding its own business and plowing along in flight, is suddenly set upon by the

*The most common flycatcher of open country, the eastern kingbird perches in a characteristic still-hunting posture.*

kingbird demon; the raven peers over its shoulder with what looks very much like panicked glances as its nemesis keeps bopping it from above and behind. During attacks, the kingbird may raise its red crown feathers, otherwise rarely observed, and open its mouth, exposing its red gape. To an intruding birder being thus dived upon, "the effect is dramatic," wrote researcher Michael T. Murphy, "and has caused at least one human to nearly lose his grip and fall from a tree." Yet, though they fiercely defend their nests even against people at times, kingbirds often seem surprisingly tolerant of smaller birds—even other nondisplaying kingbirds—in the nest vicinity, especially after hatching occurs. Until hatching, however, nesting females do not even tolerate their own mates nearby. Nevertheless, except during the breeding season, these are extremely gregarious birds, voicing their easily identified chittering calls both from perches and on the wing. During migrations and on the winter range, they often associate in flocks that may number into the hundreds.

Eastern kingbird breeding range, the largest of any North American flycatcher, occupies most of the continent from the Canadian boreal forest to the Gulf. The birds migrate in spring and fall.

*Spring.* Flycatcher migration in spring usually coincides with the first large insect hatches on their routes. Thus most kingbirds arrive at their northern breeding sites in early May. Most have been en route since mid-March, having moved north along the east coast of Central America and Mexico from their South American range. Males precede females by a few days, traveling by daytime in small flocks of 5 to 12 birds, feeding in open fields.

*Philopatry,* fidelity to the previous year's breeding site, is strong in this species, stronger in males than in females. As a result of their return to the same territorial area each year, pairs tend to remain monogamous for life, though nest failure or absence of a former mate on the territory results in female dispersal. Evidence indicates that polygamous extrapair copulations also occur. Kingbird trios are fairly common and often remain stable over a season; they form when a third adult, either male or female, appears at the nest, attaches itself to the territory, and remains tolerated by the mated pair. One researcher suggests that this third adult may be an unmated first-year bird (possibly a previous offspring) "prospecting" for a territory.

The territory, typically about a half acre in size, has ill-defined boundaries, the defense of which apparently depends more upon behavioral cues from intruding kingbirds than upon any rigidly enforced territorial lines. A radius of about 30 yards around the nest becomes the focus for most activities, though feeding frequently occurs off territory as well. Previously mated pairs tend to bond again quickly; a new female, however, must overcome initial attempts by the male to chase her off. Wing-fluttering displays—a rapid series of shallow wingbeats in which the bird seems to walk on air—commonly occur between mates when they meet throughout the nesting season; a series of chatter calls from both partners accompanies these displays. The so-called dawn song of territorial males is given in predawn darkness and also in the evening. This song differs from the birds' other sounds in its repetitive alternation of 2 complex phrasings: "t't'zeer, t't'zeer, t'tzeetzeetzee." Following territorial chasing of a larger bird or a boundary conflict with another kingbird, the male flies up 100 feet high or so, if he is not already aloft, then descends via a tumble-flight display—a variable but dramatic series of twists and jerks—and glides back to his perch.

Females do the nest building, accompanied everywhere by the male, who usually perch-guards near the nest when the female is absent. She may begin several preliminary nests before completing a final one. Most nesting on the northern range begins by early June.

EGGS AND YOUNG: usually 3; eggs creamy white or pinkish, brown spotted, often wreathed around blunt end. INCUBATION: by female; 14 to 18 days; hatching synchronous; nestlings altricial, orange colored for about a day, then fading to dark gray. FEEDING OF YOUNG: by both sexes; large insects, fruits. FLEDGING: 16 or 17 days; fledglings usually begin sustained flight several days later.

*Summer.* The territory of some birds expands after hatching occurs; with others, such as kingbirds, territory tends to shrink. Fledglings remain almost entirely food dependent on the parents for 2 to 5 weeks. The family unit remains together and highly conspicuous owing to the birds' almost constant vocal sputtering and wing fluttering. Parent birds become less hostile to territorial invaders as the season progresses. Even as parental feeding gradually declines, the adults continue to defend juveniles against predators for several more weeks. Adults raise only a single brood per year, but renesting may occur into July if the first nesting fails. Plumage molting in this species apparently does not occur in summer, an extreme exception among North American birds. Eastern kingbird families stay together (or sometimes coalesce) until migration, which peaks from mid-August to early September. Daytime migrating flocks are usually larger than spring flocks, sometimes numbering into thousands of birds as they assemble at staging areas before crossing water barriers. Some flocks apparently cross the Gulf of Mexico, but most probably fly overland. By mid-September, most eastern kingbirds have arrived in Central America and are still heading southward.

*Fall, Winter.* Most eastern kingbirds arrive at their wintering sites in western Amazonia (southern Colombia and Ecuador), also in northern Chile and Argentina, by mid-October. The degree of site fidelity *(philopatry)* in the winter range remains unknown but is probably more variable than in the summer range because of the change in food resources.

Social now, the birds often travel in nomadic feeding flocks of 10 to 20 individuals. Soon after arrival, they undergo their annual plumage molt. By early March, they are again moving northward. A question that still puzzles researchers is whether kingbird pairs that have repeatedly mated also remain together during migrations and winter.

**Ecology.** Eastern kingbirds are primarily savanna dwellers, favoring open lands thinly scattered with shrubs or small trees. They are, however, more flexible than most flycatchers in habitats they occupy; these include residential areas and roadsides, orchards, pastures, parklands, and often wetland edges and wooded shorelines. Forest clearing and agriculture have largely benefited this species. Probably kingbirds were less abundant before European settlement, occupying fire-cleared and other forest openings, dunelands, lake edges, and shrubby wetlands. During migrations, the birds forage mainly in open areas but also in pine scrub and other habitats. Kingbirds favor winter habitats—usually forest and water edges—that are more wooded than breeding areas.

Eastern kingbirds are tree nesters, though exceptions occur. They usually nest either fairly low (about 6 feet up) in the crotch of a small tree or, more frequently, much higher and well out on a horizontal limb of a large tree. The limb nests, often highly exposed to the elements, may lack overhead cover. In the fall, when the leaves are gone, these flattish nests are easy to see and identify. Although apparently fragile, they are surprisingly durable among the outer twigs of such trees as hawthorn, apple, mulberry, and Osage orange. In some areas, kingbirds tend to build on the east side of trees. Near water, commonly used nest trees include northern white cedar, American hornbeam, sycamore, and dead snags. The bulky, somewhat ragged looking nest, about 6 inches in diameter, consists of coarse stems—straw, twigs, stalks of composites—lined inside with fine rootlets, willow catkins, cottonwood and cattail down, some-

times feathers. At times the birds build atop vacated nests of American robins or inside those of Baltimore orioles. Occasionally they reuse a previous nest of their own, and they often build in the same site they previously occupied.

Eastern kingbird diet varies extremely between breeding and winter ranges. The chief food (85 percent of diet) from May to September is insects—at least 200 kinds, mainly bees and wasps, beetles, dragonflies, grasshoppers, butterflies, and moths. The bird consumes many

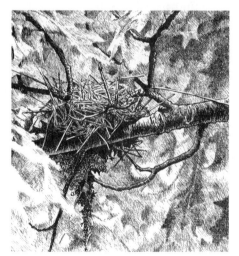

*The eastern kingbird's nest, often built in exposed, horizontal, out-on-a-limb sites, is quite durable. Sometimes the birds reuse their old nests.*

bees—at one time apiarists, calling the birds "bee martins," shot many kingbirds. One study claimed that most honeybees taken by the birds are drones, male nonworkers of the bee colony, which seems somewhat dubious. Another researcher maintained that parent kingbirds remove stingers from bees and wasps before feeding them to nestlings. Small frogs are also occasionally consumed. As summer progresses, the birds add fruits and seeds (some 40 species) to the insect diet. These include mulberries, shadbush, dogwood, and sassafras fruits, cherries, blackberries, elderberries, and nightshade berries. On the winter range and spring migration routes, fleshy fruits—especially those of yagruno macho or matchwood *(Didymopanax morototoni)*—are the chief food items.

Competition seems minimal on the breeding range. Eastern kingbirds often nest in fairly close proximity to American robins, cedar waxwings, tree swallows, and orchard and Baltimore orioles—"because all are attracted to the same nesting sites," suggested Murphy. Yet, as Murphy noted, other nesting passerines are frequently attacked by territorial kingbirds when they approach the nest tree. On the winter range, eastern kingbirds are often observed fruit foraging in association with related tropical kingbirds and fork-tailed flycatchers. Eastern kingbirds tend to be dominated by other frugivores (fruit feeders) including tropical kingbirds, social and grey-capped flycatchers, and great kiskadees. Large kingbird flocks at this season may, however, partially overwhelm territorial exclusion by other frugivores. Kingbirds have been long regarded as friends of the poultry farmer because of their readiness to attack and drive away hawks.

Predators on adult kingbirds are relatively few, owing to the birds' readiness to attack raptors and other potential prey seekers. Egg and nestling predators include tree-climbing snakes, American kestrels, American crows, blue jays, and squirrels. Brown-headed cowbirds do not successfully parasitize kingbirds, which remove cowbird eggs from their nests, indicating long evolutionary adaptation to the intruders. Pesticide use, however, can definitely threaten survival of these birds, especially those that nest in orchards where spraying is routine.

**Focus.** Eastern kingbird eggs were once prized by egg collectors for their elegant colors and spotted patterns.

"With its small clutch, large space requirements, and heavy dependence on flying insects," wrote ecologist Richard Brewer, "the kingbird is potentially vulnerable to several kinds of environmental abuse." Evidence of significant decline exists in eastern and southern North America, where habitat loss and natural plant succession have widely occurred. (I have noted a rather striking decline of eastern kingbirds in certain local Michigan areas where the birds seemed abundant just 3 or 4 years ago; none of the usual reasons given for such declines seem obvious.) These effects have been balanced to some extent by significant increases of kingbird populations in the central and western areas of its range. Most researchers believe that eastern kingbird abundance has remained fairly stable, on the whole, over the past 2 decades. Researcher Eugene S. Morton has pointed out that the eastern kingbird's terminal tail band is a feature similar to that of other gregarious frugivores, such as cedar waxwings. He suggested that such markings may constitute social cues and clues, aiding the birds in finding fruit crops during spring migration by enabling them to spot each other quickly.

"Length of life varies greatly among individuals," wrote Murphy, "and net result is that a few individuals fledge many young over their lifetime, whereas many others produce only a few or no young before dying" (a statement that could as well apply to many bird species). Based on banding records, males seem to survive longer (2.7 years on average) than females (1.6 years). The difference may be related to higher rates of female dispersal from known breeding sites and possibly greater stress on older females. Seven years is the longevity record thus far in this species.

The name *kingbird* apparently derives from the dominating habits of *Tyrannus* species.

# 11

## Loggerhead and Northern Shrikes
### *(Lanius ludovicianus, L. excubitor)*

Shrike family (Laniidae), order Passeriformes. Physical differences between the 2 shrike species are relatively slight and not easily seen. Both are big-headed, gray, robin-sized birds with black masks, wings, and long tails. In flight, they show white crescents on the wings and white edging on sides of the tails. Their hook-tipped bills are similar to those of raptors (see illustration, Falcon Family), and sexes look

alike. The loggerhead's mask, a broad black band, encloses the eyes; the northern shrike's black mask is narrower, broken above the bill by white, and rarely extends above the eye. The northern's hooked bill is also longer, its head shape flatter. Both shrikes utter a variety of harsh call notes, as well as musical thrasherlike and mockingbird-like phrases and repetitions. Thoreau described the northern shrike's voice, all in one passage, as "a mere hoarse breathing," "a shrill hissing," "a very decided mewing, clear and wiry," and "a high gurgling jingle." "Unless you saw the shrike," he lamely concluded, "it would be hard to tell [from its sounds] what bird it was." The chief identity factor for observers is the

*Subtle differences distinguish the northern shrike (top) from the loggerhead shrike (bottom), mainly the size of the black mask. Breeding ranges also differ.*

season in which the shrike appears. In the northeastern and north-central United States, loggerheads are mainly summer birds, northern shrikes are winter birds. The possibility of overlap exists only during spring and fall migrations.

**Close relatives.** The shrike family consists of 30 species world-wide, most in Africa; 26 of the 30 are *Lanius* species. The loggerhead is the only exclusively New World shrike. Several loggerhead sub-species range across the continent; in eastern North America, the resident subspecies is *L. l. migrans.*

**Behaviors.** The most raptorlike of songbirds, shrikes bear the hooked bill of hawks but, though their feet are strong and sharp-clawed, they lack the talons of these predators. Thus, though they occasionally seize bird prey in the air with their feet, more often they drop the prey by a blow with the bill; then, on the ground, they sever the victim's neck vertebrae with several bites. The shrike's notched mandibles, called *tomial teeth,* resemble those of falcons. Shrikes typ-ically still-hunt from wires or exposed perches, standing in a hori-zontal posture. Loggerheads, calculated one researcher, spend about 80 percent of daytime hours perched. They drop when they spot prey on the ground or dart out to snatch a flying insect, often flying low and swooping upward when landing at a perch. They also hunt by hopping on the ground or through branches, flushing smaller birds into the open, where the shrike can pursue and strike. On the ground, a stereotypical movement, similar to that of northern mock-ingbirds, is a sudden raising of the wings half open, exposing the white wing patches and perhaps startling hidden prey.

"Being both passerines and top-level predators," shrike researcher Reuven Yosef wrote, "these birds occupy a unique posi-tion in the food chain." Shrikes are best known for impaling their prey on barbed wire or a thorn, or sometimes wedging it in the fork of a branch. A shrike may eat the impaled prey immediately as it hangs on the "artificial talon" or may cache it there, returning later to its larder thorn or fork to feed on the carcass. Shrikes impale their prey head-up and feed on it from the head downward. They gulp their prey, later (also like raptors) disgorging pellets of indigestible fur, feathers, and bones. Shrike vision is comparable to that of hawks and owls.

Shrikes live solitarily for most of the year except when nesting; they do not flock or associate with other birds. Two general populations of loggerheads exist: the nonmigratory residential birds that remain fairly common in the southern United States; and the migratory population, which is classified as threatened or endangered throughout most of its breeding range. The loggerhead's wide breeding range spans Canada's central prairie provinces to southern Ontario and south to the Gulf coast and Mexico.

The northern shrike breeds in a narrow band across Alaska east to Labrador and in northern Eurasia, southern Asia, and northern Africa; in Europe, this shrike is known as the great grey shrike.

*Spring.* Northern shrike breeding biology remains much less researched than that of loggerheads, owing to the northern's remote arctic nesting areas. Probably both species share many aspects in common. In some places in some years, shrikes engage in a prenesting behavior called *group meeting,* in which several of the birds call and display together for minutes at a time. Courtship behaviors include male feeding of the female and display flights back and forth about 20 feet in front of her. Noted for claiming larger territories than other passerines of similiar size, shrikes do not leave their territories during the breeding season and, where they reside year-round, perhaps not at all. Yet shrikes are neither territorial aggressors nor defenders, at least early in the season, and they exhibit little or no defense of a nest containing eggs. When nestlings are present, however, parent birds noisily confront an intruder, even striking and pecking humans on occasion. The ruckus occasionally attracts neighboring shrikes, which may cross territorial boundaries to join the attack.

Loggerheads in the southern breeding range remain on or near their territories year-round. In some areas, pairs stay together and maintain territories throughout the year; in others, each loggerhead individual occupies a feeding territory until late winter, then males begin to expand their territories while females often coalesce theirs with a neighboring male's. Northern-range loggerheads are very early migrators; most apparently arrive on their breeding range in early March.

Most northern shrikes remain on their arctic range year-round. Some of them, however, irregularly move southward in fall and winter and occupy a winter range. About every 4 years or so, large numbers of northern shrikes migrate southward in *irruptions.*

Loggerhead breeding territory ranges in size from 20 to 30 acres, sometimes more, often less. The site return *(philopatric)* rate for loggerhead males is much higher, according to several studies, than for females. Females may also vacate or switch mates during a breeding season if nest failure occurs. One 1982 study disclosed that territory size shifted during the breeding season; largest during incubation, it decreased by several acres when nestlings were being fed, increasing again when they fledged. Other studies have concluded that the better the short-grass breeding habitat, the smaller the loggerhead territories. In the East and Midwest, peak loggerhead nesting begins in late April.

Asynchronous hatching may lead to differential feeding of nestlings, in which the oldest, most aggressive youngster grabs the most food. Active cannibalism of younger by older nestlings and fledglings *(siblicide)* has been observed in loggerheads.

---

EGGS AND YOUNG: 4 to 6; eggs grayish or greenish white, blotched with brown and olive, often wreathed at larger end. INCUBATION: by female, which is fed on the nest by male; about 16 days; hatching asynchronous (within 48 hours); nestlings altricial. FEEDING OF YOUNG: by female for first 4 to 5 days, from food brought by male; later also by male; insects, spiders, pieces of small vertebrates. FLEDGING: about 18 to 20 days; young birds begin flying about a week after fledging.

---

*Summer.* Young shrikes typically fledge before the onset of summer. They huddle quietly in dense foliage near the nest, erupting into noisy activity when a parent arrives with food. When threatened by an intruder, they scatter and dive into the foliage, freezing still. Parent birds now defend not the nest but the vicinity of the fledglings, continuing to feed them for 3 or 4 weeks. Soon, as the juveniles begin to fly, they exhibit awkward hunting behaviors, carrying leaves or sticks, and catching beetles and grasshoppers. From 20 to 30 days of age, they begin impaling and wedging captured prey items; at about 40 days, they can capture and kill mice.

Data thus far do not firmly establish whether loggerheads are single or double brooded; presumably northern shrikes, in their short-season breeding range, are single brooded. Some studies seem to show loggerheads as double brooded in the northern states, but researcher Reuven Yosef stated that loggerheads are usually single brooded and that "most late [that is, summer] nests are apparently renesting attempts following an initial nest failure." He excepted loggerheads on the southern, year-round range, which "have additional broods more often."

Many loggerheads on the northern range begin their annual molt in July; others may not replace flight and body plumage until after fall migration. Likewise, some may depart the breeding range by early August ranging to late September, "the date probably influenced by the occurrence of double-brooding," noted Michigan shrike researcher Janea M. Little.

*Fall, Winter.* Migratory loggerheads—that is, those in the northern range, generally areas with 10 to 30 days of snow cover per year—wing southward mainly in September, sometimes into early October. The birds travel individually, not in flocks, during daytime, spanning only short distances at a time. Loggerheads east of the Rockies move mainly south of latitude 40 degrees N to the Gulf, while loggerheads farther west migrate to southern Texas. The highest winter concentrations center in Texas and southern Alabama. Year-round resident loggerheads usually remain on their breeding territories through winter.

Northern shrikes are a different story. About every fifth winter in the East, a substantial influx of them appears, usually in October and November. During years between, their appearance seems more irregular. Sometimes they range only into the northern states, in other years much farther south, even into Texas and southern California. Northerns seldom appear, however, where average minimum January temperature rises above 20 degrees F. What causes this periodic influx? Despite much research that has attempted to link such winter irruptions (which may also include snowy owls and several finches, among other species) with periodic "crashes" of arctic food resources, the connection is still mostly theory, tenuous at best; as yet, nobody really knows why it happens. Specimens taken in winter during irruptions show most of the invaders to be juveniles of the year, but since the highest percentage of most winter bird populations consists of juveniles, this evidence seems unhelpful. Winter bird atlas researcher Terry Root pointed out that Christmas count data from 1900 to 1935 showed shrike invasions every 4.2 years, but that thereafter the cycle appeared to disintegrate, with eastern and western populations differing in irruption years. Because of their lack of winter philopatry, it seems doubtful that northern shrikes maintain regular feeding territories, though some observers report the use of habitual perches in winter. Migrant northerns usually depart their wintering areas in March.

Some, if not all, shrikes undergo a partial molt of body plumage only (frequently limited to the throat), peaking in February and March.

**Ecology.** Breeding habitat of loggerheads is open country with short grass, interspersed with shrub or fence perches. Pastures, fields, mowed roadsides (one study concluded that "roadside surveys are a proven method for evaluating [loggerhead] shrike densities"), cemeteries, and golf courses are common locales, and territories frequently abut fence lines or utility poles and wires. Winter habitats are much the same, including hayfields and pastureland, though in some areas the birds frequent more shrubby and open-forest sites. "In my experience," wrote ornithologist James Granlund,

*A typical loggerhead shrike nesting site might be a red cedar savanna, with the nest hidden in the dense foliage of the cedars.*

"southern and northern loggerhead habitats vary dramatically. In the south, they are extremely flexible, nesting commonly in subdivision and suburban areas. In the north, they require sandy soils, expanses of open fields, and dense trees, such as junipers, for nesting." Northern shrikes favor open spots in deciduous and coniferous woodlands, muskeg, willow brush, and open shrubland south of the tundra. They show strong preference for forest edges, especially the northern and altitude limits of spruce forest growth. "Typically a [northern shrike] breeding habitat is a contrast of densely wooded and very open areas," according to one report. Winter habitat for migrant northerns parallels that of loggerheads.

Shrike nests are bulky for the size of the bird, measuring about 6 inches across. The open cups consist of weed stems, bark strips, twigs, and rootlets, lined with softer materials—grasses, plant fibers, feathers, bits of fur or cloth. Shrike nests, of low thermal conductance, provide a high degree of insulation. Loggerheads often nest in the same types of thorny tangles they use for larders—hawthorn, Osage orange, and multiflora rose. Red cedar and apple are also favored nest trees; one study found that nests in red cedars fledged more young than nests in other trees. The female loggerhead builds the nest from materials collected by both sexes over a period of 6 to 11 days, usually placing it in dense foliage 8 to 15 feet high. Occasionally the birds reline previous nests for usage or use them as foundations for new nests. Later-season nests tend to be placed higher in deciduous trees than earlier

*Loggerhead shrike nestlings appear almost ready to fledge in this thicket nesting site.*

attempts. Northern shrikes frequently nest in brushy growths of black spruce, shrub willows, and alders.

Both shrikes are predatory, our only exclusively meat-eating songbirds. Though primarily insectivorous, they capture and eat almost any creature of a size they can handle. For loggerheads, insects—mainly large beetles and grasshoppers—make up more than half of the summer diet. Shrikes "de-sting venomous insects, such as bumblebees," wrote researcher Sarah A. Sloane, "by rubbing their abdomens against a perch and squeezing out the poison in the manner of African bee-eaters." In winter, small mammals such as voles and ground squirrels may compose up to three-quarters of the diet. Frogs, lizards, snakes, and invertebrates such as spiders and crayfish are also taken, as well as road-killed carcasses and carrion. Northern shrikes, probably reflecting the resources of their high-latitude range,

feed to a larger extent on rodents, mainly voles and lemmings, as well as small birds, which they knock out of the air by a rap of their heavy bill. Young northerns are not agile enough to capture many birds and depend mainly upon rodent prey; thus rodent cycles of abundance may affect juvenile survival rates until the onset of winter. In heavy winter snow cover, northern shrike prey shifts largely to small birds. Shrikes are associates of spiny trees and shrubs such as hawthorn, Osage orange, black locust, crab apple, and multiflora rose. Such plants provide the impaling stations, or *larders,* where shrikes cache their prey. The birds almost always impale larger prey items before eating, but they do so with smaller prey only sometimes. They may visit and feed at their larders frequently or may leave some items impaled for weeks without

*An impaled frog is only one type of prey stored in the shrike's larder, often the thorn of a hawthorn tree. (Drawn from a photograph by Janea Little.)*

eating. Research indicates, however, that most impaled prey is eventually consumed. "Impaling probably evolved as a feeding adaptation," wrote Reuven Yosef, "because it enables shrikes to immobilize larger prey than they could otherwise handle." For loggerheads, at least, larders also apparently function as territorial markers and mate attractants. Since loggerheads in Florida remain on their territories all year, "they may have little need to stockpile food but a great need to advertise territory," Sarah A. Sloane suggested; "farther north, the need to cache food may be primary." Sloane cited impaling behavior as possibly an example of an "exaptation, a behavior that arose in one context but now functions in another."

Competitive interactions are relatively infrequent, though shrikes chase almost any bird that appears on the territory, and they dominate most encounters with kingbirds, meadowlarks, and other species that share their habitat. Shrike researcher Tom J. Cade noted "the terrific impact a pair of shrikes exerts on the nesting of other small birds. . . . I have never found other birds nesting successfully closer than 200 yards from a shrike nest. . . . Wherever they settle, shrikes appear to render about 320 acres of prime nesting habitat marginal for breeding by other passerine birds," both by direct predation and other birds' avoidance of the shrike vicinity. Thus a single pair of shrikes may exercise a definite control on local numbers and breeding distribution of other birds. Northern mockingbirds are known to steal from shrike larders, as do crested caracaras and burrowing owls in the southern range. An ecological congener to shrikes is the American kestrel, a raptor that hunts in the same habitats and kills its prey the same way. Kestrels compete at times with loggerheads, but they usually occupy warmer areas in winter than northern shrikes favor. At least one researcher believes that the periodic winter irruptions of northern shrikes result primarily from competition with other shrikes for sparse populations of small bird prey in the far north. Theoretically, most of the migrants consist of young birds of the year, which are less able to compete for this resource and thus migrate southward in large numbers seeking food.

Shrike predators are numerous and account for a significant amount of mortality, especially during the fledgling phase. Among birds that attack fledglings are scissor-tailed flycatchers, American robins, eastern meadowlarks, common grackles, and brown thrashers, plus several raptors. Adult shrikes lie low when any bird-eating raptor enters their territory. Falcons and small accipiters (kestrels, merlins, and sharp-shinned hawks) are probably the adult shrike's main predators. Predators on eggs and nestlings include black-billed magpies, American crows, blue jays, Brewer's blackbirds, and raptors, mainly northern harriers, merlins, and red-tailed hawks. Several arboreal snakes (bull, indigo, rat, and corn snakes), raccoons, weasels, and feral cats are also common shrike predators. Brown-headed cowbirds occasionally parasitize loggerhead nests. The linear habitats favored by loggerheads—that is, roadsides and hedgerows—often function as travel corridors for many organisms, thus becoming areas that also attract predators. The preference for roadway habitats also results in many collisions with vehicles, especially by low-flying juvenile birds.

**Focus.** Miss Lee, my seventh-grade science teacher, introduced me to the northern *shriek* (whereas the dictionary pronunciation rhymes with *like*), and for the next decade or so I referred to these still-unseen birds as shrieks. Later I learned that she wasn't so far off after all: *Shrike* and *shriek* originate from the same Anglo-Saxon root, and presumably some of the harsher raspy call notes gave these birds their name. *Loggerhead* is another term for "blockhead," referring to the bird's disproportionately large head. Both species have long been known as "butcher birds" for their predatory habits (*L. excubitor* means "watchful butcher").

Loggerhead shrike populations have undergone slow decline in the Northeast since the 1940s and precipitous decline in this region since about 1965. Forest clearing and agricultural development probably led initially to a wider distribution and greater abundance of this species, spreading from the "deserts, shrub steppes, and southern savannas [that] may represent the historical core areas of its distribution," one research team wrote. Because of its presently flexible habitat usage, some researchers believe that the loggerhead probably inhabited eastern "oak openings and barrens, prairies, and pine savannas and barrens," as ecologist Richard Brewer opined. Others believe that loggerheads were probably rare or absent in the Northeast before settlement of the continent, just as they are today.

Reasons are difficult to pinpoint, though unquestionably agricultural conversion to row-crop production, the use of pesticides that reduce insect food resources (especially on the winter range), and low nesting success where populations drop below an optimal point have combined to place stress on this species. In Indiana, reported one researcher in 1990, loggerheads still occurred only in a section of the state where Amish farmers maintained hedgerows free of pesticides and herbicides. "Although [loggerhead] shrikes seem to have declined more steeply than their habitat," researcher Janea M. Little suggested, "their requirements may be more specific than we realize." She cited several studies indicating that loggerheads foraging mainly in mowed or grazed fields produce more fledglings than pairs foraging in cultivated fields or unmowed grass. The loggerhead shrike is currently rated an endangered or threatened species in all of the northeastern and Great Lakes states and eastern Canada, and it is listed "of special concern" elsewhere. Largest declines are associated with the migratory populations. Much research remains to be accomplished before specific management programs for the restoration of this species can be knowledgeably undertaken. A question recently raised in some quarters, however, is "how aggressive should management agencies and programs be in preserving or restoring a species that did not historically occur in an area and that only arrived as a result of human alteration of the landscape—especially when such interference may be disruptive to other environmental aims and decisions?" "That's a good question," remarked Brewer, "but the answer is often biased based on whether an agency would like to restore a subspecies or not. . . . It wouldn't be surprising if a state wildlife division had little interest in a puzzling passerine like the loggerhead shrike." Shrikes, in short, pose policy problems.

Old World falconers and hawk trappers used tethered northern shrikes, relying on their vision as early-warning indicators to signal approaching falcons. Early American naturalists, however, had a tough time accepting the shrike for what it is. John Burroughs labeled it "a feathered assassin" and a "Bluebeard among songbirds." Even Thoreau, usually impervious to anthropomorphic value judgments, found its predatory behaviors somehow "not birdlike." In

1850, hired guns on Boston Common shot northern shrikes by the score during one winter to protect newly introduced house sparrow populations from predation (see *Birds of Forest, Yard, and Thicket*). In today's intellectual climate, which tends likewise to value judgments, albeit more positive ones, shrikes are seen as valuable insect predators—farmers' friends.

The longevity of shrikes is not well established. Loggerheads have lived to 6 years and northerns (in Europe) to 12, but these ages are probably extreme. In North America, the maximum recorded life span for northerns is about 3 years—"simply a result of low frequency of banding," judged one report.

## 12

## Eastern Bluebird *(Sialia sialis)*

Thrush family (Muscicapidae), order Passeriformes. Recognize the eastern bluebird by its sky blue upper parts and robin red breast and belly. Females are somewhat duller in color than males. When perched, bluebirds appear somewhat hunched, about 7 inches long. The musical "chur-a-lee" song, sometimes described as a pure contralto and voiced by both sexes, carries far; other sounds include a "chir-wi" flight call, soft gurgling notes, and an alarm chatter.

**Close relatives.** The only other *Sialia* species are the western and mountain bluebirds *(S. mexicana, S. currocoides),* which inhabit western North America. Some 450 thrush species exist worldwide. North American family members include the *Catharus* thrushes (the veery and gray-cheeked, Swainson's, hermit, and wood thrushes) and the American robin *(Turdus migratorius).* (See *Birds of Forest, Yard, and Thicket.)*

**Behaviors.** Bluebirds often perch on wires, fences, or low branches, periodically sailing to the ground and capturing an insect. More infrequently they catch insects on the wing or glean them in the treetops. Casual bird observers cherish the bluebird not only for its colorful plumage, gentle mien, and chortling song but also for a domestic lifestyle that seems to coincide neatly with human family values. Actually, bluebirds exhibit an often confusing array of domestic arrangements, the more startling as research brings them to light. Little evidence exists, for example, that bluebird monogamy lasts beyond a single season, and findings now indicate that in many cases, it endures hardly that long. Matings fairly commonly occur outside the primary pair bond. From 9 to 25 percent of bluebird nestlings, blood type studies reveal, show biological parentage from an adult other than the incubating female or her mate. Such cases of multiple parentage in a brood can only result from less than total mate fidelity by either parent or from egg dumping in the nest by another female. Both of these reproductive strategies are known to occur in bluebirds. "Divorce" among bluebirds can occur after an unsuccessful first nesting, usually a result of harsh weather or nest predation. The birds rapidly abandon sites of nest

The eastern bluebird, wearing "the sky on his back," in Thoreau's phrase, exhibits a characteristic hunched, neckless posture that can be observed even when the bird is too distant for its colors to be visible.

failure, even though such sites may be otherwise optimal. In such cases, the pair sometimes stays together and renests elsewhere; often, however, the pair may split and travel some miles away, the male to establish a new territory, the female to find another mate. Thus nest-site fidelity *(philopatry)*, so common in most species, seems to depend in bluebirds mainly on the degree of nesting success at that site.

Bluebirds are also among those species that utilize nest "helpers"—usually one or more juveniles from the previous seasonal brood or an unmated adult bluebird that lingers at the nest and helps feed the current nestlings. Such systems of *cooperative breeding,* seen to a much greater degree in such species as common ravens, American crows, and scrub jays, may develop when certain environmental pressures (in this case, the number of available cavities for nesting) limit opportunities for younger birds to breed and tend to force birds into group parentage systems. Nest helpers also gain experience for their own future parental roles.

Eastern bluebird breeding range extends eastward from the Great Plains to the Atlantic and from southern Canada to the Caribbean and parts of Mexico and Central America. The birds migrate to and from about the northern half of this range (above latitude 40 degrees N).

*Spring.* Eastern bluebirds reside year-round in their southern range, and nesting commences there in February and March. Each 10 degrees of latitude farther north translates to about 3 weeks later in time for the onset of breeding activity. In the northern range, eastern bluebirds begin arriving in March, with migration peaking in early to middle April. Sometimes the male moves several days ahead of the female; other times the pair arrives together. Spring snowstorms may descend upon migrating bluebirds with devastating results.

Some studies indicate that a relatively small percentage of first-year bluebirds return to their natal sites to breed. Males establish territories of 2 to 25 acres, depending on habitat resources and bluebird population density. Territory centers on a nest cavity in a tree or nest box, and territory size usually shrinks as the season advances. Episodic chasing and grappling with other bluebirds occur as the birds defend their sites. The fullest intensity of male song, sometimes voiced up to 20 times per minute, occurs before a female arrives on the territory. When she appears, his song rate slows to 5 to 10 times per minute. He moves from perch to perch, often flying in lopsided or fluttery fashion, and lifts and quivers one or both wings while perched. Another stylized courtship maneuver is landing at the cavity entrance, perching there, and rocking head and shoulders in and out of the hole. When a female joins him and enters the hole, the birds may be said to be paired. Courtship feeding, in which the male brings food to the female, is another common behavior. Aggressive encounters reach a peak during nest building and egg laying, the period when nest cavities are most vulnerable to takeover by other bluebirds or house sparrows. Female bluebirds fight fiercely against female interlopers.

Yet bluebirds rarely battle intruders of the opposite sex, and this—together with a population of unmated adults termed *floaters*—sets the stage for extrapair matings while the nominal mate is absent.

Apparently, to judge from DNA analyses, a paired male frequently mates with a single floater, which then invades the nest of the paired female and lays an egg. "Because bluebird nest sites are in short supply," suggested researcher Patricia A. Gowaty, "perhaps the only way some females can successfully reproduce is to be opportunistic—to lay their fertile eggs in nests holding some other bluebird mother's eggs." Another theory suggests that male nonaggression toward a female territorial intruder may pay off with survival benefits in the long run: If he opportunistically mates with her, he increases the evolutionary advantages of producing extra offspring.

First-brood nestlings in the North usually fledge in May. The pair typically remains together for a second nesting, beginning in late May, if the first nesting was successful. A pair may begin renesting in the same or another nest site as soon as 3 or 4 days after the first brood fledges.

EGGS AND YOUNG: typically 4 or 5; eggs glossy, pale blue or white. INCUBATION: by female, which is occasionally fed at the nest by male; about 2 weeks; hatching synchronous; altricial young. FEEDING OF YOUNG: by both sexes and (especially in second broods) by occasional nest helpers; caterpillars, beetles, grasshoppers, sometimes berries. FLEDGING: 16 to 20 days; most fledge within a period of 2 hours.

*Summer.* Many eastern bluebirds raise 2 broods throughout most of their northern range (often 3 in the South), but many also raise only a single brood. Second-brood nestlings usually fledge in late June. First nestings, in which 75 to 95 percent of the nestlings typically survive to fledge, usually prove more successful than later ones, which may fledge only 55 percent or so of nestlings. The male continues to feed first-brood fledglings for 3 or 4 weeks, sometimes more, while the female incubates the second brood. Territorial defensiveness rapidly declines after hatching, becoming almost nonexistent as nestlings and fledglings are fed. Birds still raising young in July and August are probably renesting after a previous nesting failure.

Juvenile plumage resembles the female bluebird's except that the breast is brown spotted until the molt of body plumage in late summer, when juveniles acquire adult coloration. The annual molt of adult birds also occurs in late summer. The final family group of the season often remains together, feeding and wandering until migration. During this period, they often return to the nest site. "Parents and offspring from one or several broods gather," wrote naturalist Connie Toops, "investigating the cavity inside and out. Sometimes one or more of the birds will carry a few pieces of grass or pine needles into the box, as though reinforcing the idea that this is a place to nest."

*Fall, Winter.* Many, if not all, eastern bluebirds that reside north of latitude 40 degrees N migrate south, traveling from late September through early November in small or medium-size flocks in daytime. Those few that occasionally remain in the northern range over winter tend to be experienced adult birds. Eastern bluebirds on the winter range usually remain in loose flocks of 5 to 10 or more birds, sometimes associating with other fruit eaters, including American robins, cedar waxwings, and purple finches. During cold nights, several may roost together in nest boxes or other shelters, sometimes huddling in warmth-sharing clusters. By March, many northern-range bluebirds are moving northward, while overwintering and southern-range bluebirds are establishing territories.

Eastern bluebird winter range spans the southeastern and south-central United States, with individual birds moving into Mexico, Central America, and the West Indies.

**Ecology.** Eastern bluebirds favor neither forest nor completely open field habitats but something in between—a semiopen or savanna mixture of small trees or shrubs, such as open oak or pine woodlands, old fields, pastures, orchards, even golf courses and suburban lawns. "Relatively poor, sandy soils apparently contribute to favorable habitat conditions," wrote one researcher. Vital to bluebird habitat are elevated perches for visual food finding—fence posts, wires, low or sparse ground vegetation, scattered trees or shrubs— and, for nesting, cavities in trees, fence posts, or nest boxes. In fall and winter, because of the birds' diet change from insects to tree and shrub fruits, they often occupy somewhat more wooded or marshy

habitats. Before European settlement in North America, eastern bluebirds probably frequented forest edges and openings created by fire,
storms, and beaver floodings.

What would cavity-nesting wildlife do without woodpeckers? As
cavity nesters, eastern bluebirds do not excavate holes themselves
but adopt cavities created mainly by woodpeckers. Often these holes
have been long vacated by woodpeckers, some species of which
excavate new holes every year (see *Birds of Forest, Yard, and
Thicket*), but since many birds and some mammals vie for nest cavities, the work of woodpeckers is always prime real estate for wildlife.
Today, however, after precipitous decline and partial restoration of
bluebird abundance, most eastern bluebirds probably nest in
human-built nest boxes, the placement and maintenance of which
have become a major environmental activity for naturalists. The nest
within the cavity, built solely by the female, consists mainly of dried
grasses and weed stalks, lined with finer grasses or unlined. Building
may not begin for a week or more after the cavity is claimed; actual
construction usually takes 4 or 5 days. Throughout incubation and
brooding, the female engages in a behavior called the *tremble-thrust,*
in which she pokes her bill into the nesting material and shakes it,
perhaps dislodging parasites and organic debris toward the base of
the nest. Nests average about $2^1/2$ inches inside diameter and about
2 inches deep. When bluebirds take over a vacated nest box or one
currently used by another bird, such as a tree swallow, they do not
clean out the contents but bury the previous nest along with any
eggs or nestlings it may contain with fresh materials.

Choice foods include ground beetles, grasshoppers, crickets,
caterpillars, spiders, and snails. In summer and fall, eastern bluebirds add many fruits to their diet, mainly berries. The winter diet is
almost exclusively frugivorous—fruits of dogwoods, eastern red
cedar, bayberry, Virginia-creeper, and sumac, plus wild grapes and
multiflora rose hips are widely consumed. Ecologist Richard Brewer
reports observing bluebirds capturing insect naiads from shallow
streams in winter.

Competition, as in most cavity nesters, largely consists of con-
tention for suitable nest sites. Probably the most frequent contest for

bluebirds occurs with tree swallows; each species is known to invade nest sites of the other on occasion. The swallows are most aggressive in late April and early May when searching for nest sites and when many bluebirds are already incubating. Bluebirds, on the other hand, tend to seize tree swallow sites in later May and early June before beginning their second broods. When such invasions successfully occur, each species simply builds a nest atop that of the other. Yet each seems widely tolerant of the other when both are nesting. In recent years, a popular—though still controversial—method of providing housing for both species while discouraging invasive takeovers is the pairing of nest boxes; each box is placed 15 to 25 feet from the other, with 250 to 300 feet separating each pair of boxes. Such pairing has several advantages: With increased tree swallow populations, pairing allows some boxes to remain available for bluebirds, since tree swallow territorialism prevents other tree swallow pairs from nesting nearby; bluebird pairs likewise will not nest in both of the closely adjacent boxes but can easily defend their single nest box from a tree swallow pair; and tree swallow neighbors closely adjacent to a bluebird pair help defend both boxes from other competitive invaders such as house wrens and house sparrows. Most bluebird nest boxes cannot be sparrow proofed. Placement of the boxes at least 200 yards from buildings, however, reduces house sparrow competition. European starlings also compete for nest cavities; bluebird nest boxes with $1^1/2$-inch entrance holes successfully prevent their invasion. White-footed and deer mouse and squirrel usage of nest boxes generally occurs in winter and thus rarely competes with bluebird nesting. Bluebirds and tree swallows do not compete for food to any large extent, since tree

*Sumac fruits remain on this shrub or small tree over winter, providing a reliable, if not preferred, food for bluebirds and other frugivores.*

swallows feed aerially and bluebirds feed mainly from the ground. Eastern and mountain bluebirds, where they overlap ranges in the Great Plains, rarely hybridize. The rapid transition from eastern to western and mountain bluebird range occurs within only 2 degrees of longitude (100th to 102nd meridian).

Bluebird predators include all the aforementioned competitors at times, especially house wrens and house sparrows. Other occasional bird predators include American kestrels; Cooper's, sharp-shinned, and red-tailed hawks; and shrikes. Bull and rat snakes, raccoons, opossums, and domestic cats raid unprotected nest boxes at times. Brown-headed cowbird parasitism is rarely a problem in bluebird nest boxes since the entrance holes are too small to admit them. Blowfly larvae infest many, if not most, bluebird nests, especially during second nestings; the larvae parasitize nestlings at night but seldom weaken them so much as to cause death unless the infestation is very severe. In Ontario, a 1994 study indicated that blowfly infestation followed by house wren and house sparrow predation were the main causes of bluebird nesting failure there, but other studies seem to show that blowfly parasitism does not affect fledging success. Paper wasps and ants occasionally invade nest boxes, the latter when a broken egg or dead nestling attracts them.

**Focus.** Ever since English naturalist Mark Catesby first identified "the blew bird" in America in 1731, this species has been a popular "birder's bird." The bluebird, waxed researcher Lawrence Zeleny, "is American idealism personified—a flying piece of sky, a living poem, a crystal note, an emblem of nature's moral conscience." Early colonists called it "blue robin" for its resemblance to the European robin. Naturalist John Burroughs claimed that bluebird arrival in New York and New England signaled the rise of sap in sugar maple; and bluebird song, according to one folktale, inspires the full bloom of apple trees. The "bluebird of happiness" and bluebirds flying "somewhere over the rainbow" suggest the symbolic load this bird carries in addition to "the sky on its back," as Thoreau wrote. Missouri and New York have named it their state bird, as Idaho and Nevada have claimed the mountain bluebird. Hardly another bird is so uncritically adored by casual observers, yet it is astonishing how

many people have never seen one. Indeed, most of an entire genera-
tion of Americans missed out on bluebirds, for during the decades of
their precipitous decline (1950s–70s), the birds became rare throughout much of their range. Today, thanks to hard work by people
unwilling to let the species perish, it seems well advanced on the
comeback trail.

The number of bluebird societies that exist throughout the United
States also attests to the popularity of this bird. During the nineteenth
century, bluebirds were probably about as numerous as robins today.
A combination of starling competition, scarcity of cavity nesting habitats, blanket pesticide applications, and several harsh winters were
primarily blamed for the decline. Publicity campaigns led by the North
American Bluebird Society brought awareness of the bluebird's plight
and inspired direct action to help recover bluebird populations. To
that end, bluebird nesting programs, which employed a variety of nest
box designs, and bluebird trails, with several to many nest boxes
placed and spaced in good bluebird habitats and regularly monitored
by volunteers, headed the recovery efforts. A Transcontinental Bluebird Trail project, launched by the North American Bluebird Society in
1999, aims to place nest box networks across the continent. "Strategic
placement of nest boxes,"
wrote researcher Ben
Pinkowski, "remains the
principal conservation
measure for bluebirds."
These projects plus fortu-
itously kinder weather
and reductions in pesti-
cide use have paid off,
restoring bluebird populations in many areas to
levels of stable abun-
dance. From 1966, when
breeding bird surveys
began, to 1996, the latest
figures, eastern bluebird

*Bluebird nest boxes, often established along "bluebird
trails," have probably helped restore populations of
this charismatic bird in many areas.*

populations increased 103 percent. Northern bluebird populations always will, however, be subject to periodic crashes—probably about once every 10 to 15 years—because of harsh weather, which results in widespread insect decreases and consequent bluebird starvation.

As in all blue-plumaged birds, the bluebird's blue—unlike the colors produced by pigments in most bird plumages—is an optical illusion governed by the physics of scattered light waves from reflective cells in the feathers. Thus the intensity of light shining on a bluebird (or blue jay or indigo bunting, among others) largely determines how blue it looks. Worn or molting plumage can also affect the blue appearance.

Eastern bluebirds sometimes survive for 6 or 7 years, but the typical adult bluebird averages about 2 years old. After the bird's first year, during which mortality is highest, its chances for survival increase.

The North American Bluebird Society (P.O. Box 74, Darlington WI 53530-0074; www.cobleskill.edu/nabs) continues to provide information and aid to persons who want to establish and maintain bluebird trails and nest boxes.

# 13

## Sedge Wren *(Cistothorus platensis)*

Creeper, wren, and gnatcatcher family (Certhiidae), order Passeriformes. All wrens have slender, slightly down-curved bills and cock their tails upward. Next to the winter wren, the sedge wren (formerly known as short-billed marsh wren) is the smallest North American wren, at 4 inches or slightly more. Identify it by its streaked back and crown and its buffy undertail plumage. Sexes look alike. Its chattering trill is a sequence of notes that ends with a staccato burr; one observer likened the gritty song to "rattling a bag of marbles."

**Close relatives.** The only other *Cistothorus* wren in North America is the marsh wren *(C. palustris)*. Apolinar's wren and the merida wren *(C. apolinari, C. meridae)* inhabit the Andes. Some 75 wren species all reside, except for one, in the New World, but North American species total only nine. These include the house wren *(Troglodytes aedon,* see *Birds of Forest, Yard, and Thicket)*, the winter wren *(T. troglodytes),* and the Carolina wren *(Thryothorus ludovicianus)*. Family members also include the American tree-creeper (brown creeper, *Certhia americana*) and the blue-grey gnatcatcher *(Polioptila caerulea).*

**Behaviors.** The sedge wren shares many behavioral traits with its close relative the marsh wren (see *Birds of Lake, Pond and Marsh)*. Like marsh wrens, sedge wrens are *polygynous* breeders (2 or more females per male), build dummy nests all over their territories, and with fierce competitive instincts, often raid and destroy nests of neighboring sedge wrens and other bird species. Unlike marsh wrens, however, they do not exhibit strong nest-site fidelity *(philopatry)* from year to year. Their song repertoires lack the variability of marsh wrens, thus they do not countersing by matching song types. Also, their distribution is more patchy and irregular than the marsh wren's.

A sedge wren's presence in any given year is unreliable at best; the species is notorious for suddenly showing up in almost any season, then disappearing. One early May day in northern Michigan, a sedge wren sang boisterously in a site where I had never seen one before. I have not seen one there since; this is a fairly typical sedge wren experience. In places where they do not settle in for the season, they usually remain shy and inconspicuous, fluttering in mothlike fashion only short distances before dropping back into the grass. Their social relations are also variable. Often only one or two breeding pairs are present in a marsh or sedge meadow; in other places, several pairs may nest semicolonially.

Sedge wrens breed from central Canada eastward, encompassing the northern half of the United States. Breeding Bird Survey data show them most numerous in early summer from Manitoba south through Minnesota and Wisconsin. Disjunct populations also exist year-round in parts of Central and South America.

*Spring.* Philopatry is not one of this bird's strong suits—it may or may not return to areas in which it previously nested. The birds usually arrive on their northern breeding range from early to middle May and often begin nesting in June, although nesting may occur from May through September. The sedge wren male builds several to many unlined dummy nests in its territory, which spans about a half acre and which it

*The sedge wren, one of the most puzzling and anomalous of birds, is also one of the fiercest bird neighbors in its sedge meadow habitat.*

maintains largely by song. A female selects one of the nests and lines it before laying eggs.

   Much remains unknown about sedge wren courtship and territory and how these and its polygynous breeding habits may or may not differ from those of the marsh wren. Polygyny occurs at levels of 30 to 50 percent in many breeding areas, sometimes much less. A polygynous male rarely hosts more than 2 females on his territory; the first is called the *primary female,* the next is called the *secondary.* Their nesting schedules are not simultaneous but sequential; usually a secondary female begins nesting 2 to 6 weeks after a primary begins, a period roughly concurrent with incubation and nestling stages for the latter. The role of *courting centers*—areas on the territory that provide the focus of song and nest-building activities, as in marsh wrens—remains uncertain for sedge wrens. Some studies even seem to indicate that in sedge wrens, such behaviors do not always indicate actual breeding activity, thus throwing a rather large monkey wrench into the careful methodology of breeding bird censusers.

---

EGGS AND YOUNG: 6 or 7; eggs white. INCUBATION: by female; 12 to 14 days; hatching synchronous; nestlings altricial. FEEDING OF YOUNG: mainly by female; insects, spiders. FLEDGING: 12 to 14 days.

---

   *Summer.* Sedge wren females apparently raise 2 or even 3 broods throughout most of their range, but not necessarily with the same male; perhaps this sequential breeding, plus polygyny, accounts for the late-summer nesting known to occur. Most summer nesting, however, occurs earlier, between mid-July and early August. Sedge wren males continue making dummy nests and also maintain fairly continuous song through summer, sometimes even at night. Fledglings, reported one observer, "move about among the sedge and bushes of the marsh like little mice." Parent birds continue to feed them for several days; then the juveniles join and remain in sibling flocks until migration. The annual molt, occurring mainly in August, produces richer browns than the spring plumage.

*Fall, Winter.* Fairly early fall migrators, some sedge wrens, presumably juveniles or unmated adults, may begin moving southward as early as July. Peak travel occurs in later August and in September. Most sedge wrens winter in Florida and along the Gulf coast into northeastern Mexico. A prenuptial molt of body plumage occurs in late winter or early spring.

**Ecology.** Sedge and marsh wrens rarely coexist in the same habitats. Sedge wrens favor drier, denser portions of the marsh, even upland fields at times. They tend to occupy rank sedge and grass growth rather than cattails in standing water. Stands of canary-grass and river-bulrush provide common nesting habitats. In winter, sedge wrens frequent rice plantations, both freshwater and saltwater marshes, grassy meadows, and prairies.

Bog and fen edges, wet meadows, pastures, fields of asters and goldenrods, and lush hayfields frequently host nesting sites. Sedge wren nests are smaller, more globular in shape, and lower placed than marsh wren nests. A woven ball of grasses and sedges about 4 to 6 inches in height, well camouflaged in the vegetation, seldom stands more than a foot or two off the ground. The well-hidden side entrance measures about an inch in diameter. Sometimes nests appear "to be started by drawing down the tops of the sedges to begin the outside of the ball," reported one researcher. Another reported that unlined dummy nests usually stand higher and more visibly than the brood nest, which the female lines with plant down and feathers.

Sedge wren diet, mainly insects, consists largely of true bugs, beetles, caterpillars, ants, grasshoppers, crickets, mosquitoes, and spiders.

Competition drives the sedge wren's aggressive behaviors. Like the marsh wren, it is noted for wreaking havoc on nests of other birds, destroying eggs and killing nestlings—not a predator as such, but a fierce, intolerant vandal that tries to "ethnically cleanse" its territory, driving out all its neighbors, even other sedge wrens at times. Undoubtedly sedge and marsh wrens—"fascists" of the avifauna—bear significant impact on the nesting success of other passerines in their habitats. Marsh wrens may nest in wetter parts of marshes adjacent to the drier habitats of the sedge wrens, but the species seldom compete.

*Long-tailed weasels frequent sedge wren habitats, often becoming common predators of many grassland and sedge nesting species.*

Predators include a variety of creatures—snakes, raptors, crows, and almost any hunting mammal abroad in the fields and marshes. Raccoons, skunks, weasels, minks, and foxes are probably the foremost.

**Focus.** Probably few bird species exhibit such opportunistic breeding strategies as sedge wrens. The only stable element in their reproductive milieu appears to be habitat, and even this seems variable within the basic parameters. Sedge wrens show much less rigid attachment than most birds to the structural elements of bird life history, such as seasonal timing, mating system, and site stability.

Sedge wrens began to decline throughout their range during the 1970s; Ohio now lists it as an endangered species, Indiana as threatened. Nobody knows the precise reasons for such declines; experts usually blame them on habitat loss and degradation, and no doubt this explanation remains at least partially valid for sedge wrens. Fragmentation of large marshland areas may also be a factor. Plainly, however, the species has not yet been sufficiently studied to warrant statements of certainty.

Although Breeding Bird Survey data show a slight trend of increase in sedge wren numbers during the past couple of decades, the exceedingly patchy, elusive populations make such figures sus-pect, probably "influenced by the erratic movements of this species," one report cautions. Characterized by high mobility during the breeding season—first arrivals can occur as late as mid-July, and May residents may be gone by July—and low site fidelity between seasons, sedge wrens are the bane of bird censusers. Yet where they thrive for a season, sedge wren nesting success—that is, the number of fledglings raised—often soars, approaching 70 percent.

Sedge wren longevity remains unknown.

# 14

## Swallow Family (Hirundinidae), order Passeriformes

This bank swallow's wing, superbly gauged for lift and glide, exemplifies the long-pointed, streamlined shape of all swallow wings.

Almost 90 swallow species occur worldwide, 6 in eastern North America. Short, flattened bills; long-pointed wings; weak feet; gregarious behaviors; and swift, agile flight characterize these insect predators. Their anatomy and aerial feeding habits give them some resemblance to swifts, an unrelated family. Most swallows are colonial or semicolonial nesters. Their young are altricial. In addition to the accounts that follow, other northeastern species include the northern rough-winged swallow *(Stelgidopteryx serripennis)*, cliff swallow *(Hirundo pyrrhonota)*, barn swallow *(H. rustica)*, and purple martin *(Progne subis)*. All are migrants.

SWALLOW FAMILY (Hirundinidae)

## Tree Swallow *(Tachycineta bicolor)*

Identify this 5- to 6-inch-long swallow by its metallic greenish blue upper parts; clear white chin, breast, and belly; and notched tail. Sexes look alike, except that yearling females show mixed brown and greenish blue plumage on the back. Juvenile tree swallows are brown above and white below, with a dusky, incomplete breastband. Calls include various twittering notes associated with courtship and a liquid "chee-leep," mainly voiced in flight.

**Close relatives.** Eight other *Tachycineta* species reside mainly in South America. These include the violet-green swallow *(T. thalassina)*, mangrove swallow *(T. albilinea)*, white-winged swallow *(T. albiventer)*, white-rumped swallow *(T. leucorrhoa)*, and Chilean swallow *(T. leucopyga)*. Bank swallows *(Riparia)* and a group of South American hole-nesting swallows also appear closely related.

**Behaviors.** Seldom seen on the ground, tree swallows usually perch on bare branches, power lines, nest boxes, or other above-ground sites in the open. Tree swallows tend to circle and glide more than most swallows, readily diving at the head of a person in the nest vicinity, swerving aside with a raspy note. Mobbing and diving potential predators are common behaviors in nesting areas. Yet these birds do not fly especially fast, typically less than 20 mph.

Mainly aerial feeders, tree swallows sometimes fly long distances from nests to prime feeding areas such as over-water sites or open acres sheltered from wind. They are social birds for most of the year, sometimes semicolonial nesters, yet are fiercely territorial and protective of individual nest sites. Although most pairs remain seasonally monogamous, *polygyny* (a single male pairing with 2 females, each with her own nest) occurs at about 5 percent frequency.

Tree swallow breeding range extends across North America, from the arctic treeline south to the middle tier of states. The birds are migrators.

*Spring.* As the earliest swallow migrants, tree swallows typically arrive at their breeding sites from mid-March to early April. I thus noted their arrival in my notes of a recent April 14: "Tree swallows returned, exuberantly, about mid-AM, circling, dipping, vocalizing as if greeting the area anew, checking it all out. As they course around and over the cabin, their note might be described as a chewed or chewy chirp." Older birds precede yearlings. Females, especially, exhibit highly variable rates of *philopatry* (fidelity to previous nesting areas), though the birds usually return to sites where breeding has been successful. "Occasionally," one research team wrote, "a pair breeds together for several consecutive years in the same or a nearby nest site . . . most likely a result of each individual having strong site fidelity rather than long-term pair bond."

Migrating by daytime in small, loose flocks, males usually arrive a few days before females. The birds pair soon after female arrival, exhibiting several courtship behaviors, though many females seem to "play the field" for several days after initial pairing. The pair may examine several potential nest cavity sites, and soon the male establishes a territory, which extends to distances of up to 25 feet or so from the nest site. Some 12 different call notes have been identified, plus a male dawn song and day song, repetitive phrasings of 1- and 2-note series, usually given while perched at the nest site. The male hovers and flutters near the female, and the pair bows toward each other and touches bills. Courtship displays continue until incubation begins. A social display of apparent exuberance, if nothing else, is *towering,* in which a bird circles high over its home range; other tree swallows join, calling softly as they wheel high in the air before dropping to their nest sites.

*Often a tree swallow seems much more possessive of an empty nest box it has just claimed than of a box full of nestlings—one of the many paradoxical behaviors of this species.*

Tree swallows are slow to begin nesting, usually in May. Nest building, done by the female, can encompass several days to 2 weeks, and egg laying may not begin for a week or more after nest completion. In contrast to the frenetic nesting activities of many birds, tree swallows seem deliberate, almost casual, in their timing and sequence of nesting events. Nest building usually occurs only during the morning. Both sexes fiercely compete for and defend nest sites, grappling in midair, on the ground, even over water with intruding tree swallows. Territorial disputes, attacks, and chases commonly occur before incubation begins. The birds' fierceness extends to other occupied nests; a male tree swallow moving in to replace a dead or missing male will often kill nestlings of the widowed mate before breeding with her and claiming the same nest site. Before and sometimes even during incubation, tree swallows may completely abandon the nesting area for up to several days. Eggs already laid do not seem to lose viability. This behavior may be related to a temporary lack of aerial insect food during cold or wet weather; the birds may fly 20 miles or more to forage elsewhere. This volitional abandonment of territory for such lengthy durations—thus far seen in no other North American bird—is a remarkable adaptation for a bird dependent on aerial insect prey.

Tree swallows have been subject to much field research. The more they are studied, the more complex their social relations appear. For example, the yearling female, so distinctive in plumage (the only North American female passerine bird that does not gain full breeding plumage in a year), has been found to assume an important backup role in breeding. She arrives 2 to 3 weeks later than adults, just after pairs have settled on their territories. Although she is sexually mature, her migration timing has placed her at a competitive disadvantage with older females. She thus becomes part of a population of "floaters," wandering, unpaired birds (about 25 percent of female tree swallows in a given area) that constantly revisit already occupied nest cavities throughout the nesting season. She approaches these nests with a distinctive flutter-flight, hovering with shallow wingbeats; if she finds the nest resident absent, she may immediately claim the site and proceed to defend it as her own. The male partner of the displaced female generally does not respond aggressively to such a takeover, apparently accepting any female present on the nest as belonging there. The juvenilelike plumage of the invading female, as well as its submissive flutter-flight display, may permit it to approach active nests without challenge.

In checking my own tree swallow nest boxes, I occasionally find other evidence of puzzling domestic events. One of the strangest situations I encountered occurred in the spring of 1996, when I found a tree swallow sitting on 3 of its own eggs in the lined portion of a nest box crammed with house wren sticks; several hundred feet adjacent, a nest box contained 6 house wren eggs lying in the feathered nest of a tree swallow. The root cause of such anomalies probably lies in the birds' intense competition for nest cavities, which are often in short supply. Occasionally, nesting groups—a male and two or more females—may tend or occupy the same nest cavity. Being dived upon by a trio of tree swallows when checking my nest boxes became a fairly common occurrence.

EGGS AND YOUNG: 4 to 6; eggs white. INCUBATION: by female; 14 or 15 days; hatching asynchronous, over 1 to 2 days. FEEDING OF YOUNG: by both sexes; insects. FLEDGING: average of 3 weeks.

*Summer.* Tree swallows raise only 1 brood per year. After fledging, juveniles continue to be fed by parents for several days. Sometimes juvenile tree swallows attempt to pirate food at still-functional nests of other tree swallows *(kleptoparasitism)*. Researcher Michael P. Lombardo's 1987 "exploratory-dispersal" hypothesis suggested that such visitors are exploring potential nest sites for the next year. (The relatively low frequency of yearling philopatry in this species would seem to argue against this thesis.)

Annual molt of flight and body feathers begins in July, sometimes before nesting is completed, continuing through October. After fledglings become independent, young and adults alike usually abandon the breeding area, often flocking and roosting together in open marshy habitats where aerial insects are abundant. To persons who have witnessed them, the evening preroosting aerial displays—"tornadoes of tree swallows," Roger Tory Peterson described them—are spectacular events. Hundreds or thousands of tree swallows gather over a marsh roosting area, swirling down from the sky in a funnel cloud of birds similar to the evening flights of chimney swifts into smokestack roosts (see *Birds of Forest, Yard, and Thicket*). Such roosting flights can occur during any season except spring.

Premigratory flocking begins in August, sometimes earlier. Large flocks—up to millions along the Atlantic coast—may gather with much noise and confusion in marshes or on power lines. Some researchers have described "mass examinations" of nest boxes by tree swallows during this period—an extension of Lombardo's hypothesis? Flocks may remain on the northern range into October, however, making this species the latest of fall migrant swallows.

*Fall, Winter.* Tree swallows migrate in daytime, moving in much larger flocks than in spring (many more birds now exist). Again, they sometimes investigate potential nest sites during fall migration. Migration peaks during September. Two main migration channels exist: Most tree swallows east of the Great Lakes travel along the eastern seaboard, wintering from New Jersey south to Florida and the Caribbean. Midwestern and Great Plains populations move down the Mississippi flyway, wintering on the Gulf coast and south to Venezuela. Local populations also winter south of San Francisco on the Pacific coast. A certain field near Chiapas, Mexico, hosts up to a million tree swallows that roost there from December through March. Tree swallows may occasionally linger over winter in parts of New England and Long Island owing to their dietary versatility. Often in fall and winter, tree swallows roost communally with other swallows, including bank, barn, cliff, and northern rough-winged swallows and purple martins.

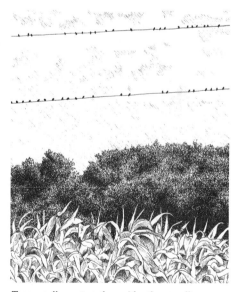

*Tree swallows, together with other swallow species, often gather on power lines in summer as they stage for migration.*

Tree swallows are about half molted when migration begins in late summer, and they complete their annual molt by October or November. Most tree swallows are en route northward by late February or early March.

**Ecology.** Tree swallows require open areas, but they may frequent several habitat types within that designation: fields, marshes, open bogs, shorelines and dunes, savannas, pastures, roadsides, and hedgerows. Often they favor open country near lakes or ponds, but not invariably; my own heavily used tree swallow nest boxes stand on a dry upland savanna miles from open water. The most important components of tree swallow breeding habitat are nest cavities—standing dead trees in ponds or wetland margins, or nest boxes within or adjacent to open areas for foraging. Beavers indirectly benefit tree swallows by creating ponds, flooding out trees that die, become excavated by woodpeckers, and ultimately serve tree swallows. The birds frequent the same types of habitat in winter, except that cavities are unneeded.

Tree swallows never excavate their own tree cavities but "recycle" the work of woodpeckers. The tree swallow's semicolonial nesting habits probably owe as much to the spacing of cavity sites within a habitat as to social preference of the birds. Most tree swallows favor a spacing of at least 30 to 50 feet from their nearest neighbor, though occasionally they nest much closer together; they also prefer substantial open space around the nest site. Eastern bluebird nest box programs, which have widely benefited that species, have probably also resulted in tree swallow population increases (see Eastern Bluebird). Tree swallows seem to prefer south-facing cavities for nest sites. Most nests within cavities consist mainly of dried grasses, sometimes other plant materials as well. Some tree swallows, however, collect very little nesting material. In my own nest boxes, a scant-covered, practically bare floor during tree swallow occupancy is not uncommon. A characteristic of many tree swallow nests is a lining of feathers—often quite large ones—in and around the nest cup. These are not the swallows' own feathers but those of other species, usually added after egg laying and incubation begin. The male collects them, and the female places them so that the quill ends stick into the nest and the feather tips curl over the eggs, covering them when the bird leaves the nest. Collected feathers are mostly white contour feathers, sometimes from waterfowl (probably collected from water), gull rookeries, and poultry yards. Almost any size and color of bird feathers may be used; I have seen ruffed grouse tail feathers in nests, and the birds will even collect from torn feather pillows. Researchers speculate that feathers in the nest may provide added insulation and a barrier to moisture and skin parasites. Occasionally tree swallows occupy rural mailboxes, wall crevices, and even holes in the ground as nest cavities.

*Tree swallows often occupy bluebird nest boxes. The feather nest lining is characteristic, though sometimes the swallows add few materials to the cavity.*

Tree swallow diet mainly consists of flying insects captured over land or water, rarely from water or ground surfaces. Some 40 percent of the insect diet consists of flies, with lesser amounts of beetles, ants, grasshoppers, dragonflies, stoneflies, mayflies, and caddisflies. During winter and early-spring migration, at least in northeastern coastal areas, tree swallows become almost exclusively frugivorous (fruit eating), with especially heavy consumption of *Myrica* fruits (wax-myrtle and bayberry species). While many birds consume *Myrica* nutlets, tree swallows probably depend upon them to a larger extent than most; the birds readily digest the waxy coating of these fruits, which in these areas may form the entire diet for long periods in winter. Tree swallows also occasionally eat fruits of red cedar, Virginia-creeper, and dogwoods plus seeds of sedges and bulrushes.

This ability to turn vegetarian in the absence of insects enables tree swallows to adapt more efficiently than most other swallows to cold spells and the vagaries of weather.

Competitive interactions abound for most hole nesters, and tree swallows are no exception. They contend for nest cavities not only with each other but also with purple martins, great crested flycatchers, northern flickers, eastern and mountain bluebirds, house wrens, European starlings, and house sparrows. The wrens, flickers, and sparrows are known to destroy tree swallow eggs and nestlings on occasion; bluebirds usually successfully defend their nests against tree swallows, which may occasionally kill bluebird nestlings. Food competition appears insignificant, but competition with other tree swallows for nest-lining feathers may become intense at times. Aggressive "feather chasing" among tree swallows often seems to show elements of play behavior: A bird may repeatedly drop its feather, then retrieve it, attracting other swallows to the chase. Feather chases may also occur after the breeding season, leading one researcher to speculate that "chases for feathers may possibly serve some social function in addition to acquiring feathers for the nest."

Bird predators on tree swallow eggs and nestlings include northern flickers, American kestrels, American crows, and common grackles. House wren and house sparrow predation is probably a secondary result of nest cavity competition. Rat snakes, chipmunks, weasels, raccoons, deer mice, and feral cats also raid tree swallow nests. Flying or perched tree swallows are vulnerable to sharp-shinned hawks, American kestrels, merlins, peregrine falcons, great horned owls, and black-billed magpies. Nest parasitism by brown-headed cowbirds, as for most cavity-nesting species, seldom occurs. Nestlings, however, are frequently parasitized by blowfly (*Protocalliphora sialia*) larvae, which rarely kill them but may reduce vigor and growth rates. The larvae attach to the nestlings at night, sucking their blood, then hide in the nesting material during the day. Hypothermia or starvation from a lack of flying insects may result from abnormally cold weather during the nestling stage. "Weather, pesticides, draining of wetlands, elimination of fruits, and local shortage of nest sites aggravated by competition with introduced species [starlings and house sparrows]," according to one researcher, covers the gamut of threats to tree swallow populations.

**Focus.** Availability of cavity nesting sites is probably the chief limiting factor on tree swallow breeding populations. Over the past few decades, regional eastern and central populations appear relatively stable or increasing, and the birds have also extended their breeding range southward. How much of this abundance owes significantly to human placement of nest boxes remains unclear. Opinions differ; some researchers believe that, although nest boxes may tend to increase local populations of tree swallows, the number of tree swallows annually fledged from nest boxes probably does not exceed 2 or 3 percent of the total; others consider the percentage much higher. Birders erect relatively few nest boxes specifically for tree swallows; usually the swallows occupy boxes intended for wood ducks or eastern bluebirds. Nest-box interiors should be roughened or grooved to facilitate the bird's exit; tree swallows often die when they become trapped in smooth-walled boxes.

When I check my nest boxes in spring, I find that tree swallows claim their sites soon after their arrival; they often vigorously defend them weeks before actual nesting begins, which invariably occurs only after bluebird nesting has begun in some of the adjacent boxes. A defending swallow often remains perched atop its nest box as I approach, not flying up until I stand at arm's length, then circles overhead and dives at me. Later in the season, when nestlings are present, the birds seem much more tolerant of intrusion. It remains unclear whether they have become somewhat habituated to it by then or have eased defense because of diminished territorial impulses—maybe both.

Thoreau, who called this species the "white-bellied swallow," noted its tendency to perch on wires; he identified the birds as "among the phenomena that cluster about the telegraph."

Average life span of tree swallows is about 2.7 years, with maximums of 8 to 11 years. Only about 20 percent of fledglings survive their first year, after which annual survival ranges from 40 to 60 percent.

## Bank Swallow *(Riparia riparia)*

Known as the sand martin except in the United States, this 5-inch-long swallow (the smallest in North America) is brown above, with a distinct brown, horizontal chest band between white throat and belly. Many show a pale rump and an irregular brown spike extending from the chest band down the belly center. The slightly forked tail and erratic, zigzag flight patterns also help identify it. Sexes look alike. In flight, the birds utter dry "bee-zeet" or raspy twittering notes.

**Close relatives.** Three other *Riparia* species exist. The Congo martin *(R. congica)* and banded martin *(R. cincta)* inhabit Africa, while the plain martin *(R. paludicola)* resides in both Africa and Asia. In North America, the bank swallow most resembles the northern rough-winged swallow *(Stelgidopteryx serripennis)* in plumage and habitats.

**Behaviors.** In contrast to northern rough-winged swallows, bank swallows rarely appear solitarily. They are among the most social and gregarious of passerine birds, not only nesting in colonies but also frequently foraging together, coursing over lakes, ponds, or open fields. Colonies vary in size from only a few pairs to 100 or more. Owing to the tendency of their nesting sites—sand or gravel banks—to erode quickly, colonies are often short-lived and do not remain in a given locale for more than a few years.

Descriptions of bank swallow flight seem to vary with the observer. Many accounts claim that they tend to fly lower with more twisting, erratic motions than other swallows, with wings held closer to the body when sailing. Other, equally reputable viewers conclude the direct opposite: that bank swallows more often glide, exhibiting *fewer*

*The bank swallow's distinct chest band distinguishes it from all other North American swallows.*

twists and turns than other swallows. Swallows remind us that birding is a fundamentally subjective pursuit.

Bank swallow breeding range encompasses most temperate regions of the globe. In North America, it ranges from the treeline in Alaska and northern Canada to the southwestern United States, but only to Alabama and South Carolina in the East.

*Spring.* Bank swallows, being exclusively aerial insect feeders, are among those migrants whose spring travel is timed by the occurrence of first insect hatches along its migration routes. Thus Great Lakes and New England bank swallows seldom arrive before mid-April, more northern populations not until May. Migrating flocks usually proceed up the seacoasts and river valleys. They often return to the previous year's colony site, but sometimes—depending upon the condition of the vertical gravel banks containing last year's nesting burrows—they do not stay.

If they do stay, males claim a site and begin digging a burrow. When the tunnel extends almost a foot, males attempt to attract females, often by circling and hovering around the new burrows. They "poise on beating wings before the face of the bank," wrote researcher Leonard K. Beyer, "holding their position for a few seconds and then wheeling away out over the nearby fields, only to

*A typical bank swallow colony shows rows of holes lining the upper portion of a sand bank. Sometimes a kingfisher pair also occupies a burrow in a bank swallow colony.*

return soon again to repeat the performance." Territorial squabbles frequently occur, as burrows are sometimes dug less than a foot apart. After pairing, mates excavate new burrows together; if they encounter an obstacle rock or large root, they often abandon their efforts and begin a new burrow. Pairs, which are probably only seasonally monogamous, sometimes claim and occupy old burrows but usually dig new ones each year. Since unmated males continue to dig solitarily, most bank swallow colonies show more holes than are actually occupied. During courtship flights, the birds chase, dart, and dive, buzzing and chittering, sometimes carrying, dropping, or passing a white feather back and forth in flight.

Nearest-neighbor pairs within a colony tend to breed synchronously, with all birds arriving simultaneously at more or less the same stage of nesting, incubation, and care of nestlings. In larger colonies, however, synchronous breeding appears to radiate from the middle of the colony toward the ends. Thus the colony as a whole breeds asynchronously. In another colony of the area, however, the timing may differ considerably.

Coloniality in this species is said to benefit the birds by reducing the likelihood of predation on any individual bird or nest (W. D. Hamilton's "selfish herd" theory) and by possible function of the colony as an "information center," though at least one recent study seems to discount this function.

EGGS AND YOUNG: typically 5; eggs white. INCUBATION: by both sexes; about 2 weeks; hatching synchronous. FEEDING OF YOUNG: by both sexes; insects. FLEDGING: about 3 weeks.

*Summer, Fall.* Bank swallows raise only a single brood per year. After fledging, juveniles often return to the nest burrow, and parents continue to feed them there for several days. Sometimes a youngster will scramble into the wrong burrow, often to be evicted by the adult occupants, which seem to recognize their own young, probably by vocal sounds. Later the juveniles return to burrows only for the night. By mid-July, colonies are largely abandoned, and juveniles tend to assemble in *creches,* groups of nonrelated juvenile offspring.

Sometimes these creches consist of mixed swallow species; juvenile bank, rough-winged, and tree swallows all look similar in pattern and brownish plumage, so that line of swallows you see on a wire in summer doesn't necessarily consist of siblings or even colony neighbors. Juveniles at this time also exhibit certain behaviors that ornithologists William Brewster and Frank M. Chapman labeled "premature exhibition of the procreative and nest-building instincts." The young birds engage in pseudocopulations and also pick up bits of grass and other materials, then fly to a perch and drop them. Probably such behaviors in young birds are not rare; many researchers now believe that juveniles of many species perform these same sorts of incipient behaviors.

Molt of body feathers in this species begins before southward migration, but flight feather molt occurs after the birds arrive on their winter range.

From mid-July through August, premigratory mixed populations of bank and tree swallows merge and flock in large coastal marshes and move into the river valleys. Few are seen inland past August. Some bank swallows linger along coastal areas of the northern range, but most have vacated by the end of September.

*Winter.* Central and South America are the winter destinations of bank swallows. In South America, the species mainly resides east of the Andes from Venezuela to northern Argentina, Paraguay, Peru, and northern Chile. Many Eurasian populations winter in Africa.

**Ecology.** Farmlands, grasslands, marshes, and open water areas are the typical foraging habitats of this species at all times of year. The chief limiting factor in the breeding range is the presence of near-vertical earthen banks of the correct consistency for digging nest burrows, and bank swallow distribution is consequently often transient and patchy.

Bank swallows usually excavate their nest burrows near the top of the bank. Stability of the soil is important, as is ease of excavation. Pure sand, as in dunes, is usually too loose and clay soil too hard to permit successful digging. A mix of sand and silty materials, as exists in most glaciated regions of the country, seems to provide the best substrate. Banks cut by stream erosion frequently provide desirable sites, probably almost the only ones before European settlement of the country. Subsequent road building, gravel pit excavations, and construction embankments have vastly increased the number of potential sites for bank swallow colonies. During the lumbering period of the nineteenth century, observers reported bank swallow colonies occupying large sawdust piles around sawmills. The birds excavate their tunnels straight into the bank, averaging 3 to 5 inches per day, by chiseling with their bills and kicking out the loose dirt behind them. Using their tails as supports while they dig, they work in brief bursts of activity interrupted by numerous time-outs for flying and foraging. An observer watching the colony during this period will see plumes of dirt thrown from holes as the birds dig; fresh windrows of excavated soil amass beneath the holes. Most burrows extend 2 to 3 feet, some up to 5 feet, in length. Usually the tunnel floor is flat, the ceiling somewhat arched. The holes measure 1 to 2 inches across, and the nest chamber at the end about 5 or 6 inches across. The flimsy nest itself consists of grass stems, weed stalks, rootlets, pine needles, bits of wool and fluff, and usually a rim of loose feathers collected and added after incubation begins. In North America, the feathers are mainly from mallards and American black ducks, easily collected from water surfaces in many bank swallow habitats, and from chickens in poultry yards. Two-week-old bank swallow nestlings often rush to the tunnel entrance as a parent approaches on the wing with food. "It is quite a sight," naturalist Charles Nelson wrote, "to see an entire cliff come alive with young swallows popping in and out of their holes while relentlessly chattering for food." Sometimes birds tunnel adjacent burrows so close together that the burrows coalesce inside, and thus 2 nest chambers come to lie side by side.

Flying insects provide almost the total diet of bank swallows in all seasons. About 25 percent consists of muscid flies (housefly types) and tipulid flies (crane flies), a greater percentage of flies than most flycatchers consume. Other items include winged ants, treehoppers, leafhoppers, aphids, beetles, mosquitoes, dragonflies, and moths. The birds feed at an average height of 50 feet, but often much lower.

Competitors are relatively few. House sparrows and European starlings sometimes try to take over nesting burrows, with varying success. Bank swallows usually seem to dwell peaceably with belted kingfishers (see *Birds of Lake, Pond and Marsh),* which excavate solitary nest holes in the same habitats, and a swallow pair occasionally adopts an old kingfisher burrow for its own. A solitary pair of northern rough-winged swallows—noncolonial hole dwellers but not excavators—sometimes resides amid a bank swallow colony. (Rough-wings often perch on roots protruding from the bank; bank swallows seldom do.) Territorial competition among bank swallows for tunnel sites often becomes noisy and intense in early spring, and "feather fights," in which birds chase and contend for a feather, are commonly seen.

Foremost nest predators include skunks and badgers, which often dig into the burrows from the horizontal ground surface above the tunnels, as well as weasels. The species roster of birds mobbed by bank swallows provides an index of potential nest predators: American kestrels, blue jays, crows, house sparrows, and occasionally kingfishers. Snake predation, it would seem, might afflict this species, but few, if any, records of it exist. Accipiter hawks probably capture adult swallows. Brown-headed cowbirds, nest parasites, rarely invade bank swallow burrows to lay eggs. Bank cave-ins sometimes destroy entire colonies of nests, as does bulldozer work at colony sites.

**Focus.** Bank swallows are notoriously difficult to track and count from year to year owing to their ephemeral breeding sites. North American data, however, suggest generally stable populations. An exception exists in California, where bank swallows are listed as threatened, their range in the state having declined about 50 percent since 1900. This decline has resulted from extensive flood control work along virtually every river and natural waterway in southern California, plus increased land disturbances along the coast.

Bank swallow colonies usually exhibit a fairly high rate of nesting success; about 70 percent of eggs finally produce fledglings, on the average. This high annual production probably compensates to some extent for the chancy durability of suitable bank habitats from year to year. Probably far fewer bank swallow colonies existed in presettlement times than today, owing to the relative scarcity of suitable streambank habitats. Earth-moving machinery and the human impulse to dig, channel, shift, and amend landscapes has benefited the bank swallow in most areas.

Most bank swallows live only 2 or 3 years at most, though longevity records of 6 and 8 years exist.

## 15

## Horned Lark *(Eremophila alpestris)*

Lark family (Alaudidae), order Passeriformes. This 7- to 8-inch-long ground bird exhibits a distinctive head pattern of black sideburns, yellow throat, yellow or white eyebrow line (depending on subspecies), and two small feather tufts, or "horns," on the crown, usually erect in males but not always readily seen. The body is sparrow brown with whitish underparts and a black patch on the upper breast. On the bird flying overhead, the black tail is conspicuous. Sexes look alike, except that females appear slightly smaller and lighter in appearance. The bubbling, musical song, heard mainly in early spring, spills forth in a high-pitched, tinkling chant of rapid chittered and slurred notes; common call notes sound like "su-weet."

*Common but easily overlooked, the horned lark often forages in flocks along farm country roadsides.*

**Close relatives.** The lark family consists of 91 species, mainly native to Africa and Eurasia. The horned lark is the only native North American species; the only other *Eremophila* is Temminck's lark *(E. bilopha)* of North Africa and the Middle East. The next closest relatives include the Eurasian skylark *(Alauda arvensis)* and the crested lark *(Galerida cristata),* another African species. Meadowlarks are unrelated blackbirds. Taxonomists have subdivided the horned lark species into 21 subspecies ranging across the continent, divisions based primarily on differences in coloration and size. "Variation in back color," maintains one researcher, "is strongly correlated with the color of the local soil."

**Behaviors.** With this family we enter the superfamily Passeroidea, the oscines or true songbirds, comprising 6 bird families in which singing (though an arbitrary definition) is most highly developed. As ornithologist Gary Ritchison wrote, "Singing by male passerines clearly has more kinds of functions than simply territorial advertising and mate attraction. However, discovering such functions requires detailed studies of song use throughout an entire breeding cycle because even subtle changes in singing behavior may convey information." All of the remaining accounts in this book are of songbirds.

The horned lark's numerous subspecies indicate that much is happening genetically with this species, which is undergoing rapid evolution. Most larks, including the horned, walk rather than hop; as in many ground birds, the claw on the hind toe, or *hallux,* is very long and almost straight, and the wings appear fairly long and pointed. In flight, the birds tend to undulate, beating the wings 3 or 4 times, then folding them against the body for the space of 1 or 2 beats. Except during the breeding season, horned larks

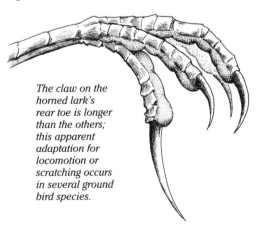

*The claw on the horned lark's rear toe is longer than the others; this apparent adaptation for locomotion or scratching occurs in several ground bird species.*

are highly social and gregarious, often feeding and moving together in sizable flocks. Migration in this species occurs during the daytime, but its occurrence throughout much horned lark range is irregular and ill defined; northernmost populations, however, are definitely migratory worldwide.

Horned lark breeding range spans the continent, except for the southeastern United States, and from arctic tundra southward into Mexico, with isolated populations in northern South America. The birds also breed in Eurasia; called shorelarks, they are divided into 2 populations by competition with the Eurasian skylark, one group residing in Scandinavian and Siberian tundra regions, and the other in the Balkans, the Middle East, and Mongolia.

*Spring.* Among the earliest-nesting North American birds, horned larks are frequently incubating eggs by early spring, and by May in the far north. In temperate latitudes, the birds continue to initiate nests through June, sometimes into July, for a total of 2 or 3 broods. Pairs remain monogamous for a breeding season, possibly longer, but if a mate dies or disappears, another partner readily replaces it. When feeding nestlings, a parent bird usually lands 50 or 60 feet away from the nest, then walks to it; after feeding the young, it walks 12 to 15 feet away before flying. Females also perform fluttering distraction displays.

EGGS AND YOUNG: usually 3 or 4; eggs gray, heavily brown spotted. INCUBATION: by female; 11 or 12 days; hatching synchronous; altricial young; nestlings show a distinctive gape of yellow-orange with black spots. FEEDING OF YOUNG: by both sexes; insects, isopods, earthworms, seeds. FLEDGING: 9 to 12 days; juveniles fly in 2 to 3 weeks.

*Summer.* Parent birds often continue to feed young, even as they begin foraging on their own, for a week or so after fledging. Adults also feed stray juveniles from other nests that may wander into their territory. Adult pairs soon begin renesting at a different site in the territory. Juveniles, in the meantime, gather in small groups, some by late April, moving and feeding together. Singing has usually ceased by late June. In August, at the end of the breeding season, all the birds undergo a complete plumage molt.

*Fall, Winter.* Far-northern horned larks vacate their breeding range in September and October, moving southward. The birds sometimes engage in brief bursts of fall singing. Southern populations mainly reside year-round, but horned lark winter range extends from the Gulf to southern Canada, the southern Great Lakes, and New England. In Michigan, I have seen roadside flocks in January. Migrational passage of the various subspecies and geographical populations, as ornithologist James Granlund points out, "makes differentiating the return of the resident birds difficult to assess." Winter-range horned larks are not territorial, frequently forming large or small flocks, sometimes mixing with other species.

Pair formation in resident populations begins in January, when males begin forming territories and start to sing. Migratory populations begin pairing later, from March to May. Territory size averages 3 or 4 acres, less or more depending upon the population density and quality of habitat. In a given breeding site, territories seem quite uniformly dispersed. Territories typically condense in size as the season advances and more territorial males arrive and compete for space. Defended until the last nestling fledges, the territory encloses all courtship and nesting and most feeding activities, though later in spring and summer, some feeding may occur outside the territory.

Males skirmish over territories mainly in the air, rising 30 or more feet, pecking and clawing each other, then settle to a song perch. Male courtship displays include a strutting parade in front of the female with erect horns, drooping wings, spread tail, and ruffled black chest patch; and a spectacular song flight, in which the male climbs steeply 500 to 800 feet, then glides down, voicing his chittering, tinkling song. Then he repeats his climb and song or plunges with closed wings to the ground. Song flights may last less than a minute to several minutes and usually occur around noon and sunset.

On the ground, males usually sing from slightly elevated perches—rocks or clods or mounds of dirt or snow. Two song types—intermittent and recitative—vary in duration; recitative song sometimes rambles on for more than a minute. Singing begins an hour or so before sunrise and sunset, ceases soon after sunrise and before dusk, and resumes at odd intervals during the day.

**Ecology.** Horned larks favor open, bare ground or short-grass areas. In early spring, plowed fields, bare fallow land, and row-crop stubble are common breeding habitats. The birds usually abandon fields where substantial plant growth occurs during spring or forgo renesting in them. During summer and fall, horned larks often appear on beaches, dunes, and short-mowed areas such as airstrips. In snowy weather, they frequently gather along plowed roadsides.

The nest, a slight cavity scratched out by the female's bill and feet, often lies adjacent to a tuft of grass or next to a rock on the windward side. She lines the 3- to 4-inch-diameter shallow cup with grasses, rootlets, and shredded cornstalks, then usually with finer materials such as grasses, down, and feathers, though some nests have no lining. *Pavings,* characteristic of horned lark nests, include such items as pebbles, earth clods, corncobs, or cow dung placed beside the nest, forming a "patio" or "doorstep," though it is not always used as an approach. The pavings cover the dirt excavated from the nest. Nests, even though lying entirely open and unconcealed, are so well camouflaged that an observer usually finds one only by accident, rarely by deliberate searching.

Horned larks consume seeds all year, but they feed their young almost exclusively insects—mainly grasshoppers, beetles, and caterpillars—plus other small invertebrates. Grasses, usually foxtails *(Setaria),* predominate in the seed diet; others include common ragweed, pigweed, smartweeds, and waste grains—corn, wheat, and oats. Seeds are usually gleaned from the ground, though the birds occasionally perch and feed on a seed head of a plant. Freshly manured fields are common winter feeding areas. In some western areas, horned lark flocks sometimes raid flower and vegetable seed crops and sprouting vegetable and grain crops.

Few, if any, competitors exist. Horned larks sometimes chase chickens and vesper sparrows from the nest area. The birds become habituated to human proximity, and their preference for heavily grazed areas makes them virtual *commensals*—that is, direct beneficiaries—of feeding cattle and sheep. Especially in fall and winter, horned larks often join mixed flocks of other passerine birds in the seed-eating, ground-feeding *guild,* a group of species that share a community resource. American tree sparrows, dark-eyed juncos, Lapland longspurs, and snow buntings are common flock and guild associates. As for all ground-nesting species, predators are numerous. Falcons, owls, and shrikes attack adult and nestling horned larks. Weasels, skunks, ground squirrels, raccoons, and domestic cats seize adult birds and raid nests. American crows, meadowlarks, shrews, voles, and deer mice also devour eggs and nestlings. Early-spring snowstorms cause some nestling mortality, and spring plowing probably destroys much of the initial nesting in some areas. Brown-headed cowbirds usually do not parasitize early-season nests of horned larks, which incubate eggs before the cowbird breeding season begins, but cowbirds sometimes invade later-season nests, laying 1 or 2 eggs in them. In contrast to the eggs of most foster parents, however, horned lark eggs often hatch sooner than the cowbird eggs, and the lark nestlings develop faster and fledge sooner, outcompeting the cowbird young. Horned larks do, however, raise a certain percentage of cowbird nestlings.

**Focus.** The ancestral breeding range of the horned lark was probably the eastern Great Plains, and this area continues to center peak populations. Land clearing and agriculture expanded horned lark range eastward to the Atlantic coast during the eighteenth and nineteenth centuries. During the past half century, however, much former farmland in this region has reverted to woodland, thus decreasing horned lark habitats, and the birds have significantly declined. Nevertheless, horned lark populations remain relatively stable countrywide.

Thoreau, who laboriously identified it with his cumbersome "spyglass," labeled the horned lark "quite a handsome bird." Juvenile horned larks, especially, can be difficult to identify as such, often being confused with Lapland longspurs in late spring, Sprague's pipits in spring and summer, or Eurasian skylarks. The geographically variable subspecies show much diversity in plumage tone and coloration but not in basic plumage pattern.

The longest surviving horned lark on record lived about 8 years. Probably half that age or less is typical.

## 16

## FINCH FAMILY (Fringillidae),
## order Passeriformes

This is the largest bird family, comprising almost 1,000 species worldwide, some 150 in North America. It includes the rest of the species accounts in this book. This family lumps several large groups that not so long ago held family status in their own right—and still do in some taxonomic classifications. In the Monroe-Sibley DNA classification system used in this book, however, they have been "demoted" to tribes.

Common traits of the entire family are difficult to generalize; kinship has been established by DNA similarities rather than by physical or behavioral likenesses. Most finches are seed eaters with stout bills adapted for seed crushing; wood warbler bills, however, are slender and sharp pointed, adapted for insect foraging.

The remaining species accounts in this book all belong under the subfamily headings Fringillinae (redpolls) and Emberizinae, which includes the tribes Emberizini (sparrows and buntings), Parulini (wood warblers), and Icterini (blackbirds and meadowlarks). The young of all of these species are altricial; hatching may be either synchronous or asynchronous.

FINCH FAMILY (Fringillidae) - Subfamily Fringillinae - Cardueline finches (Tribe Carduelini)

## Common Redpoll (Carduelis flammea)

Redpolls belong to the subfamily of finches Fringillinae, also known as cardueline finches (tribe Carduelini). Carduelines are also called winter finches because most are irruptive migrants from the North, appearing in the continental United States and at winter yard feeders in irregular years and abundance.

The common redpoll is goldfinch size (about 5 inches long), fork tailed, and streaked with gray-brown. Its most distinctive marks are a bright red forehead patch and a black chin and throat. Most adult males show a rosy pink wash over the breast and pinkish rumps. Short, conical bills, as in other carduelines, are adapted for seed crushing. Rattling call notes in flight also identify redpolls, along with a wheezy, goldfinchlike "swee-eet?" Thoreau noted their "jingling twitter and occasional mew." The spring song is trilling and juncolike.

*The common redpoll's black chin and pinkish hues identify this here-today-gone-tomorrow winter finch; numerous in some winters, it scarcely appears in others.*

**Close relatives.** Thirty-one *Carduelis* finches range worldwide. North American species include pine siskins *(C. pinus);* American goldfinches *(C. tristis,* see *Birds of Forest, Yard, and Thicket);* lesser and Lawrence's goldfinches *(C. psaltria, C. lawrencei);* and hoary redpolls *(C. hornemanni).* Almost 140 cardueline finches exist. Other North American species include the rosy-finches *(Leucosticte);* purple and house finches *(Carpodacus purpureus, C. mexicanus,* see *Birds of Forest, Yard, and Thicket);* Cassin's finch *(C. cassinii);* pine grosbeak *(Pinicola enucleator);* crossbills *(Loxia);* and evening grosbeak *(Hesperiphona vespertina).* Worldwide, cardueline finches also include the serins and canaries, seedeaters, greenfinches, siskins, linnets, rosefinches, bullfinches, and hawfinch.

Four common redpoll subspecies exist, the most numerous in North America being the common or mealy redpoll race *(C. f. flammea).*

**Behaviors.** In the northeastern United States, we see redpolls only in winter, and not every winter. Along with pine and evening grosbeaks, purple finches, and crossbills, this irruptive winter finch appears at irregular intervals that are probably keyed to seed crop size in the breeding range. Large-scale migration in these species is not invariable but adaptively timed depending upon a variable resource.

Common redpoll flocks feeding in open fields display constant, restless movements and chatter, incessantly flying up and settling down, rarely remaining for long in one spot. As one observer wrote, "Instead of relying upon a sentinel or the alarm call of an observant member of the flock, the redpolls take no chance, as it were, but fly up with pulselike precision." They wheel in unison low over the fields, undulating like goldfinches. In more sheltered spots, however, they seem considerably less frenetic; individuals appear less tied to the flock and calmer.

Redpolls not only tolerate but thrive in winter's coldest weather. Experiments have shown that they are able to survive colder temperatures than any other passerine birds. A special adaptation in the esophagus, a bilobed pouch called the *esophageal diverticulum*, allows these birds, along with crossbills and evening grosbeaks, to "pack a midnight snack." Before nightfall, the birds load up their sacs with seeds, thus providing themselves with nourishment during the night or during stormy periods when they cannot feed. Researchers have identified 3 distinct phases of redpoll feeding behavior: First, redpolls knock seeds, often from birch catkins, to the ground; then they gather the fallen seeds from the snow and store them in their diverticula; finally, they fly to a sheltered spot, often deep in coniferous foliage, where they regurgitate and shell the stored seeds, eating them in safety from predators.

Redpolls frequently bathe, often in icy water or snow. Socially, the birds exhibit a rigid dominance hierarchy; males are dominant over females—even low-status males over high-status females—except during the breeding season, when the situation reverses and females become dominant. Many observers have noted the tameness of these birds—their relatively fearless disregard of humans. Sometimes one will even land upon a quiet watcher.

Common redpoll breeding range spans the boreal forest regions of North America and Eurasia, central Europe, and the British Isles.

*Spring.* Redpolls that have wintered south of the breeding range usually move northward in flocks of 25 to 100 or more in early spring, often associating with hoary redpolls. They exhibit little site fidelity *(philopatry)* to previous nesting areas.

Resident flocks on the breeding range begin singing in early March. Singing peaks just before the flocks break up and pairing occurs, mainly in April. Courtship and pairing are apparently female instigated. Females crouch and twitter in front of now-subordinate males, which stand and bow. "Each female," reported researcher William Dilger, "clearly singles out a certain male to which she behaves in a particularly aggressive manner. These are the couples between which pair bonds are formed." If territorialism exists in this species, researchers have found scant evidence of it. Males continue to sing incessantly after pairing, keeping apart from each other, yet nests are often closely spaced, sometimes semicolonial. Peak nesting occurs in June.

---

EGGS AND YOUNG: 4 or 5; eggs pale green or bluish, purple spotted mainly at large end. INCUBATION: by female; 10 or 11 days; hatching mostly synchronous; last egg may hatch a day later than others. FEEDING OF YOUNG: mainly by female, sometimes from food brought by male, occasionally directly by male; regurgitant, insects. FLEDGING: about 12 days.

---

*Summer.* A summer day in the Subarctic consists of about 20 hours of daylight, and birds remain active almost around the clock. Frequency of redpoll brooding and feeding of young heavily depends upon the temperature, which even in July may range between 40 and 80 degrees F. The warmer the day, the less time the female must brood the nestlings and the more frequently she can hunt and bring food. Insect prey also becomes more active and available on warmer days. Thus the long days probably compensate breeding bird populations in some measure for the short seasonal warmth.

Most redpoll pairs raise only a single brood, but occasionally they produce a second, usually in July. At least some females sequentially pair with more than a single mate *(polyandry)*, sometimes abandoning fledglings from the first nesting as they begin a second. In such cases, the first male partner provides sole care for the young.

The complete annual molt in August produces a slightly gauzier look than the breeding plumage, owing to the new grayish feather barbules and whitish edgings. Toward late summer, redpolls wander widely in aggregated family flocks.

*Fall, Winter.* Although most of us see redpolls only during their occasional irruptive invasions, lesser numbers do migrate southward every fall. These migrants, moving in flocks of 20 or 30 birds, travel mainly in October through December, often along river valleys or lake lowlands. Flying 30 to 50 feet overhead, they constantly utter high "chit-chit" notes as they pass. In nonirruption years, the highest winter concentrations usually occur in the northern Great Plains, with lesser peaks in the northern Great Lakes and New England. Winter flocks exhibit no site fidelity and wander widely.

In irruption years, flocks numbering into the hundreds and thousands of birds stream southward, their quest for food pushing them even into the central tier of states, sometimes farther. Recent findings also indicate considerable east-west migratory movements. One winter day, a flock of at least 100 common redpolls descended on my yard feeder, a twittering turmoil of activity, the motions of the birds so nervous and incessant that they seemingly weren't even eating, although they were probably fast-loading their storage diverticula. They remained in the vicinity for a day or so, then disappeared as quickly as they had arrived, and I never saw another redpoll all winter. These "here today, gone tomorrow" episodes are fairly typical of redpolls.

Northward movement of migrant redpolls commences in late February. Redpolls achieve their breeding plumage as the buffy feather tips wear off, thus accenting the contrasting color patterns.

**Ecology.** Common redpolls inhabit as breeding range the stunted, shrubby margins of the boreal coniferous forest where it meets the tundra, as well as mountainous elevations that duplicate this habitat; semibarrens, subalpine, or taiga are other terms for this broad band of northern habitat that circles the globe. Typical winter habitats include fields, shrubby thickets, and coastal dunes, as well as suburban yards with feeders. The birds seek night shelter in densely foliaged conifers.

Common redpoll females usually build the nest 3 to 6 feet high on the branch of a stunted spruce or in a crotch amid a willow or alder thicket. Nests average 3 or 4 inches across, a foundation of small twigs on which rests a loose cup of finer twigs, rootlets, lichens, and dried grasses. A thick lining of molted ptarmigan body feathers, mostly white, completes the lining "into which the female can sink almost out of sight as she sits on her small eggs," wrote biologist Roland C. Clement. Plant down and lemming fur sometimes substitute for feathers. Depending on the shelter, redpoll nests may quickly blow away once abandoned or may survive the winter winds. Redpolls occasionally reuse previous nests.

Mainly a seed eater, the common redpoll specializes in tree seeds on its breeding range, especially seeds from birch and alder, along with willow catkins. Its seed diet broadens considerably in the southern winter range, where it consists mainly of weed seeds—ragweeds, pigweed, smartweeds, timothy, foxtail-grasses, whitlow-grass *(Draba)*, buttercups, and sedges, among others. One study concluded that common redpolls consume seeds or plant parts of 41 genera. "Seed crop size is the prime moving and synchronizing force behind [irruptive] invasions of boreal seed-eating birds," concluded an exhaustive 1976 study of winter finch patterns. The study found that a synchronous global pattern of seed-crop fluctuations exists in several species of high-latitude trees, with irregular time sequencing of 2 to 5 years. A year of seed abundance fosters bird survival and abundance; a following year or two of seed scarcity increases competitive interactions, resulting in sometimes massive migrations southward. During the breeding season, redpolls also eat insects, mainly ants and flies, and spiders.

Large winter flocks of redpolls that suddenly descend on area fields may compete, if only briefly, with other seed eaters for possibly limited seed crops. Competition with the visually similar hoary redpoll rarely occurs, since the hoary favors treeless tundra habitat. Some researchers believe that food competition among common redpolls always lies behind irruptive behaviors: When the swollen populations resulting from an ample food year compete for cyclically diminished food resources the next year (or years), they must seek food elsewhere and thus migrate in huge numbers.

Redpoll predators include small falcons and accipiters such as American kestrels and sharp-shinned hawks, and probably also northern harriers and short-eared and hawk owls. Jaegers and northern shrikes are also frequent predators. At winter yard feeders, domestic cats often find redpolls easy prey. Redpolls appear especially vulnerable to epidemics of salmonellosis, a virulent, highly contagious bacterial disease that has wiped out thousands of winter finches. Wrote an Alaskan observer during one outbreak, "the disease's appearance was first reported in a newspaper story about sick cats," which "were finding dead or dying birds, eating them, and becoming ill." Yard feeder droppings and debris apparently host the bacteria; feeder sanitation is the only real defense.

**Focus.** Common and hoary redpolls can look so much alike in certain plumages that identity problems frequently ensue. Although some researchers believe that both redpolls are simply color morphs of a single species, data seem to support that each is indeed a separate species. Common redpolls are generally more heavily streaked than hoaries, which show white breasts and rumps. Juvenile hoaries and adult commons, however, may appear almost identical. Probably the best field marks separating the species are head and bill shapes, which require close-up views: The common's bill is longer and narrower, its forehead sloping, whereas the hoary shows a steeply angled forehead and a short, stout bill. Other, more minor differences also exist. The two also reside in different breeding habitats.

The name *redpoll* refers to the bird's red forehead patch. Thoreau interchangeably called redpolls linarias, red-crowns, and passenger birds. A lesser redpoll, banded in Europe, survived over 7 years, but most adults probably live less than half that long.

## SUBFAMILY EMBERIZINAE

This second subfamily of finches consists of almost 80 eastern North American species, including all the remaining accounts in this book. Emberizines consist of 5 tribes that were formerly considered separate families. Each tribe differs in physical and adaptive characteristics. For that reason, the following accounts are presented under their tribal headings.

## Sparrow-Buntings (Tribe Emberizini)

Sparrows and certain buntings number more than 150 species worldwide, almost 50 in North America. These include 18 New World sparrows that reside in the Northeast, plus juncos and towhees. The lark bunting *(Calamospiza melancorys)* and seedeaters *(Sporophila)* are also emberizine finches. Birds of this tribe vary in size and form, but all have conical bills adapted for crushing seeds. Most are modestly colored, as befits their mainly ground-feeding habits. Differences in plumages are subtle, usually requiring binoculars for visual identification of a species. The word *sparrow* derives from an Anglo-Saxon word meaning "flutterer."

FINCH FAMILY (Fringillidae) - Subfamily Emberizinae - Sparrow-Buntings (Tribe Emberizini)

## Lapland Longspur *(Calcarius lapponicus)*

Measuring 6 to 7 inches long, this longspur wears a much different plumage in winter, when most of us see them, than in summer. Winter males are plain, sparrowlike birds with much streaking, a rusty half collar on the nape, and a blackish smudge on the breast. Look for parallel buffy streaking on the back, a reliable winter field mark. Females are even more nondescript, lacking the neck and breast markings. Summer males, much bolder in pattern, show a black face and chest outlined with white behind the eye; the white extends to an all-white belly streaked with black on the sides. Other markings include a chestnut nape and rear crown and a bright yellow bill. Summer females lack the black head and chest and resemble winter males. Tails of both sexes have white outer corners, most visible in flight. Males voice a musical tinkling warble, mainly during courtship. The flight call, a harsh, rattling "tickatick tickatick tsew tsew," or portions thereof, is often heard in longspur flocks.

**Close relatives.** The 3 other *Calcarius* species also reside in North America: McCown's longspur *(C. mccownii),* Smith's longspur *(C. pictus),* and chestnut-collared longspur *(C. ornatus).*

**Behaviors.** These sparrowlike ground birds derive their name from the long hind toe claw similar to that of horned larks. The claw is "presumably an adaptation for ground locomotion," wrote one researcher; exactly how it might aid such movement remains unclear. In the northeastern and north-central states, we see longspurs mainly during their migrations, usually as flocks feeding in fields. "Often the only evidence of this skulking bird," wrote ornithologist James Granlund, "is a dry rattle heard when it is flushed from beneath your feet." Flocks commonly associate with other longspur species plus horned larks, snow buntings, and water pipits, all ground feeders, at these times. Longspurs walk, run, or hop, often pausing to feed, then running on; in flight, they undulate like many other finches.

*The Lapland longspur, a ground feeder and arctic migrant, occurs in nomadic flocks during winter, when its plumage appears nondescript.*

Lapland longspurs reside in arctic breeding ranges around the globe as one of the most common and abundant birds of the tundra regions.

*Spring.* Flocks of males arrive on the arctic breeding range in April and May, usually several days to 2 weeks ahead of females. Often the ground is still snow covered, and harsh weather remains frequent and unpredictable. Longspurs in spring, like many arctic passerines, have an important adaptation that enables them to survive these exigencies, a layer of fat just beneath the skin, deposited during winter feeding. Most nonarctic migrants, in contrast, show fat deposition in the fall from summer feeding.

Breeding activity begins in early June. Males establish territories of about 4 acres by singing from shrubs or from small ground elevations. Small patches of bare ground amid the melting snow become centers of territorial activities. Conspicuous among these are courtship flights: Males rise, then glide down, voicing their bobolinklike songs. They also droop their wings, fluff themselves, and chase females on the ground while singing. Researchers have often noted the general synchrony of breeding events among longspurs across their entire range. Although weather and food availability may determine the onset of breeding, the sequence, once started, runs like clockwork. "In the North Country," ornithologist George M. Sutton wrote, "the program of the individual is virtually that of the species." Singing, mating, nest building, and incubation all proceed concurrently across the breeding range, an apparent adaptation to the short summer and compressed time intervals of nesting events. Hatching, for example, coincides with the peak summer emergence of insects, and juveniles reach independence before the emergence of adult insects ceases. Probably such synchrony does not differ appreciably from that of many other arctic resident birds. In longspurs, however, it seems particularly evident.

Female partners are not always governed by male territorialism; sometimes they place the nest outside the male territory. The male then expands his territory to enclose the new nest. Many males also continue to sing and display after pairing occurs, and some males mate with a second female *(polygyny)* after the first partner begins incubating.

EGGS AND YOUNG: 4 to 6; eggs greenish white to buff, scrawled with black and brown. INCUBATION: by female; 12 or 13 days; female rarely fed on nest by male unless food is extremely scarce; hatching asynchronous over 1 to 3 days; nestlings altricial. FEEDING OF YOUNG: by both sexes; insects, mainly crane flies. FLEDGING: 8 to 10 days; first flight at about 12 days.

*Summer.* Many longspur nestlings die from starvation (a sudden cold snap can wipe out insect populations overnight) and exposure, and fledglings are likewise often at risk. However, as one researcher noted, "it may be presumed that the advantages [of early dispersal] outweigh the dangers." The relatively early fledging in this species is probably adaptive, reducing danger from attraction of predators to nests and from nest overcrowding. The last nestling hatched often lags in development, and parents frequently abandon it when the other nestlings fledge. Lapland longspurs, like numerous species, divide the fledged brood into 2 groups, or *brood units,* each fed and cared for by a single parent. These units remain stable until the juveniles become independent, probably several weeks.

The annual plumage molt begins in early July after nesting and lasts for about 50 days. Male birds, now in winter plumage, look much drabber than in spring and somewhat resemble vesper or house sparrows; female winter plumage remains inconspicuous. By mid-July, the birds are gathering into small flocks that gradually merge into larger ones.

*Fall, Winter.* Migration peaks in late September and early October, typically in flocks of 50 to 100 birds but sometimes double or triple that size. While virtually all Lapland longspurs migrate, the number of birds that travel as far south as the United States varies irregularly from year to year, apparently depending on seed crop abundance. Flocks winter from southern Canada to central Texas—"roughly coincident with the region where winter wheat and oats are grown," according to one Christmas Bird Count analysis—with the largest concentrations settling in the southern Great Plains. The northern limit of the winter range during mild winters is about 50 degrees N latitude. Longspurs roam widely in winter, exhibiting little *philopatry,* or site fidelity; nomadic and opportunistic food seekers, they may linger for a week or more, then move elsewhere. Spring northward movements begin in late February, peaking in March and April. A combination of molting head and throat feathers plus erosive wear of the collar and back feathers in March reveals the breeding plumage.

**Ecology.** Wet meadow areas, communities of sedge, dwarf birch, and willow are the Lapland longspur's favored tundra breeding habitats. Typical plant species include the sedges *Carex aquatilis* and tussock cotton-grass *(Eriophorum vaginatum),* arctic bluegrass, and wood-rush *(Luzula confusa),* plus mosses and lichens. During migrations each winter, the birds frequent fields, dunes, golf courses, airports, and other grassy and weedy areas.

The nest, built by the female in a tussock of grass or sedge, is a slight, grass-lined depression holding a finer lining of grasses, plant down from willows, ptarmigan or raven feathers, and hair from arctic hares, lemmings, or caribou. "The nest nearly always has one conspicuous entrance," wrote ornithologist Francis Williamson, "generally on the south side."

During the breeding season, when protein must fuel egg laying and feed young birds, Lapland longspurs mainly consume insects. Crane fly eggs, larvae, pupae, and adults form a high proportion of the diet. A 1979 study indicated that each parent bird must gather 2 crane flies per minute of foraging time—that is, almost around the clock—to satisfy its own requirements plus those of 5 nestlings. Leaf beetles (Chrysomelidae), weevils, and mosquitoes also rank high, as do caterpillars and spiders. Grass and weed seeds become the foremost diet in all other seasons, though wintering longspurs in Texas also feed extensively on beetles and grasshoppers. Seeds of foxtail-grasses, crabgrasses, sedges, wheat, pigweed, and common ragweed are favored.

Competition with other species seems minimal. Other longspur species mainly inhabit drier breeding sites, as do horned larks and snow buntings. All of these birds may associate during migrations and winter. Food competition on the breeding range probably mounts only with scarcity of insects or seeds. Many researchers believe that such competition becomes the basic driving force of winter irruptions in longspurs and other finches (see Common Redpoll). Predation accounts for many nest losses. Arctic foxes, ground squirrels, and weasels account for most nest predation. Fledglings become highly vulnerable to avian predators including parasitic and long-tailed jaegers, snowy and short-eared owls, merlins, and northern shrikes. Indirectly affecting predation are brown lemming population cycles—if they exist (see Snowy Owl). When abundance of this rodent prey dips, mammal and owl predators usually shift to bird prey. Spring snowstorms sometimes wipe out thousands of longspurs.

**Focus.** In Eurasia, they are called Lapland buntings. Lapland in northern Scandinavia was the site locale of the first type specimen collected, hence the species name.

Hatching success for most arctic passerines is about 60 percent. Studies indicate that about 45 percent of year-old Lapland longspurs survive to the next year. Maximum longevity observed in this species is 6 years.

FINCH FAMILY (Fringillidae) - Subfamily Emberizinae - Sparrow-Buntings (Tribe Emberizini)

## Snow Bunting *(Plectrophenax nivalis)*

The whitest eastern songbird of all, the snow bunting measures about 7 inches long. In winter, when it appears in the United States, it looks almost entirely white in flight; on the ground, it shows a yellowish bill, tawny crown, and touches of rusty brown and black. Large white wing patches and black wing tips are distinctive in both sexes. The male in breeding plumage looks almost solid white except for a black back, wing tips, bill, and central tail feathers; the female shows less contrasting gray and white and is also speckled and streaked. Body plumage of first-winter juveniles looks quite brownish. The flight call, a clear "teer" or "tew tew" followed by a trill, is distinctive, as is the aggressive "churr call," a purring note like the noise "power lines make on cold days when the wind causes them to vibrate," one observer described it. The male song, rarely heard except in the arctic breeding range, is a musical warble. Like several other passerine ground birds, snow buntings have a long claw on the hind toe *(hallux)*.

**Close relative.** The only other *Plectrophenax* finch is McKay's bunting *(P. hyperboreus)*, which nests mainly on 2 small islands in the Bering Sea.

**Behaviors.** To those of us in the northeastern or north-central United States, "the snow bunting is the very epitome of an arctic bird," as ornithologist David F. Parmelee wrote. Flashing white wings in a restless flock, the birds frequently swirl and skim in a snow-covered weedy field before landing again. "They twist and turn in unison," wrote naturalist J. A. Haig; "when they are low over bare ground or against a leaden winter sky, the whole flock may suddenly seem to vanish, as they turn their darker backs towards the observer, concealing their snow white undersides." Flock members at the rear seem to leapfrog the fliers in front, thus creating the rolling, wavelike effect of a snow bunting "superorganism" with all parts supremely coordinated. One study indicated that only the subordinate members of the flock actually leapfrog: They continually lag behind, then fly ahead, only to be overtaken again as the dominant birds, which stay on the ground, sweep ahead. "Their cheerful calls and constant commotion" wrote Haig, "are always enough to put some sun into the gloomiest of winter days."

*Patches of rust on its white plumage mark the winter dress of the snow bunting, another arctic resident that visits us in winter.*

Yet this is not actually a very peaceful gregariousness; seen up close, fighting and bickering seem incessant. Some observers report no evident social hierarchy or status structures among snow buntings, but such a lack would seem an unlikely contrast to most flocking species. The flock's sudden, characteristic explosion into flight, then the circling and returning to the same spot, "seems to be caused by a sudden erratic movement by one or more fighting birds," Haig noted. Often a snow bunting flock contains a few Lapland longspurs or horned larks, also ground feeders.

Feeding along shorelines, snow buntings frequently behave like sandpipers, chasing the retreating waves or dipping in pools. At intervals during the day, when not feeding, snow buntings often perch in the tallest places available, such as treetops or TV antennas, usually near feeding areas. At night, the birds roost close together on the ground, facing into the wind; perch in trees (rarely); or dive into soft snow. Snow buntings frequently bathe in both fluffy and hard-crusted snow, rubbing their body plumage against the surface. They appear to relish blizzards and blowing snow, seeming "almost like chickens dusting," according to one observer. "The snow buntings and the tree sparrows are the true spirits of the snowstorm," wrote Thoreau. Snow bunting metabolism, adapted for extreme cold, shows a lower critical temperature than that of other passerines of the same size. This bird can tolerate temperatures of −40 to almost −60 degrees F.

*Spring.* Among the first arctic migrants to arrive in spring (mid-March to mid-April), snow buntings move northward in small, loose flocks of 30 or so, flying both day and night, sometimes accompanied by longspurs. Harsh spring weather may slow their arrival, and large flocks sometimes stop over at staging areas, where they feed at the edges of melting snow.

Snow buntings exhibit relatively low fidelity to previous breeding sites *(philopatry),* though they often return to the same general areas and home ranges. Migrant flocks appear sex segregated; males may arrive at breeding sites 3 weeks or more before females. These males remain in foraging flocks and may ground roost together in flocks of 30 to 80 birds. The males disperse and establish territories before females arrive, singing from rock perches, called song stones, and in flight. Territories may initially span 1,000 or more feet in diameter, shrinking to 150 to 300 feet as the season advances. Snow buntings often forage for food in a much larger home range outside the defended territory. The male's flight song display, given over the territory, both attracts potential mates and threatens potential male intruders. It consists of a steeply rising flight 30 to 50 feet high, followed by a burst of song as the bird glides downward with V-postured wings; it lands on its song stone while continuing to sing, holding its wings upright for several seconds after it lands. Most snow bunting populations show male-biased sex ratios, and arriving females may visit several male territories before settling in one. Males display their plumage to visiting females, spreading wings and tail, leading females to potential nest sites in the territory while voicing soft "zis zis zis" calls, known as swift or inciting calls.

Once pairing occurs, usually in early June, song declines to irregular frequency. Occasional males, however, continue to sing and display after pairing, behaviors apparently aimed toward extrapair copulations, which sometimes occur. These "superstud" males usually have whiter plumage than most of the monogamous males.

Snow bunting breeding range consists of high arctic tundra in North America, plus Greenland, Iceland, northern Scandinavia, and Siberia. The birds rarely breed south of 52 degrees N latitude.

EGGS AND YOUNG: 4 to 7; clutch size increases with latitude, decreases with later nestings; eggs greenish, bluish, or white, brown spotted and marked. INCUBATION: by female, which is often fed by male at nest; 10 to 15 days; hatching asynchronous over 2 to 4 days. FEEDING OF YOUNG: by both sexes; mainly insects (crane flies, midges). FLEDGING: 10 to 17 days; fledging asynchronous over 15 to 30 hours.

*Summer.* Since fledging often occurs at differential times, brood division frequently results. The male parent continues to feed the first fledglings while the female attends to birds still in the nest. Each fledgling remains with a parent until it reaches independence. It is fed for 8 to 12 days, though it can catch flies for itself 3 to 5 days after fledging. Snow buntings occasionally produce a second brood in the almost perpetual arctic daylight, but single broods are typical. Independent juveniles soon group into flocks of up to 100, feeding and roosting together. Adult birds also abandon their territories and become gregarious, often gathering along arctic coastal and beach areas. The earliest molting begins in mid-July, about fledging time, peaking in August. As flight feathers drop, adult birds often become flightless for a few days. Most of the new body plumage is variably brown tipped, giving many of the birds a darker appearance than at any other season. (Fall-plumaged snow buntings were once designated "tawny buntings.") "The fresh adult fall plumage," according to Parmelee, "is essentially the breeding dress heavily overlaid with brown above and, to a lesser degree, below." The feathers, he wrote, are "immediately sensitive to abrasion, which produces a great variety of plumages both individually and seasonally." The bill, black during the breeding season, turns yellowish.

*Fall, Winter.* Peak southward departure from the breeding range occurs in September, extending into November. Migration flocks are sex segregated, as in spring, and females depart first; females also tend to migrate farther south than males. Relatively few snow buntings, however, travel farther south than the top 2 tiers of states spanning the continent. This bird favors snow and cold; it only requires seed food that remains accessible above the snow or in wind-swept patches of bare ground. Its breeding and winter ranges even overlap in some low arctic areas. The northern limits of the winter range are, in fact, uncertain, though the greatest winter abundance occurs in open, snow-swept habitats of the Great Plains and eastern North America. Outside North America, snow buntings winter in northern through central Eurasia.

As winter progresses, the birds molt head and throat feathers. Abrasion on hard snow wears away the brownish feather tips, producing the male's black and white breeding plumage.

**Ecology.** Open, cold, and rocky describes the snow bunting's arctic breeding habitats. The birds favor rocky patches or boulder fields located near sedge meadows or dryas-lichen tundra (dryas is a trailing shrub). This is one of the few bird species that inhabits nunataks, islands of land surrounded by ice or snow, and it also often nests in association with colonial cliff-nesting seabirds such as auks and puffins. Favored winter habitats include weedy fields, grain stubble, forest clear-cuts, shores, and duneland. "A freshly manured field is probably the surest place to locate flocks on snow-covered ground," wrote Haig. Snowplowed areas such as roadsides or railroad sidings also attract them. Early arctic explorer Samuel Hearne noted that the birds "are fond of frequenting dunghills"; he boasted of killing "upwards of twenty at one shot."

Paired females may begin building nests in several sites but soon settle on one. The most typical nest site is a rock cavity or fissure, with the nest usually placed well back from the entrance. Sometimes the birds nest beneath boulder protection or in cliff faces. Where rock cavities are lacking, snow buntings prove adaptable in using barrels, cans or boxes, stone foundations or construction rubble, even large mammal skulls for nest shelter. Studies suggest that male feeding of the female during incubation—in contrast to the habits of most open-nesting arctic passerines—has evolved mainly as an adaptation to the cold microclimate of the nest cavity. The nest itself, a bulky, thick-walled structure of mosses, grasses, or both, is lined with finer grasses; fur of arctic foxes, lemmings, and snowshoe hares; hairs of musk oxen and caribou; and often the white feathers of ptarmigans, jaegers, gulls, snowy owls, and snow buntings. The nest is about 3 inches in average inside diameter and almost that deep. Occasionally snow buntings reuse their old nests, building and relining on top of them.

Seeds provide 90 percent or more of the diet, but snow buntings also consume insects, spiders, and small crustaceans (isopods and amphipods) in summer and fall. In spring, seeds of bluegrass *(Poa)* and the high-protein leaves of goose grass *(Puccinellia phryganodes)* become important foods, as do seeds of crowberry, bog-bilberry, bistort, red sorrel, purple alpine saxifrage, asters, goldenrods, and *Draba* species. Winter seed foods that rank high in the diet include foxtail-grasses, ragweeds, pigweed, sand-grass, goosefoots, oats, and knotweeds. "They have the pleasure of society at their feasts," wrote Thoreau after observing a winter feeding flock, "busily talking while eating, remembering what occurred at Grinnel Land." In the West, wheat, barley, and other gleaned grains are the dominant foods.

In its breeding range, the snow bunting's foremost competitor is probably the northern wheatear, a thrush that may vie for nesting cavities and niches. Male buntings chase them from bunting territories but usually tolerate other passerine species such as American pipits, Lapland longspurs, and hoary redpolls. One study found subtle habitat differences existing among the 4 ground-nesting passerine birds on Bylot Island in the Arctic: American pipits favored warm, sunny ravines; horned larks selected flat, bare sites; Lapland longspurs preferred well-vegetated slopes; and snow buntings occupied the ridges and rockpiles. Lapland longspurs are probably the most frequent snow bunting associates in winter.

Predators include gyrfalcons and peregrine falcons, which sometimes follow snow bunting flocks along coastal areas in the fall. Snowy owls and long-tailed jaegers also prey on adult buntings. Nest raiders include short-tailed weasels, arctic ground squirrels, lemmings, and arctic foxes. In nesting areas, the buntings may mob such predators, but they apparently perform no distraction displays. Nest predation rates soar highest in the year following high abundance of lemmings because of consequent predator abundance. Harsh spring weather causes much snow bunting mortality; starvation and exposure weaken the birds, enabling easy catches by predators.

**Focus.** Snow buntings perform the same heraldic rites of spring for the Inuit and other arctic peoples that robins and red-winged blackbirds do for those of us in the central and northeastern United States. "Only the North Countryman," wrote ornithologist George M. Sutton, "knows how welcome is the cheerful greeting of the little *Amauligak* [Inuit for male snow bunting] when it returns in the Spring." Farmers in winter, on the other hand, once regarded a restless flock of snow buntings as a harbinger of stormy weather. In spring, wrote explorer Samuel Hearne, snow buntings "are very fat, and not inferior in flavour to an Ortolan [the ortolan bunting, a Eurasian species]." The Inuit and Cree netted them for food, killing them by pinching their heads. In northern Quebec, snow bunting stew was a keenly anticipated spring delicacy. The birds were also market hunted in winter for the nineteenth-century gourmet trade.

Longevity data include banding records of birds at 4, 6, and 8 years of age. Annual adult mortality measures about 40 percent.

FINCH FAMILY (Fringillidae) - Subfamily Emberizinae - Sparrow-Buntings (Tribe Emberizini)

# White-crowned Sparrow *(Zonotrichia leucophrys)*

About 7 inches long, the adult white-crowned sparrow shows a black and white, longitudinally striped head crown; pink bill; unstreaked grayish underparts; and brown back, tail, and wings with 2 white bars. Sexes look alike. Juvenile birds, however, show buff and brown head crowns and bright pink bills. The song, described by one observer as "like an imperfect white-throated sparrow song," begins with 1 or 2 clear whistles followed by several husky trilled notes.

**Close relatives.** Four other *Zonotrichia* sparrows exist, 3 of which are North American: Harris's sparrow *(Z. querula)* of central Canada and south-central United States; the white-throated sparrow *(Z. albicollis;* see *Birds of Forest, Yard, and Thicket)*; and the golden-crowned sparrow *(Z. atricapilla)* of the West. The rufous-collared sparrow *(Z. capensis)* inhabits Central and South America.

**Behaviors.** Five subspecies or races of white-crowned sparrows exist in North America. Contrary to the usual situation regarding subspecific variations, each differs considerably in behaviors and song, as well as in distribution. Most of the information in this account relates to the familiar eastern North American subspecies, *Z. l. leucophrys.*

The white-crown's song has been variously phoneticized as "more wet wetter chee zee" or "oh gee, it was the whiz-whiskey" (phonetic transcriptions invariably reveal more about the condition of birders than of birds). In any case, this song is seldom heard by many of us, since in the United States we normally see this bird only during its migrations or in winter. And even though males do sing year-round, they vocalize most frequently in spring. "Much of our understanding of song ontogeny [song development in individuals] and geographic song variation in birds," wrote one research team, "is based on the study of this species."

White-crowned sparrows are usually fairly conspicuous when present. Not especially shy, they often associate in small flocks of 8 to 10 birds during nonbreeding seasons. White-crowns feed mainly by scratching and gleaning on the ground; sometimes, however, they jump up to snatch flies or other aerial insects. Flocks are governed by shifting dominance hierarchies. In wintering flocks, adult males dominate adult females, which in turn dominate juvenile males; juvenile females rank lowest. Subtle age and sexual differences in crown plumage seem to be the primary indicator to the birds themselves of dominance status.

Not all white-crown subspecies are migratory, but the eastern race travels far in spring and fall. The eastern subspecies' breeding range occupies much of Ontario south and east of Hudson Bay, plus northern Ontario, Quebec, and Newfoundland. The entire species' breeding range spans the far north, with outlying resident populations along the Pacific coast and south to New Mexico in the Rockies. White-crowns also occasionally appear as vagrants in Greenland, Iceland, western Europe, and Japan.

*Spring.* The relatively late white-crown migration usually peaks in mid-May, lingers into June. Preceding actual migration, a period of restlessness termed *zugen-*

*Their vividly striped heads make white-crowned sparrows more easily recognized than many sparrow species. They commonly appear in northern states during spring and fall migrations.*

*ruhe* occurs, marked by a decline in daytime activity and an increase in nocturnal activity. Migration proceeds at night, usually in small flocks or individually; the birds move across a broad front, averaging about 50 miles of progress per day. Large concentrations sometimes gather at prime feeding areas along the way.

White-crowns show directional orientation under night skies, suggesting navigational reliance on star patterns; moonlight and urban lights may disrupt this mechanism. Geomagnetic navigation may also occur; researchers have found slight amounts of the mineral magnetite embedded in the fascial tissue of head and neck muscles.

A partial molt of crown and other head feathers occurs more or less concurrently with migration. Juveniles of the previous year shed their brown striping at this time. New grayish crown stripes wear down, becoming black and white as the season advances. Migrating males precede females by 2 or 3 weeks, often to the previous year's breeding site. Many pairs apparently remate in successive years; others are monogamous only for a single breeding season. Occasional *polygyny* (a single male mating with 2 or more females) and extrapair copulations also occur. Pairs apparently do not remain together after the breeding season.

Breeding activities of white-crowns are governed strongly by the length of daylight, or *photoperiodism;* "the periods for arrival, lag between male and female arrival, time before egg-laying, and time between broods all decrease with increasing latitude," summarized one report (the same statement applies to many North American bird species). Most pairs of the eastern subspecies produce only a single brood; white-crowns that nest south of about 55 degrees N latitude often produce 2 or 3 broods.

Territory ranges in size from less than an acre to much more, depending on bird density and habitat quality. Males establish territories by singing—some 4 or 5 songs per minute—from conspicuous perches and by chasing intruders. Both sexes voice trill calls; from a female they usually elicit copulation as she flutters her wings, from a male during aggressive interactions with other males. Male song, occasionally voiced during moonlit nights and peaking in morning and evening, not only defends territory and attracts a mate but also, according to research, incites female ovarian growth and nest construction.

Nesting in the eastern race begins from early to mid-June. One observer labeled the white-crown's devious behaviors at and near the nest "more mousy than regal in bearing." When disturbed, the bird seldom flies directly off the nest but "mouse runs" inconspicuously through the grass for 10 or 20 feet before flying. When approaching the nest, it lands some distance off and steals silently to the nest. The bird performs a "broken-wing" distraction display when fledglings are present. When foraging on the ground, white-crowns hop along and, like juncos, towhees, fox sparrows, and several other finches, typically double-scratch, using both feet at once.

EGGS AND YOUNG: 3 to 5; eggs greenish, semiglossy, variably brown spotted. INCUBATION: by female; averages 12 days; hatching usually synchronous. FEEDING OF YOUNG: by female for first few days, then both sexes; mainly small caterpillars, other insects, spiders. FLEDGING: 8 to 10 days.

*Summer.* Parent white-crowns induce nestlings to fledge by stopping the food supply, though they resume feeding them for several weeks after fledging. Juveniles can fly and forage for themselves in 16 to 20 days but remain on or near the parental territory for another 2 weeks or so. The annual molt, occurring in July and August, replaces all plumage; adult birds now show new, light grayish head crowns, and juveniles appear with buffier body plumage and reddish brown head striping.

*Fall.* Late-summer zugenruhe, a period of restlessness, precedes migration in September. Females, at least in some populations, precede males. I have also encountered all-juvenile flocks in northern Michigan, usually in October. The birds travel at night, as in spring, stopping to rest and forage in daytime. Often they appear in small flocks of 5 to 20 birds or accompany flocks of other sparrow species, especially the related white-throated sparrow (see *Birds of Forest, Yard, and Thicket*). The white-crown eastern subspecies migrates generally southwestward, moving as far as central Texas; many white-crowns, however, settle much farther north. Females tend to travel farther south than males. Other white-crown subspecies winter throughout the continent and into Mexico and the West Indies.

*Winter.* Sometimes called "the western counterpart of the white-throated sparrow," the white-crown occurs relatively uncommonly east of the 100th meridian in winter, though this distribution is apparently changing. Winter populations peak along the Pecos and Rio Grande Rivers in New Mexico, in California's Imperial and Sacramento Valleys, and in southwestern Utah. Few white-crowns occur in the southeastern United States. Since about 1950, increasing numbers of white-crowns have been observed wintering in the northern states and into southern Canada. Many ornithologists believe that this trend reflects the widespread use of yard feeders, resulting in expansion of the bird's winter range. White-crowns rarely remain in winter where minimum January temperature falls below 15 degrees F. Winter white-crowns are not territorial, but first-year individuals apparently imprint on their winter home ranges, and many return there in subsequent years.

**Ecology.** Although their geographic locales differ, all subspecies of white-crowned sparrow exploit remarkably similar habitats within those locales. Necessary breeding habitat features include a patchy mixture of grass, bare ground, and dense shrubbery or small conifers for resting and roosting cover. Nearby standing or running water and tall coniferous trees also mark the habitats of some white-crown populations. Far-northern habitats consist mainly of open, stunted tree growth and brush—the taiga. Road building, clear-cutting, and farming often create new open-ground habitat for white-crowns. Breeding habitat in mountainous areas is the *krummholz,* the zone of stunted trees at the edge of alpine tundra. Winter habitat generally consists of open areas within 7 feet of hedgerow or shrub and thicket cover; the densest populations occur along rivers. The birds often visit yard feeders placed near cover. During migrations, they frequent fields and extensive lawn areas.

Nests of the eastern race, usually sited on the ground, often lie in lichen-crowberry mats concealed by overhanging branches of dwarf birch or Labrador-tea. Other sites include sphagnum moss hummocks. Occasionally nests are placed a short height above ground in a shrub or small conifer. The female builds a structure about $4^1/2$ inches across, using small sticks, pine needles, coarse grass, moss, and bark shreds. She lines the 2-inch-diameter cup with fine grasses, sedges, and mammal hairs. The pliable nest cup may expand another inch or so as nestlings grow.

Food consists mainly of insects, often caterpillars and blackflies, during spring migration and the breeding period; seeds dominate the diet the rest of the year. On the northern range before large-scale insect hatches occur in spring, white-crowns have been observed to feed on the green spore capsules of hairy cap moss *(Polytrichum)* and willow catkins. Seeds make up more than 90 percent of the annual diet; pigweeds, foxtail-grasses, panic-grasses, oats and other grains, smartweeds, chickweeds, docks, and ragweeds rank high in usage. White-crowns also occasionally consume grass blades, elderberries, and blackberries.

Competitive interactions with other species seem infrequent. The central continental subspecies of white-crowns *(Z. l. gambelii)* chases chipping sparrows and dark-eyed juncos from its territories, but it overlaps territories with fox sparrows, American tree sparrows, and common redpolls. White-crowns have occasionally hybridized with dark-eyed juncos and Harris's, golden-crowned, white-throated, and song sparrows.

Predators include shrikes and several raptors—snowy and short-eared owls, sharp-shinned hawks, and American kestrels. Snakes, crows, jays, ground squirrels, weasels, and minks may raid nests. Though brown-headed cowbird nest parasitism is infrequent, it appears to be increasing in urban-nesting populations of western white-crown races. Host white-crowns sometimes bury cowbird eggs in the nest or abandon the nest and rebuild elsewhere. Parasitized nests that hatch a cowbird nestling, however, apparently seem as likely to fledge at least one chick as nonparasitized nests. Predation apparently affects populations less than weather-related mortality. Late-season snowstorms sometimes cause nest abandonment, and first-time fall migrants along coastal areas are often blown out to sea.

**Focus.** The white-crown, labeled "the white rat of the ornithological world" by researchers who work primarily with captive birds, is the prototype species for much of what we know about geographical variation in birdsong development. "Although songs differ among the various races," naturalist Alan Versaw observed, "finer differences in dialect often occur between local populations of the same race. Birds raised near the intersection of dialects may become bilingual." Yet the songs of all races sound enough alike that all can easily be identified as those of white-crowns. Much work has gone into analysis of song acquisition in this species. Results exemplify the *auditory template hypothesis*, which holds that a brain template or model pattern governs the learning selection of sounds that a juvenile bird uses to form the song characteristics of its population or song group. The learning period, during which the juvenile hears adult white-crowns sing, is day 10 through day 50 after hatching. Sequences of so-called *subsong, plastic song,* and finally (at about day 200) stable *crystallized song* follow the initial learning period as the bird ages. The eastern subspecies, however, shows fewer small-scale differences among populations in song dialects than less-migratory white-crown races or those that migrate shorter distances.

Crucial to the structure of social dominance in white-crowns is the conspicuous *avian badge* of this species, the black and white head striping. Those birds with the brightest striping (adult males) occupy the highest dominance status, those with the dullest striping (juvenile females) the lowest.

Despite widespread creation of usable breeding habitats by means of land clearing and agriculture, white-crowns continue to decline over much of their range. Reasons remain unclear.

More than most finches, white-crowns exhibit the premigratory nocturnal restlessness behaviors known as *zugenruhe.* Yet "despite the fact that it was the first known and is the most widely distributed race," observed ornithologist Roland C. Clement, "the eastern white-crown has been one of the least studied." Probably its remoter breeding areas, compared with those of the other races, account for this disparity. Some researchers believe that the eastern race is the ancestral white-crown population; as an essentially northern species, its western races have extended southward only in mountainous and cool Pacific coastal regions.

Average white-crown life span is apparently about 16 months, encompassing a single breeding season. Banding records, however, show occasional longevity of 7 to 13 years. Mortality rate for the first year after hatching is about 70 percent.

FINCH FAMILY (Fringillidae) - Subfamily Emberizinae - Sparrow-Buntings (Tribe Emberizini)

## Savannah Sparrow *(Passerculus sandwichensis)*

About 5 inches long or slightly more, savannah sparrows are heavily streaked on both upper and lower parts. Some savannahs show a slight coalescence of brown streaking that appears as a spot on the breast, similar to song sparrows. A yellowish stripe over each eye becomes visible especially during the breeding season, as well as a whitish crown stripe. The tail, unlike the song sparrow's, is slightly notched. Sexes look alike. The lisping song is an insectlike "sit sit sit seee saaay," the final note pitched lower.

**Close relatives.** Seventeen forms or subspecies of savannah sparrows inhabit North America, including the Ipswich sparrow *(P. s. princeps)*, which breeds only in Nova Scotia, and the Belding's sparrow *(P. s. beldingi)* of southern California. The only other *Passerculus* species, the large-billed sparrow *(P. rostratus)*, resides in northern Mexico.

**Behaviors.** Although savannah sparrows are common, even abundant in most of their habitats, they are easily overlooked. In spring, amid the cacophony of birdsong, their buzzy notes may pass as background noise. They also appear inconspicuous in winter as, loosely flocked, they forage on the ground and fly up in low, erratic bursts of motion. Savannahs run mouselike in the grass when alarmed or flushed from the nest. They roost at night on the ground.

Savannahs are only seasonally monogamous throughout most of their range, but if both mates survive, fidelity to the previous year's breeding site *(philopatry)* brings them together again, and they typically re-pair in subsequent years. Polygynous populations (in which one male breeds with more than one female) also exist, most notably in Canada's Maritime Provinces. Extrapair copulations, occurring when paired females wander off territory, commonly occur. The frequency of polygyny varies among populations and years; sometimes it approaches 50 percent of males, usually much less. Savannahs walk, hop, and run on the ground, sometimes double-scratch like juncos and towhees, and occasionally leap from the ground to snatch a flying insect.

Savannah sparrow breeding range spans the continent from the Arctic south to the central tier of states; in the West, the range extends even farther south to central Mexico, possibly into Central America. Small populations also exist in Siberia. All populations migrate except year-round resident savannahs along the California coast and in Mexico.

*Spring.* Migration, often beginning in February, peaks in mid- to late April. The birds travel mainly at night, apparently using sunset solar cues in both spring and fall for directional orientation. Magnetic and stellar compasses also come into play, especially in the fall for first-time migrants (see Focus). A partial molt of body feathers occurs in March and April.

Both sexes are highly philopatric to previous territories, but males usually arrive about 1 to 3 weeks earlier than females. Yearling birds, both male and female, tend to arrive and nest later than adults. The birds typically nest within 100 feet or so of the previous nest site. Females whose mates don't show up may shift somewhat farther away. Arriving males

*The savannah sparrow remains fairly inconspicuous in its diverse, open-country habitats. It raises 2 broods through most of its breeding range.*

establish their territories by singing on shrub or tall weed perches; by winging over the territory in slow, fluttery, legs-adangle display flights; by aerial chases of other males; and by ritualized parallel walking along territory borders and bill gaping. Territory size varies from a third of an acre in optimal habitats to more than 3 acres in sparser cover. Boundaries often shift during the breeding season, however, tending to enlarge. This is because a female frequently selects a nest site near the edge of, or even outside, her mate's territory, an action that often brings him into conflict with a neighboring male. Pairs do not restrict their foraging to the territory, often feeding in adjacent undefended areas. Nesting females also defend their own territory—usually extending some 60 feet or so from the nest—from other females. Some researchers believe that female-female aggression and territorialism may impose monogamy on the resident male.

Nesting begins in May, sometimes extending into July, with peak hatching in early to middle June.

EGGS AND YOUNG: typically 4 or 5; eggs pale greenish blue, heavily brown spotted and blotched, often wreathed at larger end. INCUBATION: by female; 12 or 13 days; hatching synchronous or asynchronous (within 24 to 36 hours). FEEDING OF YOUNG: by both sexes; insect larvae, spiders. FLEDGING: about 11 days.

*Summer.* Savannah sparrows typically raise 2 broods per year, except in the species' high-latitude range. Fledglings immediately disperse from the nest vicinity, and parents divide the brood, each parent guarding and feeding 1 or 2 young. They continue to feed the fledglings for 2 or 3 weeks; females sometimes continue to care for first-brood fledglings even as they build a second nest and begin incubating a second clutch. As they become independent, juveniles tend to group in loose flocks of 3 to 8 birds and establish temporary dominance hierarchies. Even though juveniles are larger than adult savannahs, having longer wing primaries and weighing more, they remain subservient to adults in the dominance hierarchy, as do females to males. Juveniles soon aggregate into much larger, wandering flocks of 100 or so. Young males often behave aggressively in these flocks; one researcher suggested that they may be prospecting future territories.

Molting progresses from July to September; male molting seems to precede that of females, many of which may still be incubating or brooding. Feather loss gives the birds a ragged, unkempt appearance in summer. The only observable difference now between adult and juvenile birds is in the head plumage, buffier in juveniles and grayer in adults. A period of premigrational restlessness, termed *zugenruhe,* is evident in this species as flocks feed and gather in fields and coastal marshes.

*Fall, Winter.* Savannah migration peaks in mid-September, often heralded by a cold front with north winds and clear skies. Again, the birds travel mainly at night, using solar and stellar cues. Most savannahs winter from the southern tier of states down through Mexico to Honduras and the Caribbean islands; a few stragglers remain on the summer range through winter. Many savannahs exhibit winter philopatry, returning to the same areas they occupied the previous winter, though winter territorialism has not been observed. Yet one observer noted that "in flocks about to commence their spring migration, individuals vary considerably in the direction of orientation, suggesting that members of wintering flocks may be from several different breeding localities."

Winter flocks, usually relatively small, tend to be temporary aggregations, largest in early morning. Winter dominance hierarchies are believed to be short-lived in the shifting social milieu. Spring migration begins in late February.

**Ecology.** Just about any sort of open country can host savannah sparrows. Their name, incidentally, derives not from savanna habitat but from the city of Savannah, Georgia, where in 1811, early ornithologist Alexander Wilson named the type specimen. This bird was presumably a migrant, as savannah sparrows do not breed there. Favored breeding habitats include alfalfa fields and other hayfields, grassy pastures, marshes, roadsides, dunes, and tundra. The birds seem to prefer a well-developed litter or duff layer on the ground. In the far north, they feed in dwarf willow and birch shrubs and in conifers. Generally, however, they avoid tree cover. Two noted ecologists (Odum and Hight, 1957) defined the savannah as an "herb sparrow," adapted to satisfy all its food and habitat requirements in exclusively herbaceous ground cover; today we would say it belongs to the grassland ground feeder *guild,* a group of species that share a resource. The densest savannah sparrow breeding populations are found on islands, and these populations show the strongest philopatry. Numbers decline where plant succession advances to shrub stages. Migration and winter habitats include open fields, pastures, golf courses, dunes, roadsides, and salt marshes. Even in the drier parts of their range, savannahs favor moist areas such as irrigated fields or pond margins. Research has indicated this species as *area sensitive,* thriving best in large contiguous habitats rather than fragmented ones. The smallest amount of contiguous grassland habitat required to maintain a breeding population of savannahs ranges from about 2 to 25 acres.

Nests, built exclusively by females, are well concealed, often flush with the ground, and shaped with coarse grasses containing an inner cup of finer grasses. The outside diameter is about 3 inches. Often a canopy of dead vegetation hides the nest, which lies in grass clumps, in goldenrod stands, or at the base of low woody shrubs such as blueberry, blackberry, and rose canes. Some nests become almost completely covered by surrounding "tents," hoods, or mats of vegetation. Tunnel-like entrances to hooded nests may be formed by the birds or perhaps incorporate the grass tunnels of meadow voles. Females build new nests for each renesting. Distance between first and second nests averages about 50 feet.

Like most finches, savannah sparrows are primarily insect eaters during spring and summer, seed eaters in other seasons. Caterpillars, larval beetles and wasps, adult beetles, grasshoppers, and midges rank high in the diet, but the birds also consume many other insects, plus spiders, millipedes, crustaceans such as sowbugs, and snails. In some areas, they capture spittlebugs by probing the insects' frothy masses on goldenrod, and they also explore the branch tips of white spruce for moth larvae. Savannah sparrows sometimes forage extensively enough to reduce caterpillar populations significantly. The seed diet consists mainly of the seeds of grasses—foxtail-grasses, crabgrasses, panic-grasses, barnyard-grasses, and sorghum—but also those of ragweeds, chickweeds, and smartweeds. The birds also consume a few fruits, mainly wild strawberries and blueberries.

Few competitive interactions seem to exist, though savannahs occasionally chase or are chased by habitat residents including tree swallows, song and field sparrows, and northern bobwhites. In some southwestern grassland areas in winter, savannahs share habitat and food resources with vesper and grasshopper sparrows. A 1977 study established, however, that little competition occurs among these species owing to *resource partitioning:* Although all of them forage in concentric patterns around isolated mesquite trees, the distance of these "feeding rings" from the tree cover varies. Vespers feed closest, at less than 12 feet or so; grasshopper sparrows feed farthest, at about 25 to 50 feet; and savannahs forage in between, at about 12 to 25 feet. Savannah and grasshopper sparrows, which belong to the same grassland guild, also exhibit resource partitioning where they occupy concurrent breeding areas. Savannahs tend to feed around perimeter areas of grass clumps, whereas grasshopper sparrows forage more frequently on bare-ground sites. Grasshopper sparrows also nest in somewhat more open sites with less ground litter than those of savannahs.

Probably the foremost nest predators are crows, ravens, and gulls. Others include northern harriers, common grackles, rat snakes, red foxes, striped skunks, raccoons, weasels, and domestic cats. Adult savannahs fall prey mainly to raptors—screech, short-eared, and barn owls; northern harriers; sharp-shinned hawks; American kestrels; and merlins. Though not frequent victims of brown-headed cowbird parasitism, savannahs do host occasional cowbird eggs and nestlings. Occasional egg dumping in savannah nests by grasshopper sparrows also occurs.

**Focus.** Like many passerine species, annual mortality of savannahs exceeds 50 percent. Mortality is highest among fledglings and newly independent juveniles. Birds that survive their first year average 35 to 70 percent survival rates until age 5 or 6, when survival falls to less than 10 percent.

Like most nocturnal migrant passerines, savannah sparrows come equipped with a flexible orientation system, which combines interacting directional senses: magnetic star, polarized light, and perhaps sun compasses. According to one report, "visual information at sunset overrides both star and magnetic cues, and polarized skylight is the relevant stimulus in dark orientation."

The savannah sparrow was apparently, at least in several instances, the bird that a puzzled Thoreau labeled the "seringo" or "seringo-bird." The word, he wrote, "reminds me of its note—as if it were produced by some kind of fine metallic spring . . . an earth-sound."

Human activities—primarily land clearing and agriculture—have clearly benefited savannah sparrows, providing increased breeding and feeding habitats and probably extending ranges of the various subspecies far beyond their presettlement limits. In Ohio and southern Michigan, for example, savannahs did not regularly breed until well into the twentieth century. Today, however, reversion of much farmland to forest, along with widespread urban development, has resulted in savannah sparrow declines in some areas. Preservation of highly productive coastal and island habitats, which provide important migratory stop-over sites as well as genetically distinct populations owing to philopatry, is vital to this species.

FINCH FAMILY (Fringillidae) - Subfamily Emberizinae - Sparrow-Buntings (Tribe Emberizini)

# Grasshopper Sparrow *(Ammodramus savannarum)*

One of the smallest sparrows (about 5 inches long), the brownish grasshopper sparrow looks quite flat headed and shows a whitish crown stripe, striped back, white belly, and buffy, obscurely striped breast. This is the only grassland sparrow whose adult plumage lacks breast streaking, although juveniles do exhibit a prominently streaked breast. Looking closely, one may observe an orange-yellow spot between eye and bill, as well as a small yellow mark at the bend of the wing. The tail is short and, typical of *Ammodramus* sparrows, consists of short, pointed feathers that are bare shafted at the tip.

Sexes look alike. The weak, fluttery flight usually zigzags close to the ground. Males have 2 distinct songs: the primary, or "grasshopper" song, a long, dry, insectlike buzz—"tsick tsick terrrrrr" or "tip-tup-a-zeeeee"—and a sustained song consisting of a series of short, buzzy, seesaw notes. Both sexes also voice a trill call.

**Close relatives.** Seven of the total 9 *Ammodramus* sparrows reside in North America, the other 2 in South America. North American species include the seaside sparrow *(A. maritimus)*, saltmarsh sharp-tailed sparrow *(A. caudacutus)*, Nelson's sharp-tailed sparrow *(A. nelsoni)*, Le Conte's sparrow *(A. leconteii)*, Henslow's sparrow *(A. henslowii)*, and Baird's sparrow *(A. bairdii)*. Twelve subspecies of grasshopper sparrows exist, 4 in North America.

**Behaviors.** Seldom seen more than a few feet off the ground at a song perch or in brief, zigzag flight, grasshopper sparrows stay mostly hidden. Often, instead of flying, they run on the ground, sometimes for hundreds of feet. Incubating females never approach the nest directly; they always drop into the grass some distance away, then move on foot. Likewise, they run for a distance before flying when leaving the nest. Perched, the bird often appears slightly crouched, its head lower than its back. Unlike most sparrows, this species does not flock at any time of year.

Breeding distribution spans most of the continent, from the Rockies eastward and from southern Canada to northern portions of the Gulf states. Local populations also exist west of the Rockies and into Mexico, Central America, and the West Indies. Even in the East, however,

*The body shape and posture of grasshopper sparrows, which stay close to the ground, give them an almost cringing appearance. Unlike most sparrows, they seldom flock.*

grasshopper sparrow populations remain spotty and unevenly distributed, uncommon to rare throughout much of their range.

*Spring.* Only the northernmost 2 subspecies of grasshopper sparrows *(A. s. pratensis, A. s. perpallidus)* are highly migratory. Late-spring travelers, they fly at night in small groups or as individuals, typically arriving on the breeding range in early to late May. Males, which arrive first, show irregular site fidelity *(philopatry)* to previous breeding areas; banding studies indicate that rarely more than 50 percent of previous breeders reappear at a breeding site, usually less, and that eastern populations are more philopatric than midwestern ones. "Return rates to former breeding sites," wrote one researcher, "differ markedly between populations and probably between years." Yet the number of forms or subspecies of grasshopper sparrows would suggest that philopatry, and consequent geographical isolation of subgroups, has strongly guided this bird's evolution.

Upon arrival, males establish territories by primary song, by fluttering flight and wing-flicking displays, and by chasing. Since aerial or grasstop territorial conflicts have been the only ones observed, do territorial infringements ever occur on the ground? "Perhaps the grasshopper sparrow recognizes the limits of its territory only from a grasstop point of view," suggested one researcher. Males tend to establish song perches at territorial edges rather than centers. Territory size typically ranges from 1 to 3 or more acres. When females arrive several days after the males, the sustained song type becomes dominant. Male singing diminishes as pair formation occurs but resumes during egg laying and incubation, possibly soliciting extra-pair copulations; cases of *polygyny,* in which a male mates with 2 or more females, have not been reported but probably occur at least occasionally in this species.

Increased breeding densities in certain locations, such as on islands, may build to the point where populations appear semicolonial, with 3 to 5 pairs occupying 2 or 3 acres. Nesting in the Northeast typically begins in mid- to late May.

EGGS AND YOUNG: 4 or 5 in first clutch, often 3 in second; eggs cream-white, sometimes gray or purple shaded, sparsely speckled with reddish brown; markings sometimes concentrated at large end. INCUBATION: by female; 11 to 13 days; hatching synchronous. FEEDING OF YOUNG: by both sexes, occasionally also by adult and juvenile attendants; insects, mainly grasshoppers. FLEDGING: 8 or 9 days.

*Summer.* Many, if not most, grasshopper sparrow pairs raise second broods, extending the nesting season into July, although some studies seem to show that first-time breeders produce only a single brood. Females always build new nests for second nestings, and frequently the pair shifts to a new locale. In one study, 17 percent of the grasshopper sparrow nests were attended by nest helpers, mainly nonrelated juveniles and adult birds from adjacent territories whose nests had been destroyed. Attendant birds, tolerated by the parents, both fed and brooded nestlings. Such instances of *cooperative breeding* happen less commonly in this species than in some other passerines, but they rarely occur among other sparrow species. Although the duration of parental care for first-brood fledglings remains unknown, an adult typically appears with only 1 or 2 offspring in the week or so after the nestlings fledge, suggesting that parents may split up the brood between them. Juveniles become independent at 3 or 4 weeks of age and may forage in loose flocks, sometimes in bare, sandy areas where grasshoppers abound. Both adults and juveniles tend to remain in the territorial vicinity until migration.

The annual plumage molt usually begins in August, in some cases not completed until October, after migration.

*Fall, Winter.* Details of fall migration in this species are poorly documented, owing to the birds' secretive behaviors and generally solitary movements, though sometimes grasshopper sparrows appear in mixed sparrow flocks. Travel peaks in September and may extend into October. As in spring, the birds fly at night, probably using similar compass cues to those of savannah sparrows. The northern limits of grasshopper sparrow winter range remain ill defined. The range encompasses the southern tier of states, both East and West, and into Mexico, Central America, northern South America, and the Caribbean islands.

**Ecology.** Grasshopper sparrows, especially the 2 northern subspecies, favor grassland cover that is relatively sparse (but see the Vesper Sparrow account for contradictory data). Optimal habitat contains a minimum of about 25 percent bare, litter-free ground (the figure varies somewhat in different studies). Old fields, hayfields, and native prairie are common habitats, as are capped landfills and recent grassy burns. The birds tend to avoid grasslands with shrub cover, though this does not apply to all subspecies. Winter field habitats of the southeastern United States are dominated by smooth crabgrass and broom-sedge grass. Grasshopper sparrows appear *area sensitive,* at least to some degree, favoring large grassland tracts over smaller, fragmented ones. Minimum space requirements, where studied, vary between 75 and 250 acres.

The rim of the nest, built in a depression lined by the female over 2 or 3 days, typically lies flush with the ground surface, measuring about 5 inches across. Often it lies at the base of a grass clump and is domed over by overhanging grasses; a side entrance gives it some resemblance to an ovenbird's nest. Materials consist of dried grasses, with a nest lining of fine grasses, rootlets, and sometimes animal hairs.

Grasshopper sparrows feed primarily on insects during the summer, especially grasshoppers, though the name of the bird derives mostly from its insectlike song. Favored prey species include *Cordillacris, Scudderia* (bush katydids), and spur-throated grasshoppers (*Melanoplus,* among the most destructive of crop insects). The birds usually remove an insect's legs before feeding it to nestlings. Caterpillars, ants, spiders, and snails are also taken. In the East and Midwest, summer and fall seed foods, about 20 percent of the total diet, include foxtail-grasses, red or sheep sorrel, oats, and knotweeds. Winter seed fare consists largely of panic-grasses and sedges.

Probably the grasshopper sparrow's main bird competitor is the possibly dominant savannah sparrow, which occupies similar, though often somewhat denser, grassland habitats. Savannah sparrows have replaced grasshopper sparrows in some areas where that species was formerly abundant. Since savannahs appear more adaptive than grasshopper sparrows to shrub invasion, advance in plant succession may account for such replacement. In some places, the species have been observed countersinging, but aggressive interactions between them are rarely seen. In other areas, both species maintain overlapping territories. Grassland blackbird species such as meadowlarks and bobolinks sometimes chase grasshopper sparrows off their singing perches. Where several sparrow species winter together, some resource partitioning evidently occurs, with grasshopper sparrows able to forage farthest from shrub cover (see Savannah Sparrow). One study found that interspecific competition, at least during the breeding season, does not affect grasshopper sparrow populations.

Nest predators are mostly snakes—black racers, rat snakes, garter snakes, kingsnakes, and pigmy rattlesnakes—and mammals: striped skunks, raccoons, weasels, ground squirrels, foxes, and domestic cats. "Because nest density is generally low and the nest is well concealed," wrote researcher Peter D. Vickery, "nest predation . . . is likely to be incidental to other foraging activities." Hawks rather infrequently capture grasshopper sparrows, though loggerhead shrikes, when they were more abundant, quite often killed and impaled them in their larders. Brown-headed cowbirds occasionally parasitize grasshopper sparrow nests; the frequency, however, remains low in most areas, higher near forest-edge nest sites. Early-season mowing of hayfields causes many nest failures, as in other grassland species; for low ground nesters, the sudden loss of cover exposes nests to predators.

**Focus.** Local abundance of grasshopper sparrows commonly fluctuates from year to year, even in areas of prime habitat. Nobody knows why, though guesses abound. Yet the long-term trend of grasshopper sparrow decline throughout the century continues. Just since the late 1960s, populations have declined about 70 percent across the continent. The Florida subspecies of grasshopper sparrows is now listed as endangered. Though the grasshopper sparrow was once abundant in New England and midwestern grasslands, only remnant populations now exist in these regions; the bird's present distribution looks increasingly patchy and localized countrywide. This trend reflects the general decline, loss, and fragmentation of grassland habitats throughout the bird's breeding range. Whereas early land clearing, settlement, and agriculture benefited grasshopper sparrows, the subsequent conversion of pastureland to row crops and subdivisions, extensive and intensive grazing, and inhibition of fire, which has resulted in rank cover conditions and invasive shrub growth, all have played major roles in grasshopper sparrow decline. Grasshopper sparrows and other species that show uneven distributions and populations that are often not self-sustaining have increased our knowledge of population ecology. Populations may function as centers of individual recruitment and renewal, known as *sources*, or as *sinks*, centers of low reproductive success. Where practiced, certain management procedures for improving grassland habitats have been found to pay off fairly quickly for this species. These techniques mainly consist of deferred mowing until July, after the nesting season; light to moderate grazing; and prescribed burning. Grassland management practices have proved especially beneficial at airports.

Vernacular names for the grasshopper sparrow include yellow-winged and cricket sparrow. This sparrow has an average life span of just under 3 years, with a longevity record of over 6 years.

FINCH FAMILY (Fringillidae) - Subfamily Emberizinae - Sparrow-Buntings (Tribe Emberizini)

## American Tree Sparrow *(Spizella arborea)*

About 6 inches long or slightly more, the American tree sparrow is easily identified by its rusty cap, unstreaked underparts with a distinct brown spot on the breast, and 2 white wing bars. The two-toned bill has a dark upper mandible and a yellowish lower one. Sexes look alike. This sparrow voices a twittering note as it feeds in flocks, a musical, trisyllabic "teedle-eet." The male song begins with 1 or 2 high, clear notes followed by a variable sequence. It is usually heard only on the far-northern breeding range or during sunny days in late winter.

**Close relatives.** Other northeastern *Spizella* sparrows include the chipping sparrow (*S. passerina;* see *Birds of Forest, Yard, and Thicket*), clay-colored sparrow *(S. pallida),* and field sparrow *(S. pusilla;* see next accounts). The timberline sparrow *(S. taverneri),* Brewer's sparrow *(S. breweri),* and black-chinned sparrow *(S. atrogularis)* reside in the western United States. Together with Worthen's sparrow *(S. wortheni)* in

*This head profile of the American tree sparrow shows its two-toned bill, the lower mandible lighter than the upper—a useful identity mark.*

Mexico, these 8 species form the entire genus. The Eurasian tree sparrow *(Passer montanus),* introduced to America and resident in a few midwestern areas, belongs to a different family and is related to the house sparrow *(P. domesticus).*

**Behaviors.** Closely resembling its smaller relative, the chipping sparrow, the American tree sparrow is sometimes called the "winter chippy." It's unlikely that one would confuse them, however; the vocal efforts of each are totally dissimilar, and the species are seldom seen together in any case. Both are migrants, but chipping sparrows reside in the northern and central United States only during summer, whereas tree sparrows appear only in winter. Along with the dark-eyed junco (see *Birds of Forest, Yard, and Thicket*), the tree sparrow—if not as conspicuous as the junco, with which it often associates—is one of our most common winter birds.

Although they feed mainly on the ground, tree sparrows also perch in the brush, occasionally even in trees. These birds, social and gregarious for most of the year, typically move and forage in flocks of varying size. Flocks of 30 or 40 birds are common, but individual membership in a given flock may shift frequently. In winter, however, smaller flocks of 4 to 8 birds may remain stable through the season. Birds in a flock typically "converse" as they forage, a hallmark of tree sparrow identity. Thoreau likened the sound to a "tinkle of icicles." Tree sparrows exhibit straight-line dominance hierarchies and pecking order. They usually roost solitarily, however, on the

*Tree sparrows spend more time on the ground, usually in large flocks, than in trees or shrubs. Along with dark-eyed juncos, they become our most abundant "snow birds" in winter.*

ground or in thick coniferous foliage, although occasionally they roost communally under snow. Tree sparrows frequently bathe, even during the coldest weather, where open pools exist. Where they can't find water, they swallow snow. A common foraging habit in winter is to perch on a partially bent-over weed and peck at the seed head, sometimes bending the stalk to the ground or wing-beating the seed head, then retrieving the dislodged seeds from the snow surface. As long as they can find sufficient food, tree sparrows can withstand temperatures down to –20 degrees F. for extended periods.

The American tree sparrow's breeding distribution spans North America from Alaska to Labrador along the treeline and shrubby tundra south to Saskatchewan, Manitoba, Ontario, and central Quebec.

*Spring.* Spring migration peaks in late March and early April. This period is the only time of year when we in the northern states may hear snatches of the male tree sparrow's clear, warbling song. The birds travel in flocks at night, separating into smaller groups as they approach the breeding range. Migrants arrive coincident with snowmelt in late May and early June, some weeks earlier in the western range.

Strong fidelity *(philopatry)* to the previous year's breeding site, though not directly observed, can be inferred from the existence of song dialects for given locales. Males sing intensely upon arrival, especially in early morning and evening, and pair formation soon occurs. Pairs probably remain monogamous for only a single breeding season, but information on this, as on extrapair copulations or occurrence of polygyny, is lacking. Territories average 1 to 3 or more acres in size; they appear to consist of an inner core, where most activity occurs, and an outer circle of less activity. "Territorial behavior is concentrated in the central area in the morning when males are singing," wrote researcher Christopher T. Naugler, "with movements into the outer area more common later in the day." Size of territory gradually decreases as the season progresses. Males defend the territory by song, often from high tree perches and countersinging with territorial neighbors, and by chasing intruding tree sparrows.

Courtship behaviors include male wing fluttering and plumage puffery. Females solicit copulation from their mates by wing fluttering and voicing "whey-whey-whey" notes. Nest building usually begins in early to middle June.

EGGS AND YOUNG: 4 or 5; eggs pale blue or greenish, speckled and spotted with brown, markings often concentrated at larger end. INCUBATION: by female; 12 or 13 days; hatching synchronous (over 1 to 30 hours). FEEDING OF YOUNG: by both sexes; small caterpillars, flies, mosquitoes, other insects, masticated by parents initially. FLEDGING: 8 to 10 days; first flight about 15 days.

*Summer.* Tree sparrows raise only a single brood per season. Parent birds continue to feed juveniles for 2 or 3 weeks after fledging. As summer advances, family groups join and form larger flocks that wander and forage together. The complete annual molt occurs in August and September before migration.

*Fall, Winter.* October is the peak month of movement for these nocturnal migrants. Most travel in flocks, sometimes of mixed sparrow species. The winter range extends from southern Canada south to the central and southwestern states. Winter populations center in the midwestern wheat and corn belts—Kansas, Nebraska, Iowa, and northern Missouri.

The northern range limit is the –10 degrees F. average minimum January isocline. The birds appear generally philopatric to winter range sites, but they may also wander over areas of 6 miles or more following heavy snows. Some sexual segregation apparently occurs; males tend to winter farther north than females. Winter home range for most individuals averages about 600 to 1,000 feet in diameter.

The birds acquire their spring breeding plumage by erosion of buffy feather edges, but a partial molt of head and body feathers also occurs from February through April. Males begin singing in February before spring migration.

**Ecology.** As with many of our birds known by habitat adjectives, the tree sparrow's name bears only incidental relevance to its common sites of activity. Tree sparrows inhabit scrubby thickets and stunted trees bordering open tundra, the wide taiga of the far north. They spend most of their lives, including feeding and nesting, on the ground, though territories often include several shrubs or small trees on which the birds perch and sing. In winter, the birds occupy fields, hedgerows, and marshes and are frequently seen in flocks along roadsides and in urban residential areas, where they visit yard feeders. For roosting at night, tree sparrows favor cattail marshes, weedy fields, and dense pine foliage.

The nest, built by the female on the ground (occasionally up to 3 feet or so above ground), often lies in a grass tussock at the base of a small tree or shrub. Researcher Marguerite Baumgartner noted 3 distinct layers in the nest: an outer shell of coarse grasses, weed stems, and bits of bark and moss; an inner layer of fine grasses; and a soft lining of ptarmigan or waterfowl feathers or patches of lemming fur. According to Baumgartner, presence of the lemming fur suggests that "the birds sometimes raid this animal's old winter nests that are found everywhere above [that is, on] the ground." The outside diameter of the average nest is about 5 inches. Most nests appear completely open, but occasional nests, like those of the grasshopper sparrow, are partially domed and open on the side.

As one of the major grass and weed seed consumers among birds, a tree sparrow seldom lacks ample food. In winter, it eats about a quarter of an ounce of seeds per day. Conservative calculations figuring the number of tree sparrows per square mile during a winter period in Iowa concluded that 875 tons of weed seed were consumed annually by this species in Iowa alone—an extremely conservative estimate, researchers judged. The winter diet of about 98 percent seeds (about 50 percent grass seed) consists chiefly of sedges, yellow and green foxtail-grasses, northern crabgrass, panic-grasses, broom-sedge, lamb's quarters, redroot pigweed, sheep-sorrel, common ragweed, wild bergamot, smartweeds, goldenrods, and many others. Summer seed foods include sedges, cottongrasses, alders, pigweeds, mustards, sweet gale, cinquefoils, and various grasses. Fruits (blueberries, cranberries, and cloudberries), catkins (birch and alder), and waste grain are also consumed. Insects become prominent in the diet only as they become active in the June far-north breeding range—chiefly beetles, ants, caterpillars, and grasshoppers. The birds also consume spiders and snails. On warm winter days along streams, adult stone flies (Plecoptera) often hatch from the nymph stage and crawl on the snow, attracting tree sparrow flocks for winter morsels.

Competition appears negligible. During winter, flocks of tree sparrows and dark-eyed juncos often forage together. The winter distribution of tree sparrows is unusual among passerine migrants for its abrupt truncation above the Mexican border. Researchers have suggested that competitive interactions with the closely related chipping sparrow may in some way account for this restriction of winter range, but data remain unclear.

Information on tree sparrow predators exists only for winter. Raptors such as northern goshawks, sharp-shinned and Cooper's hawks, American kestrels, and screech-owls capture adult birds, as do shrikes, weasels, and domestic cats. In summer, wrote Marguerite Baumgartner, tree sparrows "are beyond the domain of snakes, cats, most crows, jays, and squirrels, and such competitors as English [house] sparrows,

*Foxtail-grasses (Setaria spp.), so named from the bushy seed head, grow abundantly almost everywhere. They provide a major winter seed food for many ground-feeding sparrows and other finches.*

starlings and cowbirds." The most serious bane of the tree sparrow is not man, the greatest predator (if sometimes indirectly) of most birds and mammals, but weather—"snows that cover the food supply," wrote Baumgartner, "and storms and sudden cold spells, particularly during the long migration."

**Focus.** It would be interesting to know the adaptive significance, if any, of the tree sparrow's "stickpin," the brown central spot on its breast. The only other North American birds that show similar marks are lark and song sparrows (on the latter, the mark appears as a coalescence of streaking).

Only a few sparrows spend less time in trees than tree sparrows. The bird derived its misnomer from apparently nearsighted American settlers who thought it resembled the Eurasian tree sparrow of England (the only visible resemblance is the chestnut crown of both, much smaller in the American tree sparrow); and even Eurasian tree sparrows, though they do nest in tree cavities, mainly forage not in trees but in weedy fields.

Longevity of this species is about 11 years. Based on banding returns, however, relatively few individuals live to their fourth year. About 50 percent of fledglings survive their first migration and winter.

---

FINCH FAMILY (Fringillidae) - Subfamily Emberizinae - Sparrow-Buntings (Tribe Emberizini)

## Clay-colored Sparrow *(Spizella pallida)*

Five inches long or slightly more, this pale, clear-breasted sparrow much resembles the winter chipping sparrow (see *Birds of Forest, Yard, and Thicket*), but its head markings are distinctive: a gray or white crown stripe; white brow and jaw lines sharply outlining brownish facial side patches; and a grayish, collarlike nape contrasting with a buffy upper breast. Sexes look alike, except that most males have whiter brow lines than females. The insectlike song consists of 2 to 8 leisurely, high-pitched buzzes.

**Close relatives.** See American Tree Sparrow. Clay-colored sparrows' nearest kin are the chipping, timberline, and Brewer's sparrows (*S. passerina, S. taverneri,* and *S. breweri*), all North American species.

**Behaviors.** Some birds make it easy for the casual observer; others, because of their secretive habits, their camouflaged patterns, or both, must be rigorously sought to be seen. Clay-colored sparrows belong in the latter category. Although not particularly shy, they merge into their shrub-grassland habitats, aided by their unspectacular plumage and unbirdlike vocal efforts, easily bypassed amid the background sounds of insect calls, other birdsong, and breezes stirring the vegetation.

Yet in the breeding area, clay-colored males frequently sing throughout the day, occasionally even at night, typically from a habitual perch—usually the top of a shrub or tall weed. A male often uses the same singing perch from one year to the next. Each male possesses one or two distinct *song types* that remain consistent; differences between the types exist in the number of buzzes voiced and total song length. Thus individual males make life easier for researchers of this species by reliably identifying themselves in the field.

Clay-colors forage mainly on the ground, gleaning from grasses and weeds, rarely from shrubs. Like most sparrows, clay-colors become highly social after the breeding season, often mingling with chipping, Brewer's, white-crowned, and lark sparrows. No system of dominance hierarchies has been observed in this species.

Clay-colored sparrow breeding range encompasses the northern Great Plains eastward across the upper Great Lakes, including southern Canada and upper New York State. Except during migrations, this bird is mainly Canadian and Mexican in distribution.

*Spring.* Many, though apparently not all, clay-colors undergo a full or partial molt of body feathers in early spring, either before or during migration. This molt produces the typical breeding plumage, with a reddish edging on the feathers and the white eyebrow lines.

Clay-colored males exhibit strong *philopatry,* or site fidelity, to the previous year's breeding territory; females are much less philopatric. Thus pairs seldom rebond, and females rarely nest in the same territory as the previous year. The birds depart their winter range in late March, traveling both day and night, usually in flocks of 25 to 100, sometimes many more. Migration flocks often mix with

*The clay-colored sparrow is a reliable creature of habit, both in individual song type and in its strong fidelity to previous nesting, and probably wintering, sites.*

chipping and Brewer's sparrows. Males usually arrive on their breeding sites by late April or early May, females 3 to 7 days later.

Clay-colors occupy the smallest territories of any *Spizella* sparrow, usually a half acre or less in size. Males establish the boundaries, which remain generally the same from year to year, by singing from perches near territorial edges and by chasing intruder males. Unlike most sparrows, clay-colors feed extensively off the territory, often in communal foraging areas. Nesting begins about mid-May. Nests on adjacent territories sometimes lie only 30 to 50 feet apart.

EGGS AND YOUNG: usually 4; eggs bluish green, sparingly brown spotted, often wreathed with brown markings at large end. INCUBATION: by both sexes (female 80 percent of time); 10 to 14 days; male brings food to incubating female; hatching asynchronous over 2 days. FEEDING OF YOUNG: by both sexes; insects. FLEDGING: 7 to 9 days; fledglings fly at 14 or 15 days.

*Summer.* Most clay-color pairs apparently do not attempt second nestings. One study, however, revealed that slightly more than half of clay-color pairs that had successfully fledged young birds by mid-June did indeed begin a second nest. Few, if any, such nests raise successful broods.

Fledglings typically disperse radially from the nest, secreting themselves in dense shrubs some 40 feet or so distant. Sometimes they end up in another clay-color territory, but trespassed neighbors tend to ignore both strayed fledglings and the parents feeding them.

Because clay-colors become so quiet and inconspicuous in summer, we know relatively little about their postbreeding activities. Parents continue to feed juveniles after fledging, probably for several weeks. Even late-nesting birds usually become nonterritorial by the end of July. Juveniles, now independent, gather in loose foraging flocks, often near ponds or pools. Adult birds, no longer paired, also join them.

Clay-color plumage molts are highly variable, both in timing and results. Most clay-colors probably complete their annual molt before fall migration, but many of them interrupt molting when they migrate and complete it on the winter range. The new plumage, much resembling that of chipping sparrows, often lacks the crown stripe seen in the breeding plumage. This is the season when clay-colors become hardest to identify as such.

*Fall, Winter.* Peak migration in this species probably occurs in September, finishing by late October. Clay-colors inhabit their southwestern range for about half the year. Most of the continental population travels across the Great Plains, wintering from southern Texas through Mexico to Guatemala. Clay-colors in smaller numbers winter along the east, Gulf, and west coasts. Most sparrows are night migrators, but this one moves extensively during daytime too, often accompanying small flocks of chipping and Brewer's sparrows. Winter segregation by age or sex, if it occurs, has not been observed— nor has philopatry to winter home ranges, though this seems probable.

**Ecology.** Clay-colored sparrows favor open shrubland habitats that contain grassy spaces and nearby water. Such areas include young pine plantations, regenerating burns and clear-cuts, abandoned fields, and forest edges, even parkland in cities. Clay-colors adapt well to disturbed and burned landscapes; in certain areas, they thrive where biologists have managed habitat programs for sharp-tailed grouse and Kirtland's warblers. Clay-colors feed mainly in pastures, in weedy fields, and along forest, field, road, and stream edges. On their Mexican range in winter, they frequent dry desert and scrub country.

Although clay-color females build nests in several types of sites, both on the ground and a foot or more high in shrub vegetation, the birds of a local population tend to favor a single site type. Some researchers report that later-season nests are placed higher than earlier nests, which mainly lie in grass tussocks. Other observers, however, maintain that nest timing shows no general correlation with nest height—that individual pairs, as well as entire local populations, tend to build consistently low or high within a season. The bulky nest cup, not so compact as that of the chipping sparrow, although nests placed in small shrubs or conifers may closely resemble chipping sparrow nests, consists of grasses and weed stems lined with finer grasses and sometimes hairs. The nest measures about 4 inches across. A favorite nesting shrub in some areas is snowberry *(Symphoricarpos albus)*, which grows on dry, rocky soils. Other hosts include silver-berry and rose shrubs.

Mainly seed eaters except during the breeding season, clay-colors consume a large variety of grass and weed seeds. Foremost seed foods include foxtail-grasses, panic-grasses, crabgrasses, pigweed, goosefoot, and various mustards and thistles, among many others. Caterpillars, beetles, leafhoppers, grasshoppers, ants, and spiders are frequent animal foods. The early-spring diet often includes tree buds and catkins.

Competition appears insignificant. Clay-colors are said to defend their territories against song, chipping, and Brewer's sparrows. The chief competitor of clay-colored sparrows, as of many grassland and scrub species, is plant succession, the progressive change and replacement of vegetation types that result in the transformation of habitats.

Predators, mainly upon nests, include garter snakes, loggerhead shrikes, meadow voles, white-footed mice, ground squirrels, weasels, and striped skunks. American kestrels sometimes attack flocks on the winter range. Brown-headed cowbirds parasitize a high proportion of clay-color nests, or try to do so. Sometimes the hosts accept the cowbird egg and incubate and hatch it; often, however, the sparrows simply desert the parasitized nest and build elsewhere. **Focus.** From their original Great Plains habitats, clay-colored sparrows have expanded their breeding range eastward and northward since about 1900, a trend that continues. The foremost reason for this expansion probably involves habitat changes wrought by logging and agriculture followed by plant succession on abandoned land. Small but significant declines, however, have occurred in the past 2 or 3 decades, as intensive agriculture and urban developments continue to eliminate much open shrubland in the central plains.

English zoologist William Swainson first named this bird, from a Saskatchewan specimen in 1827, the clay-coloured bunting. Audubon, thinking it a new species and finding it abundant along the upper Mississippi River in 1844, called it Shattuck's bunting after a friend. *Clay-colored* evidently refers to the paleness of the bird's plumage; its grayish nape patch is probably the only true claylike color to be found on the bird.

Longevity of these sparrows does not typically exceed 4 or 5 years.

FINCH FAMILY (Fringillidae) - Subfamily Emberizinae - Sparrow-Buntings (Tribe Emberizini)

## Field Sparrow *(Spizella pusilla)*
Recognize this 5-inch-long sparrow by its rusty cap, pinkish bill, unstreaked underparts (except for juveniles, which show a slightly streaked breast), and a whitish eye ring. Sexes look alike. The common song opens with a few down-slurred notes speeding to a musical trill, usually on one pitch.

**Close relatives.** See American Tree Sparrow. The closest evolutionary kin appear to be black-chinned and Worthen's sparrows *(S. atrogularis, S. wortheni),* both residents of Mexico.

**Behaviors.** Commonly heard in the shrubby fields, the field sparrow's *simple song* has been likened rhythmically to a bouncing Ping-Pong ball, with 2 or 3 long bounces followed by a whir of rapid bounces. Another sound, more rarely heard, is the *complex song,*

*Among the most common and engaging singers of farmland meadows, the field sparrow shows a pinkish bill, whitish eye ring, and clear, unmarked underparts.*

which alternates short and longer slurred notes, a sequence of cadences mystifying to a listener familiar with only the simple song. Both songs are voiced by territorial males, the second apparently during the height of field sparrow "machismo." Within the general song formats of both types, individual males sing subtle but distinct variations.

Field sparrows primarily forage on the ground or in low vegetation. They do not double-scratch like many sparrows. Sometimes they fly to the tops of grasses, bending them to the ground and feeding on the seed heads. They scan for insects from a foot or so high on a perch, but such "still hunting" episodes last only about 10 seconds. Field sparrows sing from elevated perches 5 to 25 feet high in the territory, usually shrubs or tall weeds.

Both breeding and winter ranges of the field sparrow extend from the Great Plains and Texas eastward to the Atlantic. Breeding range extends from southern Canada to the Gulf. The highest population densities, according to Breeding Bird Survey data, center in Missouri, Kentucky, and Ohio.

*Spring.* A partial migrant, many field sparrows remain as year-round residents in the southeastern United States. Northern breeding populations generally migrate, though scattered individuals linger in the southern Great Lakes and New England areas over winter. Migrant older males arrive on their breeding areas in late March to mid-April, younger males next, females about 2 weeks later. The birds travel at night, usually in small flocks of mixed sparrow species.

Male *philopatry,* site fidelity to the previous year's territory, is strong; females appear somewhat less philopatric. "The return percentage for females is much smaller than for males," wrote researcher Lawrence H. Walkinshaw. "This is perhaps to be expected, for the male usually accepts the first female that arrives on his territory." His mate of the previous year, if arriving later, often settles on an adjacent territory with a new mate. First-year birds are not philopatric to their natal areas. Probably most pairing, which occurs shortly after female arrival, does not repeat beyond a single nesting season. Polygyny appears rare in this species, though DNA "fingerprinting" of offspring indicates that some 10 to 15 percent of nestlings may result from extrapair copulations.

Males sing frequently and loudly upon their arrival, establishing territories of 2 to 3 acres in favorable habitat by song (often countersinging with adjacent neighbors) and by chasing competitor males. First-time males on a territory apparently try out 2 or more song types, then settle on one that closely matches a neighboring male's. Singing virtually ceases after pair formation but resumes at lesser frequency when incubation begins or if renesting occurs (as, because of predation, it often does). Nesting in the northern range begins in late April or early May.

---

EGGS AND YOUNG: 3 to 6; eggs greenish or bluish white, brown spotted, often wreathed at large end. INCUBATION: by female, which is occasionally fed by male; 11 or 12 days. FEEDING OF YOUNG: by both sexes; mainly caterpillars, grasshoppers, spiders. FLEDGING: 7 or 8 days; juveniles begin flying at 2 weeks.

---

*Summer.* One or both parents continue to feed fledglings until they become independent, in about a month. At first, fledglings remain near the nest, often staying grouped until they can feed themselves. If the female starts building a second nest (6 to 20 days after the first young fledge), the male assumes sole care of the fledglings. Sometimes, however, females desert their mates, taking some or all of the fledglings with them, and pair with new males, which then feed the first-nest fledglings. Females also frequently abandon their nests following nest predation or cowbird parasitism. Over a single breeding season, some 4 different laying periods may occur, extending into August or September. Probably most females make 3 to 4 nesting attempts on average, though up to 10 have been recorded. Predation and desertion account for most renesting attempts.

Independent juveniles forage together in small flocks of 10 to 12 birds. They may often wander into other field sparrow territories but remain unchallenged by territorial males. An important summer business of juvenile birds dispersing from parental territories apparently is to select the breeding site to which they will return in spring; they rarely return to their birth sites. As migration time nears, more of the sparrows flock together, sometimes foraging by the hundreds in feeding areas, roosting at night in the foliage of small trees and shrubs. The annual plumage molt occurs from August through October.

*Fall.* Most field sparrows residing north of a line drawn from Massachusetts to northern Kansas migrate southward in the fall. Movement, mainly at night, peaks in October. Resident field sparrows south of that line may migrate farther south or remain in the vicinity of their breeding areas.

*Winter.* Peak field sparrow populations in winter occur where minimum January temperatures rarely fall below 20 degrees F. and where freezing is infrequent. Winter range extends from southern Pennsylvania and Kansas to the Gulf and northern Mexico; the birds do not migrate from the continent. Field sparrows typically forage in small winter flocks, often mixing with chipping and other related sparrows. No data exist on winter philopatry or on dominance hierarchies in this species.

A partial molt, mainly of facial and throat feathers, begins in February and continues at irregular intervals into summer; one researcher suggested that the more or less continuous replacement of plumage in these body areas may help reduce lice (Mallophaga) infestation.

**Ecology.** Field sparrows favor old field and savanna habitats, using scattered small shrubs or trees for perches. Woodland openings and edges, power line rights-of-way, roadsides, fencerows, young conifer plantations, and nurseries are common breeding areas. Unlike several sparrow species, the field sparrow does not appear to be area sensitive and utilizes fragmented habitats, but it rarely resides near houses or in urban areas. Plant succession—the advance of tree and shrub thickets—and consequent habitat change cause the birds to vacate. Fire benefits field sparrows, which often occupy burned savanna and grassland habitats.

Like some other *Spizella* sparrows, field sparrows tend to build early nests of the season on or near the ground in clumps of grass (dried clumps of fall witchgrass are common sites) or at bases of shrubs. "Any type of dense, short vegetation in any open field or on a dry side-hill," wrote Walkinshaw, "might be a nesting site of the Field Sparrow." One 1978 study indicated that new grass growth overtopping the dead grass litter makes ground nest placement unstable, cuing the birds to build in higher sites as the season advances. Most ground nests are sited within a short distance of woody vegetation. Later nests of the season, when leaf foliage is fully grown, are placed up to 4 feet high (usually lower) in crotches of shrubs or small trees. Frequent sites of these nests include blackberry, red

*This typical field sparrow nest was built about 3 feet high in a dogwood shrub. Its placement above ground reveals that it was probably a summer nest for a second brood.*

*Crabgrasses (*Digitaria *spp.), the bane of suburban lawns, are important seed plants for wildlife, especially sparrows and other finches.*

cedar, crab apple, shrubby St. Johnswort, coralberry, honeysuckles, dogwoods, and hawthorns. The nest of dried grasses, lined with finer grasses and sometimes rootlets, averages about 5 inches across. The nest appears rather flimsy and loosely built, hardly anchored, and not very compact, with wispy ends of grass protruding on outside layers.

Mainly seed eaters, field sparrows consume primarily grass seeds, along with some weed seeds. The foremost seed foods include foxtailgrasses, crabgrasses, broom-sedge, panic-grasses, and oats. In summer, however, more than half of the diet consists of insects and spiders—mainly beetles, grasshoppers, and caterpillars. One study noted that "a trend in height opposite from that for nest placement is seen in foraging sites": Invertebrates (insects and spiders) fed to nestlings "seem to be gathered mostly from woody vegetation in May, whereas ground foraging is more important later."

Many researchers have reported field sparrows as being less aggressive than most passerine species, attesting that they seldom, if ever, conflict with other birds—except other field sparrows—in their territories. Competitive interactions appear rare. In Pennsylvania, field and song sparrow habitats overlap extensively, although song sparrows tend to build ground nests farther from shrub or tree growth than those of field sparrows. One 1978 study noted some nest-site competition with chipping sparrows in common juniper shrubs. Also evident was a degree of habitat partitioning in the junipers: The chipping sparrows usually built nests higher than 5 feet, whereas the field sparrows nested lower than 5 feet. As plant succession advances to denser shrub and tree growth, chipping sparrows tend to replace field sparrows. During fall and winter, however, the species frequently forage together in combined flocks. The field sparrow's numerous predators account for most nest failures and desertions. Nest raiders include several snakes—blue racer, milk snake, black rat snake, garter snake, and prairie kingsnake—plus blue jays, American crows, chipmunks, red and gray foxes, weasels, skunks, raccoons, opossums, and others. Brown-headed cowbirds commonly parasitize field sparrow nests, laying one or more eggs. The frequency of cowbird parasitism varies seasonally and geographically from less than 1 percent to 80 percent of field sparrow nests. Nests in May are most heavily parasitized; later nests, when cowbirds have stopped laying, remain uninvaded. Probably the less open, more wooded, and more fragmented habitats favored by cowbirds also have higher rates of parasitism. Many field sparrows abandon cowbird-parasitized nests, rebuilding elsewhere, but some incubate and hatch cowbird nestlings.

**Focus.** Since most field sparrow habitats become quickly transitional as plant succession advances, local population distributions may shift considerably over time. Thoreau, in a remarkable exposition of ecology before such a science existed, noted the occurrence of field sparrows as he set out pines at Walden: "As the pines gradually increase, and a wood-lot is formed, these birds will withdraw to new pastures, and the thrushes, etc., will take their place." Before European settlement, field sparrow populations probably occurred only sparsely in the East, being restricted to forest openings and recent burns. Land clearing and fires may have increased the species' distribution, which probably peaked during the late nineteenth century. Since then, though populations remain abundant, the species has declined (about 3.4 percent per year between 1966 and 1991), mainly owing to land use changes—conversion of old fields into row crops and residential developments—and to plant succession. High rates of predation also affect this bird's abundance. In a Pennsylvania study, only about 40 percent of functional nests succeeded in fledging at least 1 young. Field sparrow populations in some locales cannot maintain themselves by normal *recruitment—*

the annual addition of progeny—and remain stable only by means of juvenile dispersal from other areas.

The oldest field sparrow banding recoveries show a longevity of almost 7 years, but relatively few adults survive beyond 2 or 3 years.

FINCH FAMILY (Fringillidae) - Subfamily Emberizinae - Sparrow-Buntings (Tribe Emberizini)

## Vesper Sparrow *(Pooecetes gramineus)*

Recognize this 6-inch-long, streaked sparrow by its juncolike white outer tail feathers, best seen when the bird flies. A whitish eye ring gives it a wide-eyed appearance. Sexes look alike. Much resembling the song sparrow except for its grayer appearance and square-tipped tail, the vesper also sounds much like the song sparrow. Vesper song begins with 2 slurred notes followed by 2 higher ones, then a trill of musical notes; the effort sounds less bright and breezy, more minor keyed, than song sparrow song.

**Close relatives.** None; the vesper is the only sparrow of its genus.

**Behaviors.** This dusky ground sparrow, though a frequent songster and not especially secretive, is not easily seen as it forages in the grass. When it is alarmed into flight, however, its flash of white tail feathers immediately identifies it. Vesper males seek aboveground perches, usually the tops of small trees or shrubs, only for song sites.

Vesper sparrows relish dust baths, often fluffing themselves in sandy roads or roadsides or in bare patches of fields, where excavated soil mounds of burrowing mammals such as woodchucks provide dusting sites. The vesper is one of the most common "road birds," often roosting in the ruts of dirt roads at night, leaving its tracks and little dust basins in the loose sand and soil. Vespers are not known to use standing water either for bathing or drinking. Apparently, as an adaptation to their dry habitats, they obtain all the moisture they need from their food metabolism and perhaps dew.

Vesper breeding range spans the continent from British Columbia to the Maritime Provinces, extending from mid-Canada and the northern Great Plains into the central tier of states.

*Spring.* Vesper sparrows begin arriving on their breeding sites in late March, with migration peaking in April. The birds have acquired their grayish breeding plumage mainly by wear, having lost most of their brownish feather tips over winter. Vespers exhibit strong *philopatry*—fidelity to previous nesting sites—a remarkable proclivity, in a sense, for a bird that utilizes the ephemeral habitats of early plant succession. Yet, as one research team wrote, "although a particular site may have been suitable Vesper Sparrow breeding habitat for only a few years because of vegetation development, advantages gained from site fidelity evidently [are] great enough to favor evolution [of philopatry]," aiding the bird's exploitation of nesting and food resources. The same argument

*Noted for its melancholy-tinged song and attraction to bare, dusty areas, the vesper sparrow much resembles the song sparrow, both vocally and in appearance; however, it usually occupies drier, more open habitats.*

would presumably apply as well to most other philopatric grassland species.

The frequency rate of monogamy beyond a single season remains unknown; repeat pairings are probably relatively uncommon. Males sing almost continuously when establishing or reestablishing territories, which typically cover slightly more than an acre in size. Most courtship behaviors—mainly male walking, running, and hopping into the air with spread wings and tail in the vicinity of a female—occur on the ground. Nesting typically begins from early to mid-May.

EGGS AND YOUNG: usually 4; eggs white or greenish white, spotted and marked with brown. INCUBATION: by female, occasionally male also; 12 or 13 days; hatching synchronous. FEEDING OF YOUNG: by both sexes; insects. FLEDGING: about 9 days average, though variable.

*Summer.* Vesper sparrows, double brooded throughout most of their range, sometimes even try for 3 nestings, though most breeding activity has ceased by the end of July. Fledglings from the first nesting are fed mainly by the male as the female begins building another nest. Juveniles continue to be fed for several weeks, attaining full independence in a month or so. The annual plumage molt occurs in August, producing a browner appearance from darker edgings of the feathers.

*Fall, Winter.* Migration usually begins in September, extending through October. Vespers often travel and winter in small, loose flocks of 10 birds or less. Lagging vespers are not uncommon, and some may even remain in the breeding range over mild winters. Most of the population, however, winters from the southern United States to southern Mexico. Dense concentrations center especially along the Alabama-Georgia-Florida border.

**Ecology.** Vesper sparrows favor dry, sparsely vegetated, and short-grass habitats; areas of poor soil, old fields, pastures, corn stubble, and hayfields are frequent breeding sites. Orchards, pine plains, and shrub savannas may also host vespers. This is one of the few birds that nests successfully on golf courses because the countersunk nest survives the mowing of fairways. "In the forests of the north," wrote Minnesota ornithologist T. S. Roberts, "every clearing, old burned-over area, wind-fall, or cut-over region has its considerable quota of vesper sparrows." Important habitat components include song perches—fences, scattered trees or shrubs, or tall weeds. Lack of elevated song perches may limit vesper sparrow abundance in otherwise suitable habitats. A 1979 study indicated a gradient of breeding habitat preferences for vesper, savannah, and grasshopper sparrows: Vespers selected areas with low or sparse plant density; savannahs chose those with intermediate plant density; and grasshopper sparrows favored high-density vegetation. (This study contradicts some others in ranking sparrow cover preferences.) Winter habitats include tree and scrub savannas of the Southwest, though the birds avoid creosote bush areas.

Vesper sparrows build their nests, rims flush with the ground litter, in small depressions they scrape. The nest, a bulky mass of dry grasses and weed stalks lined with finer grasses and rootlets, usually lies in a grass tussock or at the base of a plant. It measures 4 or 5 inches across.

The foremost seed foods include *Cyperus* sedges, foxtail-grasses, wild oatgrasses, panic-grasses, ragweeds, smartweeds, pigweeds, and many other weed seeds. Animal food, more than half the total diet in summer, consists chiefly of beetles, grasshoppers, caterpillars, and ants.

Little, if any, competition with other bird species exists. Vespers occasionally chase song and field sparrows from their territory, but these species often nest fairly close to vespers. Vespers are also nesting associates of the rare Kirtland's warbler in its jack-pine habitats. Habitat partitioning, though subtle, may help vespers avoid conflict with other grassland sparrows. Such division of resources is also seen among vesper, savannah, and grasshopper sparrows in winter grassland habitat; in contrast to its preference for low-density nesting cover, the vesper usually forages closer to mesquite cover than the other species (see Savannah Sparrow).

Nest predators include most of the usual ground-nest raiders: garter snakes, ground squirrels, skunks, and raccoons, among others. Farm machinery (though probably not mowing) destroys many cropland nests. Accipiter hawks and shrikes occasionally capture adult vespers, and brown-headed cowbirds frequently parasitize early-season nests; most vesper sparrow nests I have found in May contained a cowbird egg. Vesper nests located near woodlots or thickets show higher rates of cowbird parasitism than nests farther out in the open. "Thickets and trees," wrote researcher A. J. Berger, "apparently provide perches and cover for female cowbirds on the

*The garter snake is a common predator of ground nests, devouring eggs and nestlings.*

alert for nest building activity." Later-season nests remain relatively unparasitized owing to the cowbirds' fairly short egg-laying period in spring.

**Focus.** Vesper sparrows probably were far less abundant before European settlement than they are today in eastern North America. Nineteenth-century forest clearing and agriculture extended their open habitats eastward from the Great Plains. Northeastern populations apparently peaked about 1900. Although vespers remain common in many areas, dramatic fluctuations in their abundance—especially since the 1960s—have occurred in other areas, and their decline has been more or less continuous over much of their range since the 1940s. Vespers are currently listed as endangered in New Jersey and Rhode Island. Much of the loss countrywide has been attributed to shrinkage of farmland habitats and changes in farming practices. The growth of corporate farming and consequent large-scale cultivation, plus the use of chemicals and pesticides, quite effectively limit seed and insect food resources for grassland birds.

Research shows that no-tillage agriculture enhances vesper sparrow reproductive success because of reduced field machinery operations. Moderate to heavy grazing and, in some places, prescribed burning also benefit these birds. One area into which vespers have expanded their range in recent years is reclaimed strip-mined land of

West Virginia and Ohio; vespers, it appears, are one of the first bird species to reoccupy these lands. Vespers tolerate high degrees of habitat fragmentation. One study concluded that less than 25 acres of contiguous grassland can maintain viable breeding populations; other studies give figures of 25 to 250 acres as optimal habitat sizes.

The name *vesper* stems from a romantic notion of naturalist John Burroughs that the bird sang more sweetly at dusk than at any other time. During spring, the birds may commonly sing after sunset, but no more frequently than several other birds. Before Burroughs indulged his fancy, the bird was more accurately labeled the bay-winged bunting, grass finch, or grass-bird.

Banded vesper sparrows have been recovered at age six, but probably half that age is a more typical longevity.

## Wood Warblers (Tribe Parulini)

Birds of the tribe Parulini, some 115 species, all reside in the Western Hemisphere. Forty warbler species (most in the genera *Dendroica, Vermivora,* and *Oporonis*) breed in eastern North America, and most of these reside for all but a few months of the year in the tropics. These small, 4- to 6-inch-long birds have slender, sharp-pointed bills. In the spring, most, though not all, show brilliant yellow plumage on some part of the body. Songs are distinctive for each species. Warblers "lisp, buzz, hiss, chip, rollick, or zip," wrote one observer; few actually warble, a trilling song description better ascribed to sparrows. The name probably derives from the group's resemblance to Old World warblers (family Sylviidae).

Migrant warblers are usually among the last bird arrivals in spring. Seldom remaining still for long, they hyperactively forage in well-defined *niches,* the roles in a habitat particular to a species, ranging from ground surface to treetops. Warbler species generally favor particular stages of plant succession, from transitional edges to mature forest. Warblers can be classified by foraging sites into 3 broad categories: those that feed primarily in trees (most warblers), in brush, and on the ground.

Today many wood warbler species are profoundly at risk, showing steadily decreasing abundance in areas where not so long ago
they thrived. Severely affected by habitat fragmentation in their
breeding range, and probably by Neotropical rain-forest destruction
as well, our dwindling warbler populations are alarming indicators of
environmental decline.

FINCH FAMILY (Fringillidae) - Subfamily Emberizinae - Wood Warblers (Tribe Parulini)

## Blue-winged Warbler *(Vermivora pinus)*

Recognize this 5-inch-long warbler by its yellow forehead and underparts; olive green back; gray-blue wings, each with 2 white bars; and
a black line through the eye. Sexes look much alike, with females
wearing somewhat duller plumage and less yellow on the crown. The
distinctive song is a 2-part, buzzy "swe-e-e-e zee-e-e-e," the first note
higher than the second; it is sometimes likened to an inhale-exhale
sound.

**Close relatives.** Eight other *Vermivora* warbler species exist.
Northeastern summer residents include the golden-winged warbler
*(V. chrysoptera)*, Tennessee warbler *(V. peregrina)*, orange-crowned
warber *(V. celata)*, and Nashville warbler *(V. ruficapilla)*. Virginia's
warbler *(V. virginiae)*, Colima warbler *(V. crissalis)*, and Lucy's warbler *(V. luciae)* reside in the Southwest, and Bachman's warbler *(V.
bachmanii)* in the Southeast.

**Behaviors.** This attractive warbler of abandoned fields and other
habitats is fairly easy to see and identify both by sight and sound. Its
dreamy, somnolent song could be mistaken for an insect's buzz.

Blue-wings conduct most of their activities close to the ground,
foraging mainly in small trees and shrubs. They commonly probe
into curled leaves, both green and dead. Their movements, often
compared to those of vireos, seem silent and deliberate, unlike the
nervous, incessant fluttering of many tree warblers. Sometimes a
blue-wing forages while hanging head-downward from a twig like a
chickadee.

Blue-winged warbler breeding range occupies only that portion
of the continent east of the Great Plains, from the southern Great

*The blue-winged warbler has become a common resident of disturbed landscapes;
it is probably much more numerous now than before land clearing and settlement.*

Lakes to northern Georgia—the area ecologists once labeled the Carolinian life zone.

*Spring.* Relatively late migrators, as are most warblers, blue-wings arrive on their breeding range in late April to mid- May. Most travel across the Gulf of Mexico from the Yucatan Peninsula, and thence up the Mississippi and Ohio River Valleys to their destinations. Males precede females by about a day. Frequency of *philopatry,* fidelity to the previous year's breeding territory, is variable. Monogamous pairing that spans more than a single breeding season is rare.

Males establish territories that, in most habitats, average from slightly more than an acre to about 5 acres in size. They vocalize from song perches atop shrubs or trees in the territory; spring is probably the only time of year, except during migration travel, that they get this far above ground. Blue-wing males emit 2 distinct song types: the characteristic 2-part "bee-buzz," the basic territorial song; and the so-called nesting song, a variable succession of short and long buzzy notes, sometimes slurring up or down and often voiced in flight. This second song, heard after pairing has occurred and nesting has begun, bears close resemblance among all blue-wings in a local population, though individual birds may sing several versions of the local dialect. The song varies geographically, however, so that even experienced birders who learn the song dialect in Pennsylvania may not recognize the blue-wing song in Michigan or Iowa.

Pairing occurs quickly once the females arrive. Males exhibit 2 types of flight displays: a slow "moth flight," with firm wingbeats, and a long, coasting glide flight. Females initiate copulation by the soliciting posture characteristic of many passerines, with lowered breast, raised tail, vibrating wings. Sexual activity appears most intense just before and during the first day of nest building, usually in mid- to late May. The birds readily abandon partially completed nests or egg clutches if disturbed.

EGGS AND YOUNG: typically 5; eggs white, finely brown spotted mainly at larger end. INCUBATION: by female; 10 or 11 days. FEEDING OF YOUNG: by both sexes; small insects. FLEDGING: 8 to 10 days.

*Summer.* Blue-wings apparently raise only a single brood per year, at least in the northern portion of their range. Details of their postnesting activities remain obscure, though parents probably divide the brood and continue to feed fledglings for about a month. Song ceases with the end of nesting in June, and the birds become elusive and inconspicuous in behavior. The annual molt, which occurs in July, produces a new, lemon yellow plumage with greenish-tipped crown feathers. Erosion of these greenish ends during winter produces the spring breeding plumage. Southward migration begins in mid-August, peaking from late August to mid-September.

*Fall, Winter.* Blue-winged warblers travel mainly to Mexico and Central America down to Panama, some also to Caribbean islands. Most migrate across the Gulf of Mexico in nonstop flight.

On the winter range, they often forage in mixed warbler species flocks. One research team reported, however, that wintering blue-wings and golden-wings seem never to become "gregarious with their own species. When they join a mixed-species flock, they appear to treat it as a territory, and drive away members of their own species." This "flock as territory" phenomenon has also been observed in worm-eating warblers.

Northward migration begins in March.

**Ecology.** This species seems to confound the usual tenets of restricted habitat selection. Blue-winged warblers, and also golden-winged warblers and to some extent common yellowthroats, range across wet and dry, upland and lowland, open and wooded habitats. Typically, however, blue-wings thrive in old fields, early shrub successions, or savanna areas of dense shrubs bordered by open grassy areas. Golden-wings are said to utilize earlier, less advanced stages of plant succession than blue-wings. Sources differ on whether blue-wings generally favor wetter or drier habitats than golden-wings. Research data, in fact, permit few general conclusions about blue-wing habitats that apply universally across the breeding range.

Blue-wing nests, well concealed on the ground, or sometimes up to a foot above ground, are bulky structures, deep and narrow, often conelike in shape—a "rather unusual and distinctive" structure, according to at least one nest expert. Attached to upright weed stalks or a tuft of grass, the nest may lie among blackberry canes, beneath a shrub, or between stump roots, often along a shaded field edge. The foundation of dead leaves, usually with leaf stems facing

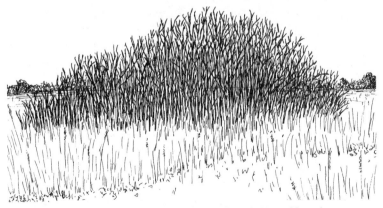

*Blue-winged warblers occupy a variety of wet and dry habitats. Many, however, favor abandoned fields that contain a substantial component of scattered brush, as exemplified by this solitary gray dogwood clone.*

outward, supports a coarse structure of dead grasses, more leaves, and bark shreds, lined with finer grasses, bark fibers, and hairs. The birds often use the bark of wild grapevines, laying bark strips across instead of around the cup, and overlaying them with fine grass stems. The nest measures 4 or 5 inches across.

Blue-wings capture most of their insect food by prying open curled leaves. Their foremost prey includes tortricid and other moths and their caterpillars, plus spiders. The birds also extract and consume spittlebugs (froghopper nymphs) from their foamy masses on plant stems.

Puzzling interactions of blue-winged and golden-winged warblers, sibling species, have fueled decades of controversy and research. Most researchers have regarded the two as competitors, with blue-wing populations gradually replacing golden-wings throughout much of the latter's range. Possible reproductive isolating mechanisms, however, seem obscure and ill defined. The blue-wing is said to be a more adaptable habitat generalist than the golden-wing. In some areas, at least, peak spring arrival of blue-wings precedes that of golden-wings, perhaps a competitive advantage. The species hybridize, producing fertile hybrids known as Brewster's warblers and the much rarer Lawrence's warblers. Each of these hybrids bears different plumage. Neither hybrid frequently breeds with other Brewster's or Lawrence's warblers; each, rather, tends to backcross with the parent species—"perhaps just because a parental species is so much more common," suggested one observer. "Because Blue-winged and Golden-winged warblers are so similar ecologically," wrote one research team, "and because they are certainly capable of hybridizing, one might expect the evolution of interspecific territoriality in these species." A principle of ecology is that 2 species competing for the same resources cannot coexist indefinitely. Yet blue-wing and golden-wing territories often overlap; the birds rarely defend them against each other. Indeed, males of each species usually ignore each other, and the frequency of hybridization averages only 5 to 10 percent. Recent researchers have, in fact, concluded that competition between the species—if indeed it exists at all—cannot account for the decline of golden-winged warblers or for their replacement by blue-wings.

Probably the same predators that prey on most ground nests—snakes, ground squirrels, skunks, raccoons, foxes, and others—likewise raid those of the low-nesting *Vermivora*. Brown-headed cowbirds frequently parasitize their nests.

**Focus.** Discovered by naturalist William Bartram and named the pine creeper by George Edwards in the eighteenth century, this bird later became known as the blue-winged yellow warbler. Its species name *pinus* misassociates it with pine trees, one of the few habitats the bird rarely uses. (Taxonomists invariably choose tradition over accuracy in nomenclature.)

*Vermivora* bills, adapted to probing into buds and curled leaves, are very straight with sharply acute tips, whereas most *Dendroica* warbler bills, adapted to gleaning and hawking insects, exhibit a decurved tip on the upper bill plus a slight notch in the cutting edge (see illustration, Golden-winged Warbler).

"Bird census techniques that use bird calls," wrote researcher John L. Confer, "face severe difficulty" with blue-wings and golden-wings. The difficulty stems from the fact that certain individuals of each species consistently give the song of the other species. Hybrid songs match those of the parent species and are not intermediate in form. Usually, however, the species' songs sound distinctly different (see Golden-winged Warbler). Some naturalists have speculated that insectlike birdsong may represent cases of evolutionary mimicry from the surrounding acoustic environment, also applying to grasshopper, savannah, and Henslow's sparrows, among others.

Probably the most notable current *fact* about blue-winged warblers is their changing distribution. Their ongoing range expansion—north, east, and west—is apparently displacing golden-winged warblers in many areas. Blue-wings historically occurred west of the Appalachians, becoming established east of that range by about 1850. Most researchers attribute their successful expansion to changing land uses, especially the creation of open and early successional habitats. But golden-wings, which often occupy the same types of habitat, have not likewise expanded their distribution. In short, much of what has passed for knowledge about these species has been guesswork at best.

Banded blue-winged warblers have been recovered at 5 and almost 6 years of age, but given the hazards of migration, weather, and predation, probably relatively few survive that long.

FINCH FAMILY (Fringillidae) - Subfamily Emberizinae - Wood Warblers (Tribe Parulini)

# Golden-winged Warbler *(Vermivora chrysoptera)*

Recognize this 5-inch-long close relative of the blue-winged warbler *(V. pinus)* by the combination of yellow wing patch and black throat and eye patch (grayish in females). Both sexes exhibit a white belly and yellow forehead and crown. The typical song is an insectlike "zeeeee-bee bee bee," the first note higher and drawn out.

**Close relatives.** See Blue-winged Warbler.

**Behaviors.** This species so closely resembles the blue-winged warbler in almost all aspects except plumage pattern that most behavioral and seasonal descriptions of the previous account equally apply (see Blue-winged Warbler). A usual, though not invariable, distinction is the song. Two male golden-wing song types include the typical 4-note buzzing song and a rapid, stuttering sequence of notes followed by a lower buzzy note. The first song type predominates early in the breeding season before nesting begins; it sometimes continues for hours, often from a high perch. This song diminishes in frequency after pair formation, the number of "bee" notes sometimes declining to just one, as in the blue-wing song. The second song type becomes more frequent as nesting proceeds, continuing until the nestlings fledge. Golden-wing territories often occupy a somewhat larger area than blue-wing territories, ranging from 1 to 14 acres in size.

*Warbler bills differ somewhat in shape. The golden-winged warbler bill (top) is sharply acute, whereas the prairie warbler bill (bottom) has a decurved tip.*

Often observed is an association between golden-winged warblers and black-capped chickadees, especially during late summer and the fall migration (other warblers may also join chickadee flocks at these times). The two species exhibit certain similarities in facial and song patterns, though not in pitch and duration of song. Their foraging habits on tree branches are similar, they often show attraction toward each other, and their territories frequently overlap. Golden-wings migrate, whereas many, if not most, chickadees reside year-round (see *Birds of Forest, Yard, and Thicket*). The research team of Millicent and Robert W. Ficken suggested that a *mutualism*—an interaction from which both derive benefit—may exist between these species: The warblers benefit by sharing the resident chickadee feeding areas and by chickadee alertness to local predators; the chickadees gain access to insects in buds that are opened by the sharper-billed warblers. "The Golden-wing may not take all the insects available from buds because the warbler is rapidly displaced by the approach of the chickadee," said the Fickens, who further suggested that the facial plumage similarities may have evolved as a result of "social mimicry." These mutual markings may trigger behaviors that facilitate mixing of the species in flocks.

Golden-wing breeding range spans eastern North America from southern Canada to the southern Great Lakes, southern New England, and south in the Appalachians to northern Georgia. Winter range extends from the Yucatan Peninsula in Mexico southward to Colombia and northern Venezuela; populations center mainly in the highlands of Costa Rica and Panama.

---

EGGS AND YOUNG: typically 5; eggs pinkish or white, finely marked with brown, mainly at larger end. INCUBATION: by female; 10 or 11 days. FEEDING OF YOUNG: by both sexes; small insects. FLEDGING: 8 or 9 days; juveniles fly at about 10 days.

---

**Ecology.** It is difficult to generalize about this bird's habitat requirements, which as in blue-winged warblers, appear to differ with the region. They span a broad variety of sites including swampy woodlands, stream thickets, abandoned fields, conifer plantations, and others. The most consistent habitat pattern appears to be a patchy mosaic of sedges or grasses with scattered shrubs and trees, plus a nearby forest edge. In some areas where both species occur, golden-wings seem to favor earlier, more open stages of plant succession; in other places, the two apparently share habitats about equally. Winter habitat mainly consists of semiopen forests, openings, and edges. Loss of winter habitat, which has been suggested as a cause of golden-wing population declines, is not supported by evidence, say recent researchers.

Nesting and food characteristics of golden-wings do not differ significantly from those of blue-winged warblers. The nest is often slightly tilted, leaf stems and bark fragments sometimes projecting a few inches above the nest rim. Favored food items include geometrid caterpillars, or inchworms, found on leaves.

The role of competition between these sibling species and its possible bearing upon widespread golden-wing declines remain unresolved matters among researchers. Some investigators detect a pattern of golden-wing replacement by blue-wings within several decades of initial contact between them. "I know of no localities with breeding Golden-wings," wrote researcher Frank B. Gill in 1980, "where Blue-wings have been established for 50 years or more." The precise mechanism of such replacement—by social dominance and interference by blue-wings, by direct competition for space or resources, by hybridization that proves maladaptive for the golden-wing genotype, or simply by habitat changes—remains puzzling. Results of recent studies seem to challenge dominance, competition, and hybridization theories as explanations for golden-wing declines. While both species appear more adaptable than most birds in utilizing a variety of habitats, the golden-wing appears less adaptable than the blue-wing when the two become *sympatric*, occupying the same geographic area. "If the present trend continues for another 100 years," predicted Gill, "it seems probable that the Golden-winged Warbler will be a very rare species, if not extinct." ("I agree," remarked ecologist Richard Brewer, "but it seems to me that if present trends continue, a whole lot of other species will be extinct too.")

Prowling mammals and accipiter hawks are probably the foremost predators, though data are skimpy. Brown-headed cowbirds parasitize about 30 percent of all golden-wing nests, reducing fledgling rates by about 17 percent. In some cases, the warblers abandon parasitized nests; not infrequently, however, they raise a cowbird nestling along with their own.

**Focus.** Breeding range of the golden-wing has fluctuated for almost 150 years and continues to change. Changes have generally consisted of retrenchment at the southeastern limits of the range and expansion at the northern and northwestern limits. In New York, for example, a northward range expansion of about 300 miles has occurred since about 1900, concurrent with declines in the southern New England states. Likewise, golden-wing distribution appears to be shifting from the southern to the more northern Great Lakes areas. The widespread distribution of autumn-olive *(Elaeagnus umbellata)*, an introduced shrub planted for game cover in some states, has reduced suitable habitat for golden-wings, according to researcher Robert B. Payne. Yet many researchers remain uncertain as to how many of these changes in golden-wing distribution owe primarily to habitat changes—given the birds' adaptability to many open and semiopen environments—or to competition from blue-winged warblers, which now inhabit much former golden-wing range (see Blue-winged Warbler). In some areas, blue-wings appear behaviorally dominant to golden-wings, but this pattern remains far from universally consistent. Also, as Payne wrote, "with Blue-winged Warblers continually entering their range, the Golden-winged Warblers may be swamped through introgression by genes of the other species." Though it is true that golden-wings have disappeared from many areas within 50 years of blue-wing invasion, in some areas of optimal habitat (despite the difficulty in defining what is optimal for these species)—notably southern New York and adjacent New Jersey—both species have coexisted for more than a century. Obviously, much remains to be learned about some extremely complex patterns of population ecology in both of these species.

Longevity and lifetime nesting success data are sparse. A banded golden-wing was recovered at almost 7 years of age, but probably relatively few golden-wings live to half that age.

# Prairie Warbler *(Dendroica discolor)*

The 4- to 5-inch-long prairie warbler exhibits bright yellow under-parts with black side stripes, a yellow rump, and olive green upper parts. Black lines through and below the eye enclose a yellow face patch. Sexes look mostly alike, except that at close range, males show chestnut marks on the back, and females have somewhat duller plumage. The song, a thin "zee zee zee zee zee zeet!" rises up the scale.

**Close relatives.** *Dendroica* is the largest New World warbler genus. Twenty-one of the 27 *Dendroica* warblers breed in North America; of these, 13 are northeastern species. They include the yellow warbler *(D. petechia)*, chestnut-sided warbler *(D. pensylvanica)*, yellow-rumped warbler *(D. coronata)*, and the rare Kirtland's warbler *(D. kirtlandii)*, among others.

**Behaviors.** All warbler bills are efficient insect-catching devices, but *Dendroica* bills differ slightly from the others, more adapted to gleaning and hawking insects than to probing for them. Unlike the very acute, sharp-pointed bill of *Vermivora* warblers, typical *Dendroica* bills have a decurved tip plus a slight notch in the upper bill, probably an aid to crushing prey (see illustration, Golden-winged Warbler).

Prairie warblers exhibit a characteristic behavioral trait of bobbing the tail when perched, a useful identity feature shared by few other northeastern birds, which include American kestrels, eastern phoebes, hermit thrushes, waterthrushes, and palm warblers. Prairie warblers also flutter their wings frequently, a behavior that may startle insect prey into movement. They also chase flying insects and glean while hovering.

Breeding range of the prairie warbler extends from southern Canada and South Dakota to the Gulf states. Populations center in the southern two-thirds of the United States.

*Spring.* A late migrant, the prairie warbler arrives on its northern range about mid-May, though it often begins its journey northward in early March. Males, arriving about 5 days before females, exhibit

*The prairie warbler, shown here on an untypical perch, frequents open shrublands, not prairies. Its tail-bobbing habit helps identify it.*

strong site tenacity *(philopatry)* to the previous year's territory. Females show much less site fidelity, and thus most prairie warbler pairings last only a single season. Males perform courtship and territorial displays consisting of chases and short, fluttering display flights. Male song, voiced from the tops of trees, may last into July; females also sing occasionally.

As incubation proceeds, about 15 percent of male prairie warblers court and mate with one or more additional females, making this species the most *polygynous* of all wood warblers. This reproductive strategy may in this case be an evolutionary response to territorial overcrowding in optimal habitats, a situation that led early observers to term these warblers colonial, or to the high rates of nest predation that occur in this species.

EGGS AND YOUNG: typically 4; eggs white, brown spotted, often wreathed at larger end. INCUBATION: by female; about 12 days. FEEDING OF YOUNG: by both sexes; mainly caterpillars. FLEDGING: about 10 days.

*Summer.* Prairie warblers usually raise only a single brood in the North but may raise a second in the middle and southern range if the first nesting succeeds. Predation takes such a heavy toll of prairie warbler nests in some areas that females may make as many as 5 or more renesting attempts following nest failures. Parents typically divide up the brood, each guarding and feeding 1 or 2 fledglings until they become independent at 40 to 50 days. Adults perform wing-quivering distraction displays when fledglings are threatened. The annual molt occurs about mid-July. Juveniles, which gather in loose feeding groups, now wear a duller version of the adult plumage, with faint jaw, eye, and side stripes. Southward migration, which begins soon after molting is finished, usually peaks before the end of August.

*Fall, Winter.* Prairie warblers winter from central Florida to the Bahamas and West Indies, south to Nicaragua in Central America. A year-round prairie warbler population resides in coastal mangrove sites of southern Florida.

Prairie warblers may associate in loose flocks with other warbler species as they forage; researcher Cynthia A. Staicer maintained the contrary, however, saying that "several lines of evidence suggest that the Prairie Warbler adopts a winter strategy of avoidance of other warblers." The birds exhibit strong winter site fidelity, but territoriality remains undetected.

Prairie warblers undergo a partial molt of head, chin, and throat feathers before spring migration, producing the vivid black markings of the breeding plumage. Chestnut markings now become visible as feather tips wear off on the back.

**Ecology.** Not a grassland bird, the misnamed prairie warbler frequents low, shrubby growth. Early ornithologist Alexander Wilson named it for the Kentucky site where he found it, a brushy upland area locally called a prairie. Two later well-known ornithologists, Ludlow Griscom and Alexander Sprunt, Jr., proposed the more appropriate name of scrub warbler for this species. In most areas, prairie warblers favor open shrub habitats—sand dunes, pine plains, old burns, abandoned farmland, and young Christmas tree plantations. ("In western Pennsylvania," wrote warbler researcher Hal H. Harrison, "northward expansion of the Prairie's breeding range seems to be by extension from one Christmas tree planting to the next.") Preferred brushy vegetation seldom stands more than 25 feet high. Prairie warbler breeding habitats generally exhibit dry, sandy soil. Winter habitat consists mainly of mangrove forest and lowland pine savanna associated with palms, as well as open brushland similar to summer sites. Labeled a winter habitat generalist by several researchers, prairie warblers in Puerto Rico exhibit preferences for pithecellobium and tamarindus trees.

Prairie warbler nests appear fairly distinctive because of the ample felted materials used. Plant down and fibers, moss stems, and feathers are compactly woven with fine grasses, dry leaves, and bark shreds, all bound with spider silk. In areas where sheep or cotton is raised, wool or cotton becomes a common construction material, and the birds also use the gray leaves of cudweed or everlastings *(Gnaphalium)*. Audubon reported that "at first sight, [the nest] seems to be formed like that of the Humming-bird . . . of delicate grey lichens . . . and skins of black caterpillars, and the interior finished with the finest fibres of dried vines." Nests, about 3 inches across, usually lie attached and concealed in the fork of a leafy shrub or small tree, commonly less than 3 or 4 feet high. Hazelnut, small jackpines, red pines, and common or ground juniper are common shrub and small tree hosts for prairie warbler nests. Female prairie warblers often build one or more dummy nests, either whole or in part, before completing a nest they actually use. Such habits, though common in wrens and a few other birds, are rare among warblers.

Prairie warbler diet consists almost entirely of insects and spiders on both summer and winter ranges. The birds devour large quantities of true bugs including aphids, plus grasshoppers, caterpillars, and spiders.

Competition with other species, so far as known, is negligible.

The foremost predators of this species include snakes, which raid many nests, resulting in numerous nesting failures. Red squirrels and chipmunks are also known predators. A common nest parasite is the brown-headed cowbird. Many prairie warblers abandon their nests after the egg-laying visit of a cowbird. Sometimes, however, the host bird builds another floor over the egg and lays her own eggs.

**Focus.** Historical breeding distribution of the prairie warbler probably centered in the Southeast, mainly in fire-disrupted pinelands and other scrublands. Northward, prairie warblers may have inhabited Great Lakes dune country and pine plains, where they still reside in irregular, scattered distribution. Although land clearing and fires created vast new areas of open habitat, perhaps leading to northward range expansion, researchers noted continental declines of this species during the 1970s, and its occurrence has become relatively more spotty in many formerly productive sites since then. Its numbers in certain pine habitat areas, especially, seem to fluctuate widely. Since suitable breeding habitats for the species appear abundant, however, some researchers believe that the loss of Caribbean wintering habitats, where many prairie warblers reside for most of the year, may at least partially account for the declines.

Longevity data remain scarce for this species. Rhode Island banders aged 1 prairie warbler a few months past a decade, but probably most adults survive only 1 or 2 breeding seasons.

---

# (Tribe Cardinalini)

---

## Dickcissel *(Spiza americana)*

Identify this 6- to 7-inch-long grassland finch by the yellowish line over its eye, its white throat, and its chestnut shoulder patch. Sexes differ: In breeding plumage, the male exhibits a yellow breast with a black bib, much like a meadowlark; the female resembles a female house sparrow, but with a white throat lined by a narrow dark streak on the side, a yellowish patch on the breast, and a bluish bill. Male song consists of a staccato, incessant "dick-ciss-ciss-ciss," "dick-dick cissel-cissel-cissel," or "chup-chup-klip-klip-klip."

**Close relatives.** The dickcissel belongs to a tribe of finches called the Cardinalini, or cardinal-grosbeaks, consisting of 42 species worldwide. The powerful jaw muscles and heavy bills of these birds enable them to feed by cracking seeds. No other *Spiza* species exists, but North American relatives include the rose-breasted grosbeak *(Pheucticus ludovicianus),* the northern cardinal *(Cardinalis*

*cardinalis),* and the indigo bunting *(Passerina cyanea.)* (See *Birds of Forest, Yard, and Thicket* for accounts of these species.)

**Behaviors.** Exceedingly social birds at all times of year, dickcissels often migrate and winter in large flocks and even nest together in loose colonies. Dickcissels, essentially grassland birds, often associate in the same habitats with the similar-looking eastern and western meadowlarks and—especially at winter yard feeders—house sparrows. (The house sparrow association may be another example of "social mimicry"; see Golden-winged Warbler.) Yet dickcissels, notorious for their erratic fluctuations and unreliable appearance, especially at the peripheries of their breeding range, arrive much less consistently from year to year than the meadowlarks. Their unpredictable, on-again off-again presence makes them an exceedingly difficult species to monitor and has fueled several generations of ornithological speculation. Where present, however, dickcissels are easily observed. Males sing from conspicuous perches, usually fence posts, power lines, or shrubs.

Dickcissel breeding range extends eastward from the Great Plains to the Appalachians and southward from Manitoba and the southern Great Lakes to southern Texas and Georgia. Except in its center of abundance, the tall-grass prairie region, populations are erratic, occurring irregularly from year to year. In Michigan, for example, the northern edge of the breeding

*Male dickcissels are incessant singers. This bird's shifting distribution and unpredictable frequency of appearance still puzzle researchers.*

range, dickcissel influxes peaked in 1973 and 1988, with several lesser incursions in between. One foremost researcher, Stephen Fretwell, stated that dickcissel populations seem to peak in 7-year cycles.

*Spring.* Dickcissels begin migrating from their South American and Caribbean wintering areas in March, but the birds seldom arrive on their northern breeding range before May—late May in some areas. Unlike most passerine species, which exhibit greater or lesser degrees of *philopatry,* or site fidelity, to previous breeding areas, dickcissels tend to shift these locales from year to year. Males arrive a week to 10 days before females; a dozen or more pairs may form a loosely colonial aggregation of nesters. Sexual chasing by males and inciting displays by females occur in early stages of pairing. Territories, ranging from 1 to almost 3 acres, typically change in size and shape throughout the breeding season, depending upon male population density. This, in turn, depends greatly upon the density of vegetation present in the habitat: Thickly vegetated sites attract many more dickcissels than sparse growth. Mated males also claim significantly larger territories than bachelors. A density of 14 to 20 males per 100 acres of habitat seems average.

Unlike males of most passerine birds, male dickcissels share none of the nuptial tasks. They remain attentive to females but usually do not help feed nestlings—which may starve in the nest if the female is killed—or fledglings. What males do is sing, loudly and long, often through the midday hours, when other birds lapse into silence, and on into the evening. Male singing may, as in red-eyed vireos, provide a vital stimulus to female incubation. Males also copulate, sometimes with neighboring females and usually at exposed perches, for *polygyny* is fairly common in this species. Given the irregular availability of suitable nesting sites in male territories, polygyny carries adaptive advantages, allowing all females the chance to reproduce. Females distribute themselves without regard to territorial males, only to adequate nesting sites. Males may mate with as many as 8 or more females in a season, but such matings are sequential, separated by periods of 4 to 8 days. A male "takes his many mates one at a time," wrote Fretwell, "attending each one until she is well into her nesting cycle, and then seeking another." Thus

no 2 females on a territory are ever in exactly the same phase
of nesting.

Another remarkable behavior of male dickcissels, usually occurring early in the nesting season, is their proclivity for making occasional distant flights off territory—sometimes far off. One study
suggested that these are basically reconnaissance flights, in which
the males visually assess habitat suitability in other areas. Males
occupying poorer-quality habitats and with few mates were found to
engage most often in distant flights. Most nesting in the northern
range begins in June.

EGGS AND YOUNG: usually 4; eggs pale blue, glossy. INCUBA-
TION: by female; about 12 days. FEEDING OF YOUNG: by female;
mainly caterpillars, grasshoppers, crickets. FLEDGING: about 9
days; first flight occurs about 2 or 3 days after fledging.

*Summer.* Dickcissel nesting may extend into August, depending
upon local conditions and habitats. Early failures caused by predation, mowing, or grazing of nest sites may result in midseason renesting and relocation of individuals, sometimes of entire colonies.
Most researchers believe that dickcissels are, with rare exceptions,
single brooded throughout most of the breeding range. Fretwell,
however, suggested that many dickcissels may actually be double
brooded, "raising their first brood in a southern location [Texas] and
their second farther north [Kansas]." Evidence for such wholesale
midseason shifts seems skimpy at best.

Female dickcissels regularly fly outside the territory to obtain
food for nestlings. Females continue to feed fledglings for about 2
weeks, more or less maintaining family groups even as large premigratory flocks form. Before the annual molt, which occurs in July and
August, the disparity between male and female activity levels
becomes physically evident: Male feathers look only slightly worn,
whereas female plumage is extremely soiled and damaged, the outer
tail feathers sometimes eroded down to their central shafts. Molting
produces a brighter plumage on males, except for the black bib,
which is obscured by the whitish tips of the new feathers.

Large communal roosts of several hundred dickcissels may form in August, frequently in overgrown fields or along weedy ditches. Migration occurs in often large, compact flocks from late August through September. *Fall, Winter.* Strays may linger on the northern range into October, and a few dickcissels often remain over winter in the Northeast; usually they are seen among flocks of house sparrows. The densest winter aggregations that remain in the United States settle along the Mississippi River valley. Most of the continental dickcissel population, however, vacates the United States, many birds flying across the Gulf of Mexico, to reside from central Mexico into northern South America. Wintering populations center in the llanos, or grasslands, of Venezuela, where, a 1995 research team wrote, almost all of the world's dickcissels "converge on a winter range that is minute compared with their vast Midwestern breeding grounds." The birds communally roost in sugarcane fields and bamboo forests, emerge each morning in tornadolike clouds, then scatter in smaller foraging flocks throughout the llanos. Dickcissels in the llanos occupy some 15 communal roosts, a single one of which sometimes holds up to 3 million birds. Recently, however, dickcissels have also wintered in areas of Central America, where they have not previously been known to winter in large numbers. The birds typically forage and roost in both large and small winter flocks.

Before northward migration, males attain their black-bibbed breeding plumage by erosion of the white-tipped breast and throat feathers, and also by a partial molt of head and throat feathers.

**Ecology.** Dickcissels favor open land with thick herbal growth; abandoned fields being invaded by small shrubs, hayfields (especially clover and alfalfa), and ungrazed tall-grass prairies are frequent habitats. Grazed pastures host fewer numbers. Although dickcissels probably resided mainly in native prairie regions and eastern forest openings before European settlement, they now thrive best in disturbed and agricultural sites. Studies have shown that dickcissel nesting success is about 5 times greater in old-field than in tall-grass prairie habitats. Each habitat type also influences dickcissel populations by the foremost predators it hosts, as detailed later in this section. In winter, the birds inhabit grasslands and rice fields.

The bulky nest, placed on or near the ground in rank growth or clumps of grass, clover, alfalfa, thistles, awl-aster *(Aster pilosus)*, or other weeds, consists of coarse stems interwoven with leaves and fibers. Finer grasses and rootlets line the nest. "The materials used seem to be those near at hand," reported one researcher, "and vary according to the immediate surroundings," with some nests largely consisting of a single grass species. The nest measures almost 5 inches across. Some nests rest a few inches above ground, loosely supported by surrounding plants. The birds also occasionally build in hedges and low shrubs up to 2 or 3 feet high, sometimes higher.

Adult dickcissels devour seed mainly during winter, when they consume vast quantities of weed and grass seeds and waste grains. Millet appears a favorite staple at yard feeders. Adult seed food on the breeding range (about 30 percent of the diet) consists mainly of foxtail-grasses, plus oats and other grains. Spiders and insects—mainly grasshoppers, katydids, and crickets, plus beetles, ants, and caterpillars—provide some 70 percent of the adult summer diet. In one study, a family group of 2 adult and 4 young dickcissels ate about 200 grasshoppers daily. The diet of juveniles, not as adept at insect catching, exhibits reverse proportions—about 70 percent seeds, 30 percent insects. Most grain consumed by dickcissels consists of waste seed. Some researchers have theorized that increased planting of large-seeded grasses such as sorghum in the Venezuelan llanos, where many dickcissels winter, may have negatively affected female dickcissel populations. Females, which are smaller than males (averaging 25 grams in weight, contrasted to the male average of 30 grams) and are unable to ingest the large seeds, diminish in numbers, leading to a skewed sex ratio and consequent nest-density decline.

The dickcissel's foremost competitor is probably the farmer who mows his clover or alfalfa in June and July. In so doing, he eliminates one of his very best insect-eating friends. First and second mowings, often destroying successive nests and nestlings, may virtually wipe out local dickcissel populations. In the llanos winter range, however, dickcissels are not considered so farmer friendly; indeed, they are treated as agricultural pests because of their raids upon rice and sorghum crops. Farmers use organophosphate pesticides against them, spraying pools where the birds drink, their feeding areas, and most devastatingly, their nighttime roosts. "By targeting one of the larger megaroosts," reported the 1995 team, "a farmer can, in a matter of minutes, not only wipe out birds perceived as pests but also unwittingly devastate a large portion of the world's dickcissel population." Contrary to the various complex changing habitat theories that try to account for dickcissel decline, recent researchers tend to attribute the bird's dire straits to episodes of avicide on the winter range. No easy solution to the dickcissel-as-pest problem exists for either dickcissels or farmers. The situation is truly competitive; dickcissels do impose economic burdens on farmers in the winter range, and long-term solutions will probably require international control strategies—nonlethal ones, it is hoped.

Predators include most of the ground nest raiders—snakes, weasels, skunks, raccoons, opossums, and domestic cats. Owls and accipiter hawks capture adults. On the winter range, predators include Aplomado falcons, merlins, and barn owls. Brown-headed cowbirds may parasitize up to 80 percent of dickcissel nests, removing 1 or 2 eggs and replacing them with their own. Tying in with cowbird impact is the conversion to large-seeded grass crops on the winter range, possibly accounting for the sex-biased dickcissel population. According to researcher John L. Zimmerman, the consequent "reduction in females and, hence, nest density increases the negative impact of Brown-headed Cowbird parasitism on recruitment [the annual increment of young dickcissels], leading to a decline in the Dickcissel population." Habitat characteristics also affect the frequency of cowbird parasitism. One Kansas study, contrasting cowbird parasitism with predation, found that cowbirds parasitized more dickcissel nests in tall-grass prairie habitat than in old-field habitats, since nest density in tall-grass habitat was relatively low; in old-field habitats, where nest density was higher, rates of cowbird parasitism proved lower. Predation rates, however, were lower in the tall-grass prairie and higher in old fields, reflecting a natural higher density of predators in old-field communities. But these "2 major factors affecting nest survival tend to offset one another so that daily nest survival probabilities are similar."

Fretwell suggested that dickcissels may have a survival or low-density population limit beyond which the species may not recover.

One notable historic example of such an occurrence—the so-called *Allee effect* in ecology—was the extinction of the heath hen (see Greater Prairie-Chicken).

**Focus.** Drought also adversely affects the fluctuation of dickcissel populations. During the 1980s, dry weather in the Great Plains breeding range was believed to have caused declines there, even as dickcissel numbers increased in the eastern periphery of the range.

The earlier history of dickcissel distribution in North America has tested the ingenuity of theorists. Dickcissels once commonly resided both west and east of the Alleghenies, including the Carolinas and southern New England, but had practically disappeared from the seaboard states by 1900. Thirty years later, dickcissels reappeared in many of these areas and expanded into maritime Canada, and northeastern populations have fluctuated at intervals since then.

Since 1966, a more general, continentwide decline of the species has occurred at an annual rate of 1.7 percent. Until recently, most ornithologists blamed habitat changes brought about by reduction in farmland acreage and by shifting agricultural practices on the breeding range, as well as pesticide use and sorghum crop production on the winter range. One prominent researcher even predicted the eventual disappearance of the dickcissel from North American avifauna owing to the practices on the winter range coupled with the effects of drought on the breeding range. Yet this is all speculation; in fact, the species has proved more adaptable to a roster of ecological changes than anyone predicted. Perhaps "the key to survival for the Dickcissel," as ornithologist Gail A. McPeek wrote, lies in its manifest ability to change its distribution.

Vernacular and former names for dickcissels include little meadowlark and black-throated bunting. No data exist on longevity in this species.

## Blackbirds (Tribe Icterini)

Not all 97 blackbird species are black, though most show some amount of black plumage. Icterines reside throughout the Western Hemisphere, reaching their greatest diversity in South America. (The so-called blackbird of Eurasia is actually a thrush related to the American robin.) Blackbirds display a broad range of physical and behavioral features. Many blackbird species walk rather than hop on the ground. Many voice harsh or shrill song and call notes, though some are among the most melodious of singers. Breeding strategies and social behaviors also vary. The sexes in many species are dimorphic, differing in plumage coloration. Most blackbirds forage by *gaping,* as do crows, jays, and starlings. Powerful jaw musculature enables them to open the bill against strong resistance, thus exposing hidden prey beneath objects or in the ground. Eye position on the head aligns with the lower edge of the upper mandible, allowing the birds direct focus into the foraging space, as well as giving them a characteristic bug-eyed appearance when viewed head-on.

Of the 22 blackbird species that reside in North America, 9 breed regularly in the Northeast. Besides the 2 following accounts, plus the mentioned relatives, northeastern icterines include the red-winged blackbird *(Agelaius phoeniceus),* yellow-headed blackbird *(Xanthocephalus xanthocephalus),* and rusty and Brewer's blackbirds *(Euphagus carolinus, E. cyanocephalus).* South American icterines include the troupials, oropendolas, and caciques. Crows, ravens, and European starlings, though they have black plumage, are unrelated to blackbirds.

FINCH FAMILY (Fringillidae) - Subfamily Emberizinae - Blackbirds (Tribe Icterini)

## Eastern Meadowlark *(Sturnella magna)*

About 9 inches long, the meadowlark exhibits brown-streaked plumage on its upper parts, plus bright yellow underparts, crossed by a broad, black crescent mark on the breast. Its sharp, awl-like bill and white outer tail feathers also help identify it. Sexes look alike, except that females are slightly smaller. The male's primary song, consisting of several clear, slurred whistles—"tee-yah, tee-yair"—and the chattering call notes, somewhat resembling those of orioles and house wrens, herald early-spring mornings and evenings in rural areas.

**Close relatives.** The western meadowlark *(S. neglecta),* a sibling species and virtually identical to the eastern meadowlark except in song, inhabits western North America, occasionally overlapping breeding ranges in the West and Midwest. Lilian's meadowlark *(S. lilianae)*, a resident of the Southwest and Mexico, is considered an eastern meadowlark subspecies by many taxonomists. Three other *Sturnella* species reside in South America. Meadowlarks are unrelated to the true larks (family Alaudidae).

**Behaviors.** Often labeled by naturalists as the most characteristic bird of the American farm, its clear, slurred whistles, as one observer noted, "are synonymous with the grasslands of eastern North America." The eastern meadowlark is easily observed wherever present. A ground feeder, the meadowlark probes for food by *gaping,* inserting its long, sharp bill beneath earth clods, cow pats, or stones, then snapping it open and dislodging prey items. Meadowlark body form and locomotion have often been likened to those of the quail, another ground bird (see Northern Bobwhite). In flight, rapid wingbeats alternate with glides, wings held stiff. Males tend to sing from the highest perches available, though they occasionally do so from the ground, at their territorial boundaries adjacent to neighboring territories. Except during spring and summer, meadowlarks are exceedingly social and gregarious, often feeding and roosting in sizable flocks.

Eastern meadowlarks occur in many geographic variations— some 11 subspecies or races across North America. *S. m. magna* is our familiar northeastern race. In South America, 5 more subspecies reside. Eastern meadowlark breeding range, including all North American races, extends from South Dakota and the Great Plains eastward to southern Ontario, Quebec, and the Maritime Provinces; southward to the Gulf coast, Mexico, and Cuba; and through Central America to Colombia, Venezuela, and northern Brazil. It is truly one of our most widely distributed American songbirds.

*Spring.* Meadowlarks reside year-round throughout most of their breeding range, but snow cover impels their migration from northern sections of the range. They return early, however, often by early March or as soon as snow melts. Peak migration occurs in April, the birds traveling by daytime (contrary to the beliefs of earlier researchers such as William Brewster, who maintained that they traveled exclusively by night) in small, unisexual flocks. Males precede females by 2 to 4 weeks. Both sexes are strongly *philopatric,* usually returning to the same territory as the previous year or an adjacent one, although few yearling birds return to their natal site. Thus pairings may reoccur in subsequent years, though the birds cannot be said to pair for life. Most males are, like many other blackbird species, *polygynous,* pairing with 2, or rarely 3, females, which proceed to nest on the territory.

Males establish territories of about 5 to 8 acres in size before female arrival. This is the period when singing becomes most intense; song exchange and chasing of territorial intruders become the foremost activities. Posturing displays include bill tilting, with the head jerked up and feathers sleeked down; tail flashing and wing flashing, showing the white tail feathers, often accompanied by a rasping "dzert" note; a fluffing-out posture, with plumage expanded, increasing the apparent body size; and the jump-flight between facing territorial males, a sudden spring straight upward about 4 feet or more, legs dangling, wings fluttering, then a flight of several yards before dropping back to the ground. Males become so randy during this period that they may even pseudocopulate with clumps of grass. When females arrive, pairing displays include male strutting, fluffing out, and jump-flights between mates. Often females give chatter calls in response to a mate's song.

Nesting in the northern range usually begins from mid- to late April.

EGGS AND YOUNG: typically 5; eggs white, spotted with shades of brown and lavender, often concentrated at larger end. INCUBATION: by female; 13 or 14 days; hatching synchronous. FEEDING OF YOUNG: mainly by female; male feeds infrequently; insects. FLEDGING: 10 to 12 days.

*Summer.* As the season advances, meadowlark territories "undergo amoeboid changes in size and shape," in the words of one researcher. These changes result from shifts in population density, in female and nesting locations on the territory, and in habitat suitability. Territorial males that attract no mates are usually displaced by paired males.

Fledglings continue to be fed for 2 to 4 weeks, often by the female unless she begins renesting with a subsequent brood; in that case, the male finally becomes parental and helps feed. Males usually chase independent juveniles of the first brood off the territory. Meadowlark females may actually lay several clutches per year, responding to nesting failures, but few manage more than 2 successful nestings with fledged young. Egg laying continues through early June, nesting into July; final broods fledge in early August. Nesting cycles of polygynously mated females on a territory are seldom synchronous; the 2 or 3 nests that may be present on a single territory exist in different stages of incubation or nestling growth.

The birds abandon their territories as the last of the fledglings become independent. Postbreeding flocks of 20 or 30 birds begin forming, and by migration time the foraging birds may number into flocks of hundreds. Juveniles look much like adults, except that instead of a black V, a cluster of dark spots marks the breast, and the yellow underparts are paler than in adults. Following the annual molt of both adults and juveniles in August, buffy edgings of new feathers veil the yellow breast. These edgings wear off by spring to produce the bright breeding plumage.

*Fall, Winter.* For all but the most northern breeding populations, summer and winter ranges of meadowlarks remain the same.

*The eastern meadowlark, one of the most common birds of rural country in North America, always makes its presence known by its distinctive song. (From* The Atlas of Breeding Birds of Michigan.*)*

The northern population migrates southward in small to large flocks, again usually in daylight hours. Some of the birds travel as far as the Gulf coastal states, mainly in September and October. Winter populations generally concentrate along rivers and lakes; Oklahoma's Red River and Oologah Lake, Alabama's Dannelly Reservoir, and the Catawba River between the Carolinas host high densities of wintering eastern meadowlarks. Small numbers, however, linger to the north, and many flocks overwinter in Atlantic coastal salt marshes, where they forage and roost. No evidence exists for winter territoriality or social dominance hierarchies. Some meadowlarks apparently wander quite randomly in winter; not all such vagrant flocks are northern migrants. Occasional resumption of song sometimes occurs in the fall.

**Ecology.** Eastern meadowlark habitats include tall-grass prairie, hayfields, open lowland areas, golf courses, airports, roadsides, pastures, and overgrown fields. The birds favor a fairly thick ground cover of grass and duff or litter. Singing perches—fence posts or scattered shrubs—are also important, if not vital, elements of meadowlark habitats. In winter, meadowlarks frequent fields, feedlots, and marshes. Eastern meadowlarks reside only where mean annual precipitation exceeds 24 inches. They avoid wintering in regions where the average minimum January temperature drops below 15 degrees F.

For nests, eastern meadowlarks seem to favor sloping rather than flat land. The nests are woven, arched structures that deteriorate rapidly after—and even during—brood raising. The female lines a 1- or 2-inch-deep dry scrape or shallow depression—usually well concealed in dense grass or other herbal vegetation—with layers of coarse grasses and plant fibers, then fine grasses. Where available, fine stems of the path-rush *(Juncus tenuis),* a dry-land rush, are often used as lining. Sometimes the female builds in the sunken hoofprint of a cow or horse. A loosely woven dome, attached to surrounding vegetation, covers the nest floor, with a 4-inch opening on the side. Openings tend to face away from prevailing winds, and most nests show conspicuous trails or runways extending 6 to 20 inches through the grass. The outside diameter of the nest is about 7 inches, and the height is about the same. Occasional nests lie

completely open; others may have lengthy entrance tunnels, sometimes up to 3 feet long. A female typically starts building nests in several sites before selecting a final one. The nest takes 4 to 8 days to
complete, and egg laying may begin before the nest is finished. Sometimes, when more than 1 female inhabits a territory, nests may be
built as close together as 50 feet, but they are usually farther apart.
Females never reuse nests, building anew for each nesting.

During the breeding season, the meadowlark diet consists of
about 75 percent insects—chiefly crickets, grasshoppers, beetles,
caterpillars, cutworms, and grubs—which make up about 25 percent
of the annual diet. Winter food consists mainly of weed seeds (ragweeds and smartweeds), foxtail-grasses, and waste grains (corn,
wheat, and oats). Occasionally the birds consume wild fruits (bayberry, chokeberry), and they also feed on road-killed carcasses of
birds and small mammals, especially during severe winter weather
when other food is not available.

The foremost competitor of the eastern meadowlark is probably
its sibling species, the western meadowlark, in areas where their
breeding ranges overlap. "These two meadowlarks," wrote ornithologist Alexander F. Skutch, "almost certainly evolved in populations of
the same ancestral species that later became isolated from each
other." Not until 1910 were meadowlarks officially divided into 2
species. Today "they meet in a long, broad zone that stretches from
the Mexican state of Jalisco to the Great Lakes in the north." These
areas of overlap developed mainly in historical times, as American
settlement spread westward. Land clearing and agriculture resulted
in the expansion of eastern meadowlark range westward into the
Great Plains habitats of the western meadowlark, even as the western meadowlark's distribution invaded the former exclusive range of
the eastern. Today a broad area of overlap exists in the Great Plains,
as well as many irregular zones of contact eastward. Western meadowlarks tend to favor drier, less fragmented grassland habitats than
the eastern, which prefer moister habitats. Where the species coexist, males of each defend their territories against the other.
Hybridization between them occurs, though at generally low frequency; hybrid offspring show low fertility rates. Most researchers

believe that western meadowlarks are the more aggressive species, having blocked the westward expansion of easterns and being more successful invaders. "High densities of the Western Meadowlark seem to exclude its eastern counterpart, but the opposite is not true for the Eastern Meadowlark," one observer noted. Another competitor may be the red-winged blackbird. In one experimental study, eastern meadowlarks raided artificial nests designed to resemble red-winged blackbird nests, puncturing and destroying the eggs. Since the egg contents remained uneaten, the hostile action apparently had more to do with neighborhood competition for resources than with predation as such. Researcher Jaroslav Picman concluded that meadowlarks "could significantly affect the reproductive success of co-occurring birds such as bobolinks, red-winged blackbirds, and savannah sparrows." The meadowlark's other main competitor is probably the farmer eager to irrigate and till for early-spring weed control, to mow early in the season, and to wash his acreage in pesticides and other contaminants.

A hawk spotted in the vicinity elicits repeated alarm whistles from meadowlarks, which freeze in place or crouch low to the ground. Nest raiders include garter snakes, ground squirrels, foxes, domestic cats and dogs, coyotes, weasels, skunks, and raccoons.

*The red fox is a common predator of ground nests. Some researchers believe that high rodent populations in a field lead to higher-than-usual rates of bird nest disturbance by mammal predators such as foxes.*

Meadowlarks are most vulnerable to predators during their first few days as fledglings; relatively few adult meadowlarks become prey for predators. High meadow vole or other rodent populations in nesting areas may attract more predators than usual; hence, some biologists believe, the higher abundance of predators may result in a greater incidence of nest discovery and destruction. Other hazards include trampling of nests by livestock, exposure to harsh winter conditions, and destruction of nests by mowing. Sometimes a threatened female, in "exploding" off her nest, scatters eggs or nestlings, in some cases damaging or destroying them. Brown-headed cowbird parasitism occurs at relatively low frequency in most areas. Autumn migrant flocks of meadowlarks were at one time heavily harvested for food by gunners in the Midwest and South.

**Focus.** Many earlier researchers likened the eastern meadowlark to the northern bobwhite; it "has the build and the walk, as well as the flight, of the quail," reported Alfred O. Gross. Marsh quail was once a hunters' familiar name for the meadowlark. "The position of the bright colors on meadowlarks," wrote blackbird specialist Gordon H. Orians, "suggests that there may be [natural] selection both for inconspicuous plumage . . . and for bright signaling colors." Other observers have suggested that the black crescent on the

*Meadowlarks exhibit much individual variation in the amount and shape of black coloration on the breast and throat, as these sample specimens show.*

meadowlark's conspicuous yellow breast may exemplify disruptive patterning, distracting a predator's eye from the bird's outline. Similar markings are seen on several other ground birds including horned larks and dickcissels (also, most notably, the yellow-throated longclaw of African savannas).

In the early 1900s, a small but vocal group disenchanted with the bald eagle's reputation advocated its replacement by the meadowlark as our national bird. The rationale was that many eagles exist worldwide, whereas meadowlarks are strictly (North and South) American birds. Others pointed out that replacing a carrion eater with a polygamist wasn't really all that patriotic a thing to do, so the idea never caught on. Six states, however, have made the western meadowlark their state bird.

Despite the western expansion of eastern meadowlark populations into the Kansas plains and the Texas panhandle since 1960, population data of the past 3 decades indicate a declining trend of eastern meadowlarks throughout their breeding range. The greatest rates of decline have occurred in New England and the other northeastern states. Most researchers attribute the decline to the loss of grassland habitat owing to changes in land use (mainly urban development and intensive farming practices). Year-to-year nesting success appears extremely variable in this species. In some studies, polygynously mated females produced significantly more fledglings than those that were monogamously mated.

The longevity record of the eastern meadowlark is about 9 years, but adult survival rates of 3 to 5 years are more typical.

FINCH FAMILY (Fringillidae) - Subfamily Emberizinae - Blackbirds (Tribe Icterini)

# Bobolink *(Dolichonyx oryzivorus)*

Roger Tory Peterson pointed out that this 6- to 8-inch-long blackbird is "our only songbird that is solid-black below and largely white above, suggesting a dress suit on backward." That conspicuous dress code—the reverse of countershading, as seen in many birds—applies only to the breeding male with its white rump and side stripe, buff-yellow nape, and black head and underparts. Females are yellowish brown, with head and side striping. Both sexes exhibit a short, conical, sparrowlike bill and stiff, pointed tail feathers resembling a woodpecker's. Male song, voiced in flight or from a perch, is a gurgling, musical spill of notes tinkling across the fields—"like several small melodious flutes playing ascending scales together," one observer described it.

*The most melodious songster of the eastern grasslands, the bobolink male reverses the usual plumage patterns of birds, wearing lighter feathers on top and darker below. (From* The Atlas of Breeding Birds of Michigan.*)*

**Close relatives.** This is the only *Dolichonyx* species.

**Behavior.** "Away he launches," wrote Thoreau of the male bobolink, "and the meadow is all bespattered with melody." Best known for its bubbling song, the "skunk blackbird," as it is nicknamed for the male's black and white patterns, is, like most blackbirds, gregarious except on the breeding territory, where at times it becomes highly aggressive toward intruding bobolinks. At any other time of year than spring and early summer, bobolinks are always seen in flocks.

Again like most blackbirds, bobolinks are *polygynous,* a breeding male pairing in rapid sequence with 2 or more females. Probably no other songbird is so strongly and regularly polygynous as bobolinks, though the percentage of such pairings in a population apparently depends greatly upon habitat quality and food abundance. Older males seem to hold the highest-quality territories and thus more often attract multiple mates. Not only do males pair with multiple females, but extrapair copulations also occur, resulting in egg clutches sired by more than one male; in DNA analyses of nestlings, some 15 percent showed multiple paternity. The gene pool in bobolinks is well mixed.

Primarily grassland birds, bobolinks nest on the ground surface, mainly feeding 2 to 6 inches above ground on seeds and insects. Nests are hard to find because the birds leave and approach them by walking for a considerable distance before taking flight or after landing. Flight on territory is mainly between song perches and the nest, though circular song-flights occur as courtship and territorial displays.

Bobolink breeding range spans southern Canada to the middle tier of states, generally between 39 and 50 degrees N latitude. Isolated populations also exist farther south.

*Spring.* One of the longest-distance migrants among passerine birds, bobolinks begin their northward journey from the Argentine pampas in March. Flying over the Caribbean and Gulf of Mexico, males arrive on the breeding range from mid-April to mid-May, older males preceding yearling males by several days, and older females following a week or so after the initial male group; younger females bring up the rear. Both sexes show high return rates *(philopatry)* to breeding sites of the previous year, especially where nesting has been successful. Re-pairing of previous mates is thus not uncommon. Yearling birds often settle within a mile or so of their natal area.

Arriving males tend to remain in flocks, foraging together for a few days before starting to establish territories. Territories range from 1 to 9 acres in size, depending upon the quality of habitat. Older, dominant males tend to occupy the central territories in a field, whereas later-arriving males claim peripheral sites. As more birds arrive, competition for space increases, territories compress in size, and conflicts heat up. Song, usually given from the highest perches in the territory, often accompanies a group of movements called *song spread:* bowed head, spread wings and tail, and fluffing of white feather tracts. *Song flights*—high, hovering, and circular flights over the territory—also expose the male's white plumage as he sings. Occasionally bobolinks sing from the ground or low perches, especially in cold or windy weather. Aerial chases and contests in which 2 males rise vertically along a territorial boundary, striking and grappling, are the most aggressive encounters. Parallel walking, a kind of boundary guard patrol, occurs between 2 males on either side of their invisible territorial line as they slowly walk and hop parallel to each other, 6 inches to 3 feet apart. Parallel walking, along with various head and body displays, may occur in bouts lasting 1 to 3 hours over a period of 2 or 3 days.

Courtship displays include low song flights; wing lifts, with the perched male holding his wings above the body for several seconds; and aerial chasing of females. Most males have 2 distinctive song types, which remain consistent and fairly similar throughout a local population. These song types differ in arrangement and phrasings of notes rather than in tonal qualities, so careful listening is required to distinguish them. Song becomes most frequent and intense just before pairing, declining as courtship proceeds. Yearling males, according to ornithologist Gordon H. Orians, probably learn "the song type of their colony during their first breeding season, because bobolinks have stopped singing by the time the young of the year have hatched." Females often pair with a male within hours of arrival, sometimes a mate of the previous year. Females appear to select mates on the basis of habitat quality rather than by song or courtship displays, which probably serve only as attention getters. Thus breeding densities— and the number of polygynous matings—depend heavily upon habitat suitability. Pairing seems to occur more or less synchronously within a population. Polygynous males often attract and mate with their second partners 3 to 8 days after their first mating.

Yet territorial lapses frequently occur. Researcher Arlo J. Raim found that groups of 3 to 5 males often gathered off their territories or even within a territory showing no antagonism, sometimes even singing. They "appeared to be essentially social groups," he reported. "Often such groups would fly around together far off the area, eventually coming back to their respective territories."

EGGS AND YOUNG: typically 5 or 6; eggs highly variable in color, gray to reddish brown, heavily blotched and spotted with browns and purples, mainly at larger end. INCUBATION: by female; about 12 days; hatching synchronous within 2 to 5 hours except for last-laid egg, which hatches 20 to 30 hours later. FEEDING OF YOUNG: by both sexes; mainly caterpillars. FLEDGING: 10 or 11 days; runts left in the nest starve; fledglings begin flying at 13 days.

*Summer.* Female bobolinks typically raise only one brood per season, though occasional double brooding occurs. If a nesting fails because of predation or other interference, the female usually renests, building anew on the same or another territory.

Male feeding attendance at nests is exceedingly variable. In many cases, the male concentrates his attention on the first brood, ignoring or rarely visiting secondary nests on the territory. Sometimes the male may switch efforts to a secondary nest when the first brood ages to a certain point. Occasionally nesting bobolinks also use nest helpers, 2 or more adult bobolinks of either sex that supplement parental feeding of nestlings. Such helpers may be yearling offspring of one or both parents or, if male, they may have sired some of the nestlings during extrapair copulations. Parents and helpers typically obtain much of the food for nestlings in home-range feeding areas off the territory. Territorial bounds rapidly fade as adults divide the labor of feeding fledglings.

Flocks consisting of several families begin forming within 6 days after fledging. As these flocks assemble, parents may still feed their young within the flock for up to 28 days after fledging. The flock now forages as a mobile unit across the breeding area. Now a second rank of adult male bobolinks—the previously territorially excluded drifters and floaters—may move in, establishing territories and attracting females whose nestings elsewhere failed, often because of hay mowing. Relatively few of these late nestings, however, succeed in fledging young. The postbreeding adults and juveniles, in the meantime, depart the breeding area, often by late July, although sometimes not until mid-August. This flock continues to roost and forage together. Song altogether ceases.

As premigration flocks increase in size, many of them move into large freshwater and coastal marshes, there to undergo the annual summer molt, which begins in late July and continues into September. Females retain their appearance, but male plumage loses its vivid blacks and whites, which are replaced by inconspicuous, femalelike brownish and buff colors. Juveniles, which also resemble females, lack the side striping and show yellower underparts.

Bobolinks migrate, beginning in August and peaking in September, mainly in mixed sex and age flocks at night, resting and feeding by day. Bobolinks in the western range travel eastward, joining with southeastern coastal migrants. According to ornithologist Alexander F. Skutch, "most Bobolinks that breed in the western United States and Canada retrace the route by which their ancestors apparently colonized this region to join eastern populations on their southward journey." Only a minority travels a more direct course through the Southwest, Mexico, and Central America.

*Fall, Winter.* During their night flight, flocks of migrating bobolinks voice characteristic "pink" notes, probably contact calls between individuals. Most bobolinks funnel into Florida, thence across to Cuba and Jamaica—once known as the "bobolink route" because of the numerous migrant flocks observed in this corridor. The birds continue across the water to South America, reaching southwestern Brazil and Paraguay in early November, many finally settling, until March, in the Pantanal region of northern Argentina. The entire round-trip migration flight of bobolinks spans more than 11,000 miles, probably the longest of any North American songbird. As with other transequatorial migrants, which actually include rather few songbird species, the bobolink's life is one of constant springs and summers in both hemispheres, breeding only in the northern. Day-length effects on the birds' reproductive physiology in both hemispheres have been widely studied. In South America, apparently, bobolinks inhabit latitudes below the equator that do not attain 15.5 hours of daylight, thus keeping the birds in a state of reproductive dormancy. No data exist on winter philopatry or dominance hierarchies; in one study, however, a group of bobolink males banded on the breeding area remained together all winter and returned together in spring.

In late January, before spring migration, bobolinks undergo another complete molt. Now males gain their breeding plumage, which is obscured at first by yellowish feather tips. These light tips wear off by early May, revealing the bold black and white patterns.

**Ecology.** Sources radically differ on details of the bobolink's historical distribution. Some say that bobolinks originally resided in the Great Plains region, spreading northward, westward, and eastward as land clearing and cultivation extended new habitats. Skutch, however, stated that bobolinks "appear to have been originally confined to the Northeast and to have followed advancing agriculture west-ward almost to the Pacific coast." Theories and guesses are rife, but nobody knows. Widespread bobolink declines have occurred in the Northeast, concurrent with declines in hay-cropping agriculture, since the early 1900s. Today in the East, bobolinks still favor clover-alfalfa hayfields, especially older ones that have not been plowed and reseeded for 8 years or so—densely vegetated old fields with high *forb* content (herbaceous vegetation other than grasses or sedges), in addition to grass. The birds prefer fields with minimal shrub cover and a fairly dense litter or duff layer on the ground. Some studies show that larger, unfragmented fields of 75 acres or so may host twice the number of bobolinks present in 25-acre fields. In the words of one research team, "fewer large grassland patches tend to contain more breeding Bobolinks than numerous smaller patches of equal total area."

Bobolink nests, extremely well camouflaged on the ground, fre-quently lie in a slight hollow at the base of larger forbs such as meadow-rue, golden alexander, and clovers; more than 80 percent of nests in one study were so situated, with few or none concealed in grass alone. The nest, constructed by the female over 1 or 2 days of intensive work, consists of an exterior wall of coarse grasses and

*Prime habitat for bobolinks is a large, unfragmented hayfield that remains unmowed until early July, when nesting is completed.*

weed stalks lined by fine grasses or sedges. The inside diameter measures about 3 inches. Nests in heavy ground litter occasionally are arched or canopied by dead grasses.

Bobolinks consume both animal and seed foods at all times of year, though insects and spiders constitute about 60 percent of the diet during the breeding season. Caterpillars, beetles, grasshoppers, and insect larvae of various kinds are the foremost invertebrate foods. Seed foods in summer include foxtail-grasses, common dandelion, cinquefoils, common yarrow, smartweeds, Canada-thistle, and docks. Bobolinks usually glean insects and spiders from the bases and stems of plants, foraging mainly in cover less than 6 inches tall. Seeds are often taken from the tops of forbs. Migration and winter foods are mainly small grains, especially those in sprout and milk stages—wild and cultivated rice, oats, and corn—plus corn tassels and weed seeds. The birds increase their feeding rate, rapidly gaining weight and depositing fat, before their long overwater flights in the fall.

Territorial bobolinks treat almost all other bird species of their habitats as competitors, chasing and diving at them. Often, however, the pursued becomes the aggressor. Dickcissels, though harassed by bobolinks early in the season, later chase them. Eastern meadowlarks and red-winged blackbirds, especially the latter, tend to dominate most encounters with bobolinks. According to one research team, bobolinks seem to avoid nesting close to active red-winged blackbird nests. Some ornithologists earlier in the century believed that eastward-expanding Brewer's blackbird populations were displacing bobolinks. In fact, Brewer's blackbird, much more of a habitat generalist than the bobolink and seldom a direct competitor, has probably had minimal effects on bobolink distribution. Foremost bobolink competitors include the farmer who mows hay before early July—bobolink nest mortality has increased 2 or 3 times over the past 50 years owing to earlier-season mowing practices—and the rice grower on the South American winter range, although rice culture has declined since 1900 along the bird's southeastern migration routes. Called "rice birds" in this region during the late nineteenth and early twentieth centuries, spring-migrating bobolinks consumed the sprouts, fall migrants the ripening seed (many local rice growers, noted one observer, "do not recognize it as the same bird that passes through the area in spring with a different plumage"), and rice growers once shot them in huge numbers as pests.

Bobolink predators are numerous. Cooper's hawks capture adult birds, and ring-billed gulls take fledglings. Nest raiders include sandhill cranes, short-eared owls, northern harriers, ring-billed gulls, American crows, skunks, cats, dogs, deer mice, and garter, milk, and yellow-bellied racer snakes. Brown-headed cowbird nest parasitism occurs uncommonly in most areas, the highest incidence in nests placed near wooded edges. Most bobolink nest failures result from predation and adverse weather or flooding. Gunners in the rice fields frequently shot the birds for food; fat and tasty after their feeding sprees, they were known to gourmands as "butterbirds." In the North, market hunters shot and sold bobolinks as "reed-birds." Because of their rice pest status, the first federal migratory bird laws that protected most songbird species excluded bobolinks, though later legislation included them. Bobolinks are still regarded and treated as major rice pests in South America, where they are often poisoned, shot, and trapped. A caged-bird market also exists there for male bobolinks.

**Focus.** Breeding Bird Survey data show significant declines in continental bobolink populations, especially during the past 2 decades. In the Northeast, widespread cutbacks in hay acreage, along with earlier mowing that coincides with the peak nesting period in hayfields that still exist, probably account for most regional changes in distribution. Effects of human attacks against "rice bird" populations in their winter range remain largely unknown.

The bobolink's song has evoked some of the most lavish paeans in nature literature. To poet William Cullen Bryant in "Robert of Lincoln," it was "Bob-o'-link, bob-o'-link, Spink, spank, spink." The name *bobolink* apparently derived from "Bob o'lincon," somebody's fanciful rendition of the bird's lyrics. To Thoreau, the bobolink seemingly "touched his harp within a vase of liquid melody, and when he lifted it out, the notes fell like bubbles from the trembling strings." F. Schuyler Mathews heard it as "a mad, reckless song-fantasia, an outbreak of pent-up, irrepressible glee." Alexander F. Skutch likened the bobolink to the skylark of Eurasia, "the nearest approach to this cel-ebrated singer among the birds of the eastern United States." "Their notes," he wrote, "seem to stream out so rapidly that they fall over each other and become jumbled." All one must do to make sense of such hyperbole is simply to hear a singing bobolink—and all will immediately be understood.

Much investigative work has gone into the bobolink's mecha-nisms of orientation and navigation during migrations. The birds seem to rely on both stellar and magnetic cues. Magnetite in the olfactory tissues (those related to the sense of smell) plus cells in the trigeminal (fifth cranial) nerve system apparently respond to changes in the earth's magnetic field.

Banded bobolinks have been recovered at ages six, seven, and nine. Many fledglings, however, do not survive their first year, and probably few adults survive beyond 3 or 4 breeding seasons.

# Selected Bibliography

In addition to listed references and others, basic sources include Arthur Cleveland Bent's classic multivolume series, *Life Histories of North American Birds* (U.S. National Museum Bulletins 1919–1958), and Bent's modern counterpart, annually produced monographs in the series *The Birds of North America: Life Histories for the 21st Century* (American Ornithologists' Union and Academy of Natural Sciences of Philadelphia, 1993–). I have also frequently consulted relevant research articles in *The Auk, Condor, Journal of Field Ornithology,* and *Wilson Bulletin,* among other professional ornithological journals.

Baker, J. A. *The Peregrine.* New York: Harper and Row, 1967.

Brewer, Richard, ed. *Proceedings of the Eighth North American Prairie Conference.* Kalamazoo, MI: Western Michigan University, 1983.

Brewer, Richard. *The Science of Ecology.* 2nd ed. New York: Saunders, 1994.

Brewer, Richard, Gail A. McPeek, and Raymond J. Adams, Jr. *The Atlas of Breeding Birds of Michigan.* East Lansing, MI: Michigan State University Press, 1991.

Cade, Tom J., James H. Enderson, C. G. Thelander, and C. M. White, eds. *Peregrine Falcon Populations: Their Management and Recovery.* Boise, ID: Peregrine Fund, 1988.

Clark, William S. *A Field Guide to Hawks of North America.* Boston: Houghton Mifflin, 1987.

Cruikshank, Helen, ed. *Thoreau on Birds.* New York: McGraw-Hill, 1964.

Dunne, Pete. *The Wind Masters: The Lives of North American Birds of Prey.* Boston: Houghton Mifflin, 1995.

Dunne, Pete, David Sibley, and Clay Sutton. *Hawks in Flight: The Flight Identification of North American Migrant Raptors.* Boston: Houghton Mifflin, 1988.

Eastman, John. *Birds of Forest, Yard, and Thicket.* Mechanicsburg, PA: Stackpole Books, 1997.

———. *Birds of Lake, Pond and Marsh.* Mechanicsburg, PA: Stackpole Books, 1999.

Ehrlich, Paul R., David S. Dobkin, and Darryl Wheye. *The Birder's Handbook: A Field Guide to the Natural History of North American Birds.* New York: Simon & Schuster, 1988.

Ford, Emma. *Peregrine.* London: Fourth Estate, 1993.

Graham, Frank, Jr. *Gulls: A Social History.* New York: Random House, 1975.

Greenberg, Russell, and Jamie Reaser. *Bring Back the Birds: What You Can Do to Save Threatened Species.* Mechanicsburg, PA: Stackpole Books, 1995.

Gruson, Edward S. *Words for Birds: A Lexicon of North American Birds with Biographical Notes.* New York: Quadrangle Books, 1972.

Hagan, John M., III, and David W. Johnston, eds. *Ecology and Conservation of Neotropical Migrant Landbirds.* Washington, DC: Smithsonian Institution Press, 1992.

Hamerstrom, Frances. *Harrier, Hawk of the Marshes: The Hawk That Is Ruled by a Mouse.* Washington, DC: Smithsonian Institution, 1986.

———. *Strictly for the Chickens.* Ames, IA: Iowa State University Press, 1980.

Harrison, Hal H. *A Field Guide to the Birds' Nests: United States East of the Mississippi River.* Boston: Houghton Mifflin, 1975.

Hay, John. *The Bird of Light.* New York: W. W. Norton, 1991.

Headstrom, Richard. *A Complete Field Guide to Nests in the United States.* New York: Ives Washburn, 1970.

Hume, Rob. *The Common Tern.* London: Hamlyn, 1993.

Johnsgard, Paul A. *The Grouse of the World.* Lincoln, NE: University of Nebraska Press, 1983.

Kaufman, Kenn. *A Field Guide to Advanced Birding.* Boston: Houghton Mifflin, 1990.

Keast, Allen, and Eugene S. Morton, eds. *Migrant Birds in the Neotropics: Ecology, Behavior, Distribution, and Conservation.* Washington, DC: Smithsonian Institution Press, 1980.

Leahy, Christopher. *The Birdwatcher's Companion: An Encyclopedic Handbook of North American Birdlife.* New York: Hill and Wang, 1982.

Leopold, Aldo. *A Sand County Almanac and Sketches Here and There.* London: Oxford University Press, 1949.

Martin, Alexander C., Herbert S. Zim, and Arnold L. Nelson. *American Wildlife and Plants.* New York: Dover, 1961.

Martin, Laura C. *The Folklore of Birds.* Old Saybrook, CT: Globe Pequot Press, 1993.

McPeek, Gail A., ed. *The Birds of Michigan.* Bloomington, IN: Indiana University Press, 1994.

Monroe, Burt L., Jr., and Charles G. Sibley. *A World Checklist of Birds.* New Haven, CT: Yale University Press, 1993.

Nethersole-Thompson, Desmond. *The Snow Bunting.* Edinburgh: Oliver & Boyd, 1966.

Orians, Gordon H. *Blackbirds of the Americas.* Seattle, WA: University of Washington Press, 1985.

Peterson, Roger Tory. *A Field Guide to the Birds.* 4th ed. Boston: Houghton Mifflin, 1980.

Peterson, Roger Tory, Guy Mountfort, and P. A. D. Hollom. *A Field Guide to Birds of Britain and Europe.* 5th ed. Boston: Houghton Mifflin, 1993.

Pough, Richard H. *Audubon Bird Guide: Small Land Birds.* Garden City, NY: Doubleday, 1949.

———. *Audubon Water Bird Guide.* Garden City, NY: Doubleday, 1951.

Raim, Arlo J. Territory and Mating System in the Bobolink, *Dolichonyx oryzivorus.* M.A. thesis. Kalamazoo, MI: Western Michigan University, 1975.

Robbins, Chandler S., Bertel Bruun, and Herbert S. Zim. *Birds of North America.* Racine, WI: Western Publishing Company, 1966.

Root, Terry. *Atlas of Wintering North American Birds: An Analysis of Christmas Bird Count Data.* Chicago: University of Chicago Press, 1988.

Rosene, Walter. *The Bobwhite Quail: Its Life and Management.* New Brunswick, NJ: Rutgers University Press, 1969.

Scriven, Dorene H. *Bluebirds in the Upper Midwest.* Minneapolis, MN: Audubon Chapter of Minneapolis, 1989.

Skutch, Alexander F. *Orioles, Blackbirds, and Their Kin: A Natural History.* Tucson, AZ: University of Arizona Press, 1996.

Smith, W. John. *Communications and Relationships in the Genus Tyrannus.* Publications of the Nuttall Ornithological Club No. 6. Cambridge, MA: Nuttall Ornithological Club, 1966.

Stokes, Donald W. *A Guide to the Behavior of Common Birds.* Boston: Little, Brown, 1979.

Stokes, Donald W., and Lillian Q. Stokes. *The Bluebird Book: The Complete Guide to Attracting Bluebirds.* Boston: Little, Brown, 1991.

———. *A Guide to Bird Behavior.* Vol. II. Boston: Little, Brown, 1983.

———. *A Guide to Bird Behavior.* Vol. III. Boston: Little, Brown, 1989.

Terres, John K. *The Audubon Society Encyclopedia of North American Birds.* New York: Alfred A. Knopf, 1982.

Tinbergen, Niko. *The Herring Gull's World: A Story of the Social Behavior of Birds.* London: Collins, 1953.

Toops, Connie. *Bluebirds Forever.* Stillwater, MN: Voyageur Press, 1994.

# Index

*Page numbers in italics indicate illustrations.*

# Also by John Eastman

with illustrations by Amelia Hansen

## The Book of Forest and Thicket
*Trees, Shrubs, and Wildflowers*
*of Eastern North America*

## The Book of Swamp and Bog
*Trees, Shrubs, and Wildflowers*
*of Eastern Freshwater Wetlands*

## Birds of Forest, Yard, and Thicket

## Birds of Lake, Pond and Marsh
*Water and Wetland Birds of Eastern North America*

Unique ecological guides to common plants and birds of
Eastern North America, featuring each species as a community
member that affects other organisms and processes.

"The amount of detail is impressive. . . presented in a readable,
easy to follow narrative."
　　　　　　　*—Eirik Blom, Bird Watcher's Digest*

"Recommended for all libraries."
　　　　　　　*—Booklist*

"A very useful reference for both amateur and professional field
biologists."
　　　　　　　*—John D. Mitchell, New York Botanical Garden*

Available in bookstores
or directly from Stackpole Books (800) 732-3669
e-mail: sales@stackpolebooks.com